The Fortune Teller's Prophecy

The Fortune Teller's Prophecy

A Memoir of an
Unlikely Doctor

Lally Pia, MD

SHE WRITES PRESS

Published 2024

Printed in the United States of America

Print ISBN: 978-1-64742-711-5
E-ISBN: 978-1-64742-712-2
Library of Congress Control Number: 2023944881

For information, address:
She Writes Press
1569 Solano Ave #546
Berkeley, CA 94707

Interior design and typeset by Katherine Lloyd, The DESK

She Writes Press is a division of SparkPoint Studio, LLC.

For Ammah and Appah,
who showed me from the start
that everything is possible.

For Tim,
who brings sensitivity, peace,
and music into my life. I love you.

For Shermila and Shanthi.
You mean the world to me.

If you fall into a dark well

Hunt for a handhold

If you slip back down, you'll know where to reach next time

And all ways lead up and into the light

The Prophecy

The first time I removed a woman's head, it took just under two minutes. The scalpel cleared the soft tissue in seconds, but separating the intervertebral disks with a chisel and hammer was more of a challenge. My brand-new job, euphemistically labeled director of the Donated Body Program at the University of California at Davis, had sounded cool at the outset, but somehow they'd failed to put in the job description that the only humans I'd be "directing" were deceased.

"I'm so sorry," I whispered as I gently lifted the back of her head to tuck in sparse gray-brown locks of hair. Averting my gaze, I whipped off the blue paper towels I'd laid on her face and double-bagged her in a large labeled Ziplock bag on the cart beside me. Her eyes were shut, but I couldn't shake my overwhelming guilt at this dastardly deed.

When I was a baby, a dumb fortune teller had sworn to my dad that I'd become a "real" doctor one day—a "doctor of doctors," no less, not a mortician and embalmer. Maybe the fortune teller knew all along what I'd end up doing. He was probably cackling right now at my plight. *Doctor of doctors* indeed . . . more like *Doctor Death*.

Muttering a string of obscenities under my breath, I carried the bagged head to my upright morgue freezer and pulled open the vertical silver door latch. Through the misty haze, four neat shelf labels mocked me. Yesterday I'd snickered as I crafted the labels. Wouldn't it be hilarious to begin a morgue tour by yanking open the freezer door to chant, "Head and shoulders, knees and toes, knees and toes . . . ?"

At the moment I couldn't even summon the vestige of a smile.

I hoisted the head up on the top shelf, swiveling it to face the back of the freezer, so I no longer had to face her accusatory countenance. I slammed the door shut and blew out a long, uneven breath before discarding the soiled, disposable lab coat and blue shoe covers. I then stripped off bloodstained gloves and headed back to my office.

One down, eleven to go. . . .

Like Charon, ferryman of Hades, I had to ship a dozen heads to UC Irvine in a few weeks. I imagined a car accident on the way to the Davis post office, with a bunch of human heads rolling out of my trunk. Sure wouldn't be fun explaining to the cops that I was no Jeffrey Dahmer.

A week into the job, I absolutely felt like a psychopath, holed up in a closet-sized, windowless office in the basement with death all around me. The back door to my office led to a series of three rooms that housed all my morgue comrades—dismembered humans on gurneys in the anatomy room, embalmed bodies on shelves in the cavernous, brooding cadaver storage room beyond, and the recently deceased in one of my two morgue coolers, like the woman I'd just decapitated.

Body part removal bothered me the most. That, plus having to make the decision whether to embalm or dismember bodies for research. Doing the work solo had already given me sweaty nightmares of dead customers sitting upright to tell me off mid-procedure. Thankfully, they never actually talked back when I worked with them, but given my enforced solitude, there were times when I almost wished they would.

Back in my office, I slumped into my chair wondering how much longer I could handle this job. Twenty-four hundred bucks a month was a veritable fortune compared to my previous job as lab assistant, where I fashioned rat chow menus. I really wanted to quit but wasn't sure I could throw away the extra three hundred dollars a month this gig promised. The evidence was incontrovertible: I had landed myself in a true dead-end job.

At age thirty-three, I was destitute, on welfare and food stamps—a single mother of two toddler girls focused on survival. How was it already 1994? I'd been living in the States for ten years and never imagined it would come to this. Many moons back, I'd held on to a much rosier future. Leaning back in the chair, I stared at the speckles on the ugly gray ceiling, closed my eyes, and exhaled.

It had all started with that darn prophecy the year I was born.

It was May 1961. A lone crow cawed, perched on the highest branch of a flamboyant tree, as Vel hurried to his taxi. He glanced back to wave goodbye to Ranee, whose lustrous ebony braids fell well past her shoulders. The pendant of her twenty-four-karat gold necklace glinted as she clutched me, her sleeping three-month-old. Vel choked up at the sight of the precious bundle, his first-born daughter.

I picture him examining the white holy ash marks on his forehead in the passenger side mirror and yet again running his hand over the sealed envelope in his inside pocket. Exhorting the driver to speed up along the country lane, he became airborne over large potholes, each landing rattling his bones.

Disembarking at the temple gates in Vaddukoddai, Sri Lanka, his heart galloped. Dozens of worshippers formed a slow-moving column that jammed the entrance. Some wore only colorful ankle-length sarongs, with white markings on their bare chests. Others were decked out in ivory embroidered silk tops with matching *vertis* falling loosely to their ankles. Dense green foliage draped the white temple walls, mixing with clusters of scarlet bougainvillea and white jasmine. Through wide-open ornately carved doors, the cool interior beckoned, a respite from the harsh sun, already showing its might. Dozens of neatly arranged dusty sandals lay to the side of the main entry-way, and Vel shook his off.

Inside were two engraved silver cups on a brass tray, one holding white holy ash, the other a fragrant yellow sandalwood paste. Vel's fingers trembled as he dipped them, sequentially, into the containers, adding white and yellow markings to his forehead. The attendant accepted his envelope and stowed it in a tall bronze urn brimming with more of the same.

In the main temple, Vel sat cross-legged on the floor behind several rows of worshippers and bowed his head in prayer. Muffled whispers, murmured prayers, and the sound of shuffling feet were the only sounds. The cloying scent of jasmine hung heavy in the air. When he looked up, an effigy of Lord Shiva stared down at him from his perch in a raised alcove. Vel dropped his eyes hurriedly.

After an interminable ten minutes, the attendant closed the doors, and a gong sounded. Floor space had run out. The last worshippers were propped against the rear wall. A hush of expectation fell over the crowd as even whispered conversations ceased.

The priest was on his annual visit from Northern India. A fortune teller of great repute, a reincarnation of Lord Shiva, creator of the universe, he had once made a prediction that a Jaffna couple's only son would die of drowning. The panicked parents sold their house by the sea and moved inland. As legend has it, one year later the little boy's ball fell into a tall rain barrel, and he tried to retrieve it. His stricken parents discovered him face down in the barrel, drowned. Reports of the fortune teller's prowess spread like lightning.

All stood when the holy man emerged from the back of the temple and glided up the central aisle as if on a conveyor belt. Vel snuck a sideways glance. His long graying hair was fastened into a bun, and his naked chest was adorned with white markings and a thin gold chain. His ribs were prominent. A knee-length, saffron-colored silk *verti* completed his outfit. He stepped onto the dusty wooden platform.

The congregation repeated the priest's softly uttered chants. After ten minutes of prayer, he gestured for them to be seated, summoning his attendant to fetch the urn containing envelopes. Placing both hands on the brim, he blessed the container. Beads of sweat clung to his forehead.

"Fellow believers, thank you for inviting me to your Jaffna Ayanur temple. Today I will pick ten envelopes and give you my predictions for your children. I will do this daily for the next seven days, so if your name is not called today, please try again. I pray for Lord Shiva to hold my hand during this process. Time is of the essence. Let us begin." He put his hand into the urn and pulled out the first envelope.

"Velayuthampillai Mahadevan, come forward," he announced. Vel stared, dumbfounded, with a roaring in his head. The holy priest was calling his name? First? What an honor! Disbelief rooted him in place.

"Velayuthampillai! Are you present?" The priest spoke louder now. He held up the card that Vel knew listed his daughter Lally's name, her date of birth, and his and Ranee's names. He raised a shaky right hand, then rose stiffly, hoping no one could tell that his knees were knocking together under his *verti*. The priest gestured for him to approach. Vel's heart pounded like the thundering of a hundred stampeding elephants as he stood, head bowed, in front of the priest.

"Welcome, Velayuthampillai, welcome," the priest offered in a soft, hissing voice, inclining his head.

Vel's eyes met those of the priest. A warm glow enveloped his body as the temple and audience melted away. He was floating in the clouds now, his soul laid bare to a compassionate, piercing black stare. In recollecting this tale in exquisite detail for dozens of years to come, Vel would say that the roaring in his ears obscured any memories of what transpired after the priest's words—words that became sealed into his heart.

"Take good care of her. Your daughter will become a doctor of doctors."

One

The Coup

"Telex, Lally! Lally, there's a telegram from your parents!" Gisela Opoku's heavy German accent hailed me, muffled by the bedroom door. I leapt out of bed in my pajamas and raced to the door, reaching for the thin, creased strip of gray paper she held out with her elegantly manicured fingers. As I read and reread the short, heart-stopping typed sentences, it occurred to me that each word had likely cost my parents dearly.

"DON'T WAIT. PICK UP VISA AND COME TO CALIFORNIA NOW. FINISH UNIVERSITY HERE. LOVE AMMAH AND APPAH," it announced in faded black capitals.

"Well, Lally, what do you think?" Gisela smiled. "No need to rush away, you know. We love having you in our house." The warmth in her smile and concern in her eyes made me swallow. She walked up behind me and laid a warm hand on my shoulder. Her floral perfume soothed my frazzled nerves. I looked up at her over my shoulder. Sunlight lit up her halo of short golden-brown hair and the dainty freckles spattered on her cheeks. She was an angel. I covered her hand with mine for a moment.

"I don't know, I don't know what to do." I reread the words on the telex.

"I understand, Lally, you don't want to give up on med school."

I shook my head, unable to speak, and blinked furiously.

"Lally, you are strong, strong girl. After the coup, you waited . . . let me see . . . almost two months for classes to start . . . two months." She squeezed my shoulder gently. "Yes, it's hard to not be with family, but you are tough girl, Lally. You start again in States, no? Your parents are telling you, come. It will be new road for you, no?"

I gave a slight nod, still not trusting my voice. She didn't get it. Without the degree I'd stayed behind to complete, I couldn't even apply to med school in America. They had a different system out there. I needed that degree. I'd be throwing three years away. An errant tear trickled down my cheek. I gripped the telex tightly.

"Give it some time. Think about it, okay? Let us know what you decide, Lally. Remember, if you want to wait longer, you have a home with us, right? Right? We promised your parents that we would take care of you till you left. We are here for you, okay? It's no trouble."

I nodded again, and the scrap of paper in my hand wavered. The pressure eased from my shoulder, and she walked out quietly, leaving a delicately scented void in her wake. The Opokus were like my second family, but they'd thought they would host me for a few weeks, not months. As far as I knew, my parents had made no financial arrangements for my extended stay here. The huge hibiscus flowers outside my window blurred into crimson splotches of blood. A huge ache of homesickness churned in my stomach for my own family, now over seven thousand miles away.

When the door clicked shut, I tossed the telex on my desk and let the tears flow freely. The dirty white cast on my left forearm clattered on the surface of the desk—the fractured middle finger extending obscenely—a reminder of my predicament. I'd been goofing off to get a laugh, fallen on the finger, and broken a bone. Now my friends' artwork and signatures extended all the way from my left middle finger to my elbow. They often joked, "Put that gun away, Lally," when I came toward them.

Last week, I'd had a close shave. I was walking back home, close to the deadline of an imposed military curfew, when the dark, stooped figure of a man approached a block away. He was across the street, but my pulse skittered when he crossed to my side for no reason I could fathom and continued to head toward me. I crossed the street, but he followed suit. Now he was about twenty feet away and still advancing. With the gloom of twilight closing in on him, I instinctively snatched up my gleaming white cast, postured it at chest level, and aimed it at the man. To my profound relief he ducked, turned around, and ran the way he'd come. I ran for my life, slammed the gates shut and latched them, then hunched over a rose bush, taking multiple deep breaths of air. Thank God for my "gun."

When my family left Ghana for California with our dog, Rocky, in April 1983, I was halfway through medical school at the University of Science and Technology in Kumasi. The Opokus brushed off offers of financial remuneration from my parents and generously opened up their home for the few extra weeks it was supposed to take me to complete final exams for a bachelor of science in human biology.

I'd worked out what I thought was the perfect plan. With my undergraduate degree in hand, I'd join the family and apply to med school in California. I'd maybe have to wait a year or so for the application process to go forward because of the switch in countries and regulations, but I planned to use the delay to acculturate to living in America. Perhaps I'd look for a job while I waited.

Little did anyone know that fate had another plan up its sleeve. Mere weeks away from my finals, a deluge of cow dung descended from the heavens. On May 16, 1983, a military coup was imposed on the country, and the army commander, Jerry John Rawlings, announced the indefinite closure of all the country's universities. The army then announced that students should form "task forces" to mobilize in agricultural areas where they could help farmers increase production. As a foreigner, I was exempt, but not my unfortunate Ghanaian medical student colleagues.

As each day of unrest and dusk-to-dawn curfews dragged by, I prayed that this military coup would be like all the others, with a quick return to normal in a few days. Summer was fast approaching with no indication that any universities would reopen. I feverishly read the daily morning papers, only to learn that the student dormitories had been evacuated. Despite all indications that this might lead to protracted unrest, I stubbornly refused to believe that the awful timing of the coup could suck away my dream of earning my first undergraduate degree. After a full two months, my optimism withered, and panic set in.

I glanced at that creased telegram, now burning a hole into the desk. If I actually took my parents' advice and flew to California now, I'd have to repeat undergraduate training in America. What if the medical school reopened just after I left the country? On the other hand, if I stayed longer with the Opokus, I'd place a financial hardship on their generosity. They never let me feel anything but a part of their family, but as each day dragged by with no classes, I felt like a burden, imposing on the rhythm of their lives.

"I'll go," I whispered out loud. Doubts flooded back in as I reflected on twenty-two years in a country I was now poised to leave.

I was barely six months old when my parents moved to Ghana from Sri Lanka, shortly after they were married. My dad was a Hindu Tamil and my mother a Christian Tamil, but they'd decided to break the mold and step aside from a traditional parent-orchestrated arranged marriage, opting instead for a love marriage. They were engaged but separated in different continents for seven years while my dad studied architecture at Nottingham University in England. My mom worked as a grade school teacher and sent her entire salary to help with my dad's expenses in England.

Tamils made up only 10 percent of the island's population, so married life gradually became a struggle when the Sinhalese, free of British rule, appeared intent on obliterating any privileges afforded to Tamils by the British occupiers. By 1958, there'd been anti-Tamil pogroms and riots, where murders of Tamils were estimated in the hundreds. Tamils fled the country any way they could. My dad jumped at the option to work for the Public Works Department in Ghana, after his sister and brother-in-law had moved there and touted the relative safety and prosperity of the country. His architectural training was apparently highly sought after in Ghana, a country that had gained its independence from Britain in 1957, only four years before they landed there—the first African country to do so.

A prominent British flavor lingered when my parents arrived in Kumasi in 1961. The stores were packed with all manner of European delights—assortments of Smarties, Cadbury English biscuits, and giant Swiss Easter eggs packed with toys and miniature chocolates that delighted me as a child.

My parents set up our first home in Kumasi, the "garden city" in central Ghana. Even though they were firmly middle-class, expatriates were provided housing that "came with the job." I spent my first ten years in a spacious colonial building with a private drive. Our home was set on about an acre of land with paved roads leading to the front and back of the home. We also had a paved badminton court by our back veranda. During holidays, my parents frequently invited friends over for dinner.

"Doctor of doctors!" my dad exclaimed one night, his voice warmed by his after-dinner Remy Martin cognac at one such Christmas party. "That's what he said. He said, one day Lally will become a doctor of doctors." His loud proclamation boomed out through the open glass door leading to the veranda. I sat perched on a chair with my two younger sisters and about a half dozen friends. A delicious cool breeze ruffled the leaves of the plants on the veranda. I'd heard my dad's tale from the moment I understood the spoken word and could have repeated every word that would follow. In fact, if I shut my eyes, I could even smell the jasmine in the temple and visualize the sweat on the priest's forehead.

I was ten years old and had been enjoying the balmy evening till I heard what my dad said. My sister Viji grimaced and shrugged at the misery on my face. My friends had heard my dad's rambling story a hundred million times, and I wanted to vanish out of sheer embarrassment. My friend Sanju shot me a knowing wink from the far side of the veranda.

"Doctor of doctors," he mouthed.

I stuck my tongue out at him, ran to the glass door, and shut it, but this only muffled my dad's loud voice.

It had been such a wonderful evening. I'd stuffed myself silly on crispy meat patties, rice, my mom's delicious Sri Lankan savory chicken curry that made our eyes water, dhal, and assorted vegetables like the grated carrot and the coconut sambal I loved. Then came dessert. My mom's specialty was tapioca and raisin pudding, made with coconut milk, cashews, and flavored with cardamom, but I'd also grabbed a couple of syrupy *gulab jamun* balls that Mithu's mother had made—my favorite. My belly was warm and full, and I'd been rolling around laughing as we went around the circle telling jokes, but during a lull in the conversation my dad had spoiled everything.

"Let's play a word game," I announced loudly to the other children. "I'll get paper and pencils." *Anything* to escape the knowing smirks.

Once inside the living room, I grabbed pencils and paper from the "Big Thing"—the armoire where we kept stationery. The room, packed with grown-ups sitting in a circle, reeked of alcohol and was hazy with cigarette smoke. The eyes of the grown-ups were fastened on my dad. I'd been told many times that a party was never a real party without my dad's stories. He delivered them in such a charismatic fashion, especially after his tongue had been lubricated by brandy. Under our golden chandelier he sat, his golden brandy glass half full, bathed in the light, with a big smile on his face. His cigarette was brandished at a characteristic angle, pointing to the ceiling, and I saw a tiny cylinder of ash that hovered, about to drop on his black dress trousers. From the gleam in his eye, I could tell that he was excited to launch into the tale yet again. My mom sat next to him with an averted head and rolled eyes. Like me, she thought it was a little ridiculous to put so much weight on a prediction made so many years back by a Hindu priest.

Government workers like my dad were provided paid trips back to Sri Lanka every eighteen months, so we were regularly immersed in our Sri Lankan roots. As ethnic trouble escalated in Sri Lanka, large numbers of our relatives fled to Australia, England, and America. A few aunts, uncles, and cousins on my mom's side remained in Jaffna, a Tamil stronghold in the north of the country.

There was often tension during summer visits to Sri Lanka. My cousin told us never to speak Tamil on the local buses. Apparently, our accents were so bad that other bus travelers might think we were Sinhalese. My poor cousin worried that this could enrage Tamils around us, and we might be attacked.

The Fortune Teller's Prophecy

When I was eleven, we took a train ride from Colombo to Jaffna on a train packed with mostly Tamils. A young boy outside the train threw a rock at the train through my open window, and it hit my neck. I guess he was Sinhalese and had been taught to hate Tamils. I didn't bleed, but it bruised my neck. For some perverse reason, I couldn't bring myself to throw that rock away. It was a symbol of hatred. I carefully wrapped it up in aluminum foil and stored it with my treasured belongings.

Ghana had a bustling, supportive, you-can-do-anything-here atmosphere in the early sixties. As a young child, I felt very safe cycling or walking around our beautiful tree-lined neighborhood. In Sri Lanka, the hired help typically lived in the home, but in Ghana, foreigners like my parents had attached servants' quarters. Servants' jobs were highly sought after by Ghanaian villagers in outlying areas because they were relatively well paid. The "servant" typically became a close, trusted family member.

Our first hired helper, Assibi, lived with us for ten years. He played games and helped with meals and chores. He babysat when my parents left in the evenings and was the older brother I'd always wanted. It was a huge betrayal when my younger sister Viji, who could barely put words together, pointed out to our parents that she'd seen Assibi sneaking out of the house with stolen items. My dad walked to his quarters for the first time ever and discovered our prized Swiss alarm clock boldly housed on Assibi's nightstand. In plain view were numerous other purloined items.

My mother called him into our living room to confront him. Assibi sidled in, dragging his feet, and he wouldn't look up. She had the clock in one hand and a long finger pointing at him.

"Assibi," she said, shaking her head, "how could you do this to us, how?" Her voice was all shaky, and I saw tears in her eyes.

"Madam, I . . . I . . ."

"We *trusted* you, Assibi, we treated you like another son. A *son!* We have *never* gone into your quarters till today. How could you do this, Assibi?"

"Madam, please, please!" To my horror he flung himself down on the floor in front of her, grabbed her ankle, and curled up as if she were his only anchor in the world. "Please, one chance. Please, madam, sorry, sorry. I won't do it again." His short black Afro curls had picked up a ball of dog hair dust from the floor. I wanted to run over and brush it off, but my legs wouldn't work.

My mom backed off and tried to pull her ankle out of his grasp, but he wouldn't let go.

"No, Assibi, no more chances." She shook her head. "Maybe I would have given you a chance if you only took our food and our things." She dashed away tears from the side of her face. "But what about Polly, Assibi? Polly?"

My ears perked up. Polly was our beloved African gray parrot. We'd had her for years. She talked nonstop and would perch on my shoulder, gently pecking at my earrings or nuzzling her head against my neck so I could ruffle her silky soft head feathers. A month back, we returned from a weekend visit, shocked to find her cage empty. Assibi told us she had flown off because the latch got loose.

"Polly?" He raised his head and let go of her ankle, sitting upright. To my disgust, I saw a glimmer of fear in his face mixed with a shuttered look I'd never seen before.

"Yes, Polly. Polly would *never* have flown away, Assibi. We know and *you* know that. When I let her out into the garden every evening she always came back. *Always.* I can't prove it, Assibi, but I know . . ." she tapped her chest, "I *know* you took her."

Assibi looked down and shook his head but didn't say a word.

"What did you *do* to her, Assibi? Sell her? *Kill her?* My next-door neighbor said some Ghanaians sacrifice parrots so they can use their red tail feathers for . . . for black magic. Is *that* what you did, Assibi? Is that . . . ?" She stumbled on the words, sobbing, and held a wall fixture for support. I wanted to hold her but was frozen on my chair like a statue. Our beloved, beautiful Polly. I'd had no idea he might have done something so awful to her. Tears slid silently down my cheeks.

Assibi vacated his quarters the next day. I cried all night for my beloved parrot—and my lost brother.

The neighbors in our quiet subdivision, all expatriates like us, formed our support community. At my international school, I befriended children from all over the globe. Like us, they'd been uprooted from their countries of origin to settle in Kumasi. They also returned to their mother countries in the summer, and we shared experiences. The alliance helped us bond, but unfortunately it also prevented true integration into the Ghanaian culture. Less than 5 percent of my elementary school classmates were Ghanaian.

Expatriates were always treated preferentially in Kumasi. In stores, hospitals, and other official gatherings, we were afforded more privileges. In addition, my mother was a teacher, and teachers were highly respected. Despite the cultural divide, I was immersed and cocooned in a warm cloak of Ghanaian hospitality. If our car broke down, it was never just our problem but a problem for anyone in the vicinity. Strangers raced up to provide help, no matter how busy they were. Someone would hail a taxi. Others would gather to push the car along and off the road. Ghana really showed me the true meaning of community.

Multiple military coups to overthrow various civilian and military governments had become a way of life. We'd had no less than four this past year since Jerry Rawlings, a lieutenant from the Ghana Air Force, had deposed President Limann at the end of 1981. For some reason, control of radio broadcasts was the first target of the army. Military marches blared out on all the radio stations for days on end. On my sixteenth birthday, a dusk-to-dawn curfew was in place, so we started the party early, and my friends crashed on couches or the floor till they could safely leave the next morning.

During my primary school years, much of the country's prosperity was snatched away by a succession of greedy rulers, and the economy slumped into steady decline. My three younger siblings were all born in Kumasi. Viji was closest to me in age, Nimi was six years younger, and my brother Vimalan (Vim), the baby of the family, was a full ten years younger than I was.

By the time I turned seventeen, most of my friends and their families had left Kumasi. Basic food supplies like flour, butter, and sugar were gone from the store shelves. Life would have been even more intolerable for us were it not for the close-knit community we had built up. Much of the time during my high school years, our eggs came from neighbors who owned hens. If my mom had waited in line to get butter, often there'd be a simple exchange of butter for flour, or something else the friend or neighbor had in excess. It was a bartering system, and it drew our community together.

Faced with the ever-present instability, danger, empty shelves, and the lack of job opportunities for four growing children, my dad applied for immigration visas for the United States. The bulk of his family had successfully moved to California and blossomed, becoming engineers, doctors, and other highly trained professionals. For years, his family urged us to leave Ghana to move to "the land of opportunity." My uncle Pathmarajah, a gastroenterologist in California, said he would act as the financial sponsor for our green card application.

Apparently it could take five years to get green cards approved so we could join my dad's sister and mother in California.

Given the severe deterioration in the country and widespread food shortages, my parents, now in their late forties, decided it was time to seek new horizons, even though this was a tough decision. My dad had designed many beautiful buildings in Kumasi, and he was hailed for his attempts to use natural materials when possible. My mom's big heart earned her hundreds of friends, and she was highly respected as a teacher at Ridge School, my old elementary school. She also taught piano and music and was an accomplished badminton player. Leaving would mean starting up all over again for both of them, with virtually no cushion of savings.

Returning to Sri Lanka was out of the question because the Tamil-Sinhalese situation we'd left behind there had further deteriorated into the start of an all-out bloody civil war. The Tamil Tigers were fighting for a separate state in the north of the country, while Sinhalese government forces were trying hard to rout them from their hideout in dense jungles, heedless of the cost to civilians caught in the crossfire. My mom opened each blue aerogram from Sri Lanka with shaking fingers, fearful for the plight of our cousins, uncles, and aunts still living in Vaddukoddai, which was in the Jaffna area.

After a four-year wait, our American green cards were finally issued in January 1983. By that time, even basics like toilet paper and toothpaste were scarce. Matters escalated on January 17, 1983, when one million undocumented Ghanaian immigrants were expelled from Nigeria, putting a further strain on Ghana's resources.

"We'll be the last Sri Lankans to leave," my dad proclaimed at breakfast, two weeks before the family prepared their move to California. "Do you know that when we first came here in the sixties, there were forty Sri Lankan families here?"

The Coup

"Yes, Appah," I groaned, and my sister Viji snickered at the expression on my face—this was something he'd repeated dozens of times. I watched the smile that played around his lips as he sipped his tea. He was so proud that we had stuck it out so long, while other close friends succumbed.

With green cards in hand, plans moved with lightning speed. They would all leave in March 1983. I would stay behind another two months with family friends to get my bachelor's degree in human biology, which was awarded halfway through medical school. I'd then fly out to America and apply to medical school out there, since I'd already have an undergraduate degree.

"I wish I was going with you guys," I grumbled at breakfast, a week before they left. I was stretched out under the stairs with my face lodged in our German shepherd's soft neck. He sighed and stretched out, as if he wished I were too. Half-open suitcases cluttered the usually pristine space under the stairway.

"You'll be there with us soon, Lally." My mom inclined her head at me, her slice of marmalade-laden toast in the air. "Two months will go by so fast, girl. By the time you join us, you'll be our first child with a degree."

On March 6, 1983, the family packed two decades of Kumasi into ten suitcases. A deep emptiness weighted my chest like an iron blanket when our servant solemnly wheeled the bags outside. Two cars had their engines running, ready to transport the five of them and the dog to the airport. I dragged my feet as I followed, well aware that I would miss their reaction as they embarked upon the biggest adventure to date—the move to America.

Rocky had his snout out of the car, and I stroked him goodbye gently, not trusting myself to look at or speak to my siblings or parents. He put his head to one side, as if puzzled that I wasn't going. I leaned forward to inhale his delicious doggy smell one last time. Tears poured down my cheeks as they shouted out final goodbyes, and the desolation and abandonment fully hit. My mother looked away down the drive, and I knew from the angle of her head that she was crying. Then gravel crunched under the car wheels as they vanished from sight. My chest was so tight with sadness that I felt I'd been stabbed.

"Sixty days," I whispered as I drove my dad's red Ford to the Opokus' house. "I'll be with you guys in about sixty days. Soon . . . very soon," I said aloud to nobody.

Back in my room at the Opokus' house, I placed the telex from my parents in my diary and headed to the living room to inform Gisela that I had decided to take my parents' advice and leave Kumasi for California. A week later, I packed my meager belongings into a small gray hard-shell Samsonite suitcase, invigorated that I was actually doing something for a change, instead of sitting around waiting for the country to come to its senses. At the same time, I wondered if it was a terrible mistake to jump ship. Maybe I should have waited a few weeks longer for the medical school to reopen.

Bidding a tearful farewell to the Opokus, with bone-crushing hugs all around, I made the four-hour trip to Accra with Reverend Mills, a pastor and family friend. He told me I could stay there with his family until I picked up my green card from the American Embassy in Accra and flew to California at the end of the week.

I cried the entire drive from Kumasi. Hot, silent tears squeezed out through clenched eyelids and drenched my T-shirt, as the blurry, dense green foliage and red laterite soil whizzed past for the last time on the long, bumpy drive. Reverend Mills gave me space to grieve without filling the space with needless chatter. Multiple images cascaded through my head. All the friends who'd departed to other countries, the overflowing warmth of the Ghanaian people, my schools, my wonderful family life despite many hardships. I also reflected on the uncertainty I would face in a strange country where I'd have to start undergraduate studies all over again, because I'd been stymied from getting my degree. Thankfully, the family had already blazed the path to California, which would undoubtedly cushion my landing.

I tried to think of bad experiences to stem the tears. I remembered the overpowering, headache-inducing, scorching heat and my three bouts with malaria. However, each time I shut my eyes, I saw instead a sea of warm, smiling Ghanaian faces filled with that overwhelming sense of can-do I'd grown to love. Rather than the terrifying chills and drenching sweats of malaria, I thought about the doctor's home visit and his smile when he assured my parents that my fevers would subside. I saw the proud smile on my math teacher's face after my perfect test result, our wacky badminton gang of teenagers, hilarious games nights with my friends, and our wild adventures on safari in northern Ghana.

Gone. All gone.

With my friends now scattered to the far corners of the globe, this was a true end to childhood. It was devastating to admit that I could never bring those days back. The daily diary entries I'd kept since I was fifteen were now the only chronicles of my life in this country. The prevailing culture of warmth, community, and regard for others would always be a part of my own character. My tears escalated to racking sobs. Reverend Mills shot me a quick sideways glance. The car hit a huge pothole, rendering my body briefly airborne, and my head bumped into the roof of the car.

"Sorry," he exclaimed. A trickle of sweat slipped down from his graying hair into his beard.

The jolt knocked me out of my self-absorption. Here I was, wallowing in my own misfortunes but lucky to have an escape route—the privilege of starting life over in America in less than one week. From all my siblings' letters, Davis, California, was a great place to live. My poor classmates, on the other hand, didn't have the luxury of jumping into an airplane to seek new horizons. Some had to do farm work in outlying areas and deal with the whimsical fantasies of the military while they prayed for classes to resume.

With my green card in hand, I'd leave behind all the disappointment, uncertainty, and stress. This would be an exciting chapter, a new start. Life couldn't possibly get any worse.

Two

Gateway

From the Millses' house in Accra, I made an appointment to pick up my green card from the American Embassy and confirmed my flights to California. They had a beautiful African gray parrot, so much like our lost Polly that tears pricked my eyes. I taught her to whistle the theme song from *Bridge on the River Kwai*. Two days later, Reverend Mills dropped me outside the American Embassy gates.

"It's just a formality, but the waiting around can take several hours. Stand by that tree over there when you're done," he said, and pointed to a shady tree just outside the entrance. "I'll be back around noon, okay?"

I nodded and smoothed out the creases in the best dress I owned—navy blue with tiny silver pinstripes—squared my shoulders, and headed to the entrance of the well-maintained white three-story building. The grounds held a sparse accumulation of green shrubs and palm trees, but the armed American guards and security fencing made my throat tighten. The huge American flag outside waved lazily in the breeze. The biggest gateway in the world and my final stop as I prepared to abandon Ghana in four short days.

My heart beat like a metronome set to presto. Although this was an uncomplicated visit, I pictured myself in the final act of

A Tale of Two Cities, walking to the guillotine. Once inside, with the harsh sunlight shut behind me, the first thing I noticed was the clockwork precision. The marines walked stiffly, like robots. They had buzz cuts and crisp uniforms, flat lines for mouths, and expressionless eyes that either bored into the back of my head or avoided my gaze completely. I sat with the sinking feeling I have when a cop is in my rearview mirror. I'm doing something wrong. If not, I will do so eventually.

After twenty minutes in line, I made it to the check-in window. The attendant stared suspiciously at my driver's license.

"Reason for your visit today?"

"Er . . . I'm here to pick up my green card. I'm flying out to California Friday."

"Please take a seat and someone will call you," he said in a mechanical voice that probably repeated those same words all day long. I wondered if he needed to be wound up. Perched on the edge of a seat, I waited two hours. It was disturbing to see desperate families dressed in their Sunday best, clutching squalling babies, all grasping at a chance for a new life across the Atlantic. Thankfully, my green card had been issued already. I was here just to pick it up.

The cold silences, hushed conversations, clicking heels of interviewees as they made their way to interview rooms, and the parade of uniformed marines with polished boots ratcheted up my anxiety. Each time a door opened, scores of eyes looked up in anticipation, then were lowered—mine included. I watched the faces of the returning interviewees, trying to predict how it had gone. A few tight smiles emerged. Most appeared tense. A distraught Indian woman in a sari came out blinded with tears, and she almost stepped on me. Her husband placed an arm around her as she sobbed. Another rejection. My bladder was near max capacity, but I was afraid they'd relegate me to the bottom of the list if I took off. Couldn't chance it, so I decided to hold on.

A uniformed marine finally approached and told me to follow him. He opened a door to a small blindingly white room outfitted with a table and two chairs. Gesturing toward a chair, he told me someone would be there soon and left. No swinging light bulb, but I idly wondered if people were tortured in there. A surveillance video camera mounted on a corner of the ceiling intimidated me at first, but as time wore on, I had to clamp down on the strong urge to make a wacky face, to see if it angered an official enough that someone might come in running.

I needed to pee badly.

Another fifteen minutes dragged on before a very serious-faced man in full uniform walked in. He had graying hair at the temples that matched his gray uniform, but most notable was that he lacked a smile. Without greeting me, he sat across the table from me and laid down a manila file. I saw my full name typed in large black letters. He opened it, cleared his throat, then sat back facing me, drumming his fingers on the table. I stared back at his blue-gray eyes.

My gut told me something was way wrong, and this sent shivers down the back of my neck. I couldn't imagine how there could be a problem. We'd all been issued green cards just a few months back, and my parents and siblings were settled in California. Today, I'd simply come to pick up my green card before I joined them there.

"Is something wrong?" My voice quavered and I tried to inject confidence, but it came out tremulous and feeble. "I've been waiting almost three hours." To my utter disgust, a tear slid down one side of my face. I angrily brushed it away.

He looked at me as if he was trying to compose a response, then he cleared his throat and took a deep breath. "We've got a problem, ma'am. I'm sorry."

"A problem," I repeated tonelessly. I opened and shut my mouth like a goldfish. My heart fell into my shoe. I remained silent, feeling a vice clamping down on my stomach. "What kind of a problem?"

"We can't issue your green card today. I'm sorry." He blinked several times but maintained eye contact.

"You can't give me the . . . what? There's a delay? I'm flying to California Friday! What are you talking about?" I was utterly terrified at the finality in his voice.

"When your father applied for a green card for the family, ma'am, I'm afraid we . . . we gave you the wrong green card. I'm sorry."

"What?" The fear began to coalesce.

"We gave you a card for a dependent. Since you're twenty-two now, you'll need an adult green card. You were a minor when your dad applied. That was four years back, ma'am."

I opened and shut my mouth. Words failed me.

"I'm sorry, ma'am . . . we're very sorry this happened, but there's nothing we can do about it."

If he said he was sorry once more, I'd throw up. I wondered what would happen if I barfed all over his shiny medals. My brain hummed with clashing and confused thoughts that spun like goldfish on meth.

"You're telling me that when the family left, you had a valid green card for me, but you gave me the wrong card?" I repeated stupidly. Clashing, discordant cymbals replaced the goldfish.

"Yes, ma'am. That's correct. You have the wrong green card. We made a mistake when we told your father you could pick it up. I'm sorry." He opened the file. "Your parents have to apply for a new green card—for you as an adult." There was dead silence while I tried to make sense of what he was saying. He flipped pages, making a sharp rustling sound, probably to avoid my eyes. The clock mocked me, ticking relentlessly. Murmured voices sounded from the nearby rooms.

"But . . . if you made the mistake, please, please, can you fix this? This was your mistake. They're all in California. I can't believe this is happening. I'm flying out Friday. I don't have anywhere to stay in Ghana any longer. They shut down my med school." Tears poured down my face, and his face wavered in and out of focus. I felt a huge weight settling on my shoulders, and inside was a hollow, cold feeling of dread. I was a cornered rat, and this was too much to process. Surely I would wake up soon.

"I'm sorry, ma'am, there's nothing we can do about it." He closed my folder, indicating the discussion was over. I didn't budge. He reached into a cupboard in the desk and handed me a box of tissues. I grabbed several and blew my nose loudly. He simply stared at me with those penetrating eyes.

"How long will it take to get another green card?" I finally got out tonelessly. My hands shook, and I placed them under the table, trapping them under my thighs. My bladder was bursting. I couldn't look at his eyes, so I focused on his chin.

"Can't say, one or two years—if you're lucky."

"What?" I couldn't for the life of me digest this. "What did you say?"

"One or two years, ma'am. It depends on how many people apply each year and how many are accepted. We have quotas, you know, for each country."

"Up to two years?" I whispered brokenly. To a twenty-two-year-old, it was a lifetime. "I can stay in California while I'm waiting, right? I'm flying Friday. I've nowhere to stay here. My university is closed. Friends put me up in Accra for a few days . . ." I stammered incoherently till my voice petered out.

"I'm sorry, ma'am. The rules are very strict. You're not allowed to visit while your green card is being processed." Through my tears I watched him squeeze his eyes together with his fingers.

"Let me get this straight," I said, with all the confidence I could muster, trying to steady my quavering voice, "you gave me the wrong green card—and now you're telling me I can't see my family? For up to two years?" My brain shut down completely, and all I could hear were all the instruments in an orchestra blaring out a single high-pitched note. I clutched my knees, desperately seeking a solution.

Oh, dear God, where am I going to wait for two years?

"That's our best approximation. It may take less time. Tell your parents to start up a new application as soon as possible."

"But I have nowhere to stay here in Ghana, no money, no nothing," I repeated helplessly, stupidly. His face swam in and out of focus.

"How about Sri Lanka—can you wait it out there? Family members there, maybe?" he asked gently.

"Sri Lanka?" I said incredulously. An image inserted itself into my mind of the gallant lion on the Sri Lankan flag soaked in the blood of all the Tamils who were being slaughtered. "No way. There's a civil war going on. It's not safe to travel. They're massacring Tamils—I'm Tamil. It won't work." I took a deep, shaky breath. My fear ratcheted up another step.

"Any other friends you could stay with? Perhaps you have friends in another country?"

I thought furiously, picking up and discarding fragmentary ideas. I had already overstayed my time with my Kumasi friends and couldn't bring myself to burden them again. When John and Judy Clayden hosted me in Scotland when I was eighteen, they'd said I was welcome to visit again—but for up to two years? What a huge imposition! I didn't know if I could ask. There was Uncle Nava, a close family friend in North Wales. It would be a tight squeeze. He had a wife, two kids, and a nephew in their tiny house.

"I have friends in Scotland, but I don't know. . . ." My voice petered out.

"Good, good." He sounded relieved and embarrassed all at

once and busied himself by straightening the paperwork. My stomach lurched as my precious forms disappeared into the envelope. "I'm glad you have at least one option, ma'am. The airlines should help you to switch your California ticket to one for England. I'm really sorry about all this, ma'am."

At least he wasn't a robotic bureaucrat. Sounded like he had a heart. But . . .

He walked me to the door. I barely made it to the bathroom in time. When I stumbled out of the embassy into the bright, blinding sunlight, it was as if a giant spatula had scooped out the remnants of my brain, leaving me with a jarring hole in my head.

I stood in the shade of a tree outside the gate to wait for Reverend Mills. Endless minutes stretched out. My sobs were now dry heaves because my tear ducts had run dry. I missed my family with a visceral, wrenching, stabbing pain in my chest, yearning for the hustle-bustle and all the laughs. I wanted my parents' arms around me and their reassurance that everything would be okay. Even if I found a place to stay, it would never be home.

I had no job, no money, no school, no family, no home, and now no *country* to call my own. Like a plastic ball repeatedly swatted into the air, I faced a sea of people who rejected me. A headache raged, clouding my vision. The intense noon heat made it worse. I dimly registered traffic whizzing by. People were living their lives, doing normal predictable things while I lived this nightmare. I could barely swallow. Sweat dripped down my back, the heat so intense it suffocated me like a thick blanket. Dizzy, I rested my back against the tree. A high-pitched siren sounded inside my head.

A blaring honking from down the road distracted me. A bus whizzed down the main road, headed my way. A crazy thought took hold for a second. A horrible, random thought. A thought

I'd never entertained before. It consumed me, like a flashing, enticing neon light that intensified as the bus approached.

If I just took two steps into the road, that bus would hit me. It was going fast. All my problems would go away forever. No more pain, no hurt, no thinking. It would be quick. I moved from the support of the tree in a trance and took a half step toward the ragged edge of the road. There was a large pothole a few feet away. Heck, I was in a pothole. A huge, gaping pothole. I couldn't for the life of me look away.

The family will be fine. They'll be fine. They'll miss me, but they'll get over it. Can't handle this.

Nothing's real anymore. Imagine the peace if I let go?

The bus continued to hurtle toward me. Now it was so close that I noticed it was packed. I focused on the driver's patterned, circular cloth hat, unable to look away.

Just a couple of steps. Do it and be done with it.

I closed my eyes to shut out the roaring exhortation. Suddenly, the cacophony went silent. The bus whizzed by in a blur. I was close enough to feel the suction of the air as it passed me. The crazy thoughts vanished, just as the bus had done. I opened my eyes and took deep, gulping breaths of redemption as I watched the bus retreat. Sunshine scorched my face, but this time I welcomed its unrelenting assault.

Three

Leaving Ghana

After the disastrous embassy meeting, time froze at the Millses' home. I rushed for the sanctity of my bedroom and shut the door behind me, then traipsed around like a wraith to diminish the roar still echoing in my head. Ten minutes later, I went downstairs and asked to place a call.

It was seven in the morning California time, but my mother picked up after the first ring. After I explained my predicament, there was a long silence. I felt the shock of my mom's disbelief as she handed me off to my dad.

"Not to worry, it's just paperwork," my dad said, finally. "It's *their* mistake, not ours, Lally. They said it could take a *year* to get here? Rubbish—"

"*Two* years, Appah, they said up to *two*—"

"Nonsense. We'll fix it up soon, don't worry, Lally, don't worry." I heard the quaver at the end of his sentence. I wondered if he actually had a plan or was simply blustering so I'd feel better.

My mom's high-pitched voice broke into the conversation. She spoke haltingly instead of her usual hundred miles an hour. I could tell that she was crying. "Don't worry, girl, you'll be here soon. We'll call the immigration office tomorrow. They'll get you out here in no time at all. You'll just have to be patient, girl. A few weeks, maybe a month at the most. Don't worry."

Rocky barked excitedly in the background. I imagined his beautiful, wise German shepherd face, with his head tilted to one side. He'd probably picked up on the tension. I wanted to hug Rocky tight around his huge neck, push my face into his warm doggy smell, and have him lick my face to assure me that everything was going to turn out just fine. I wanted to sit around the dining table with all of them in a tight haven of togetherness, to withdraw from the storm of nastiness howling around. I couldn't bring myself to say anything, and the long-distance static extended uncomfortably. I didn't know how much this international call was running and had no money to settle it anyway.

"Lally? Lally? Are you there?" The quaver in my mom's voice told me she was still in shock.

"I'm here."

"So you'll wait in Accra with the Millses?" she asked anxiously.

"Oh no, I can't. They have a full house, Ammah." I looked around the living room to make sure no one could hear me and dropped my voice. "I'd never *dream* of imposing anyway. I'm sharing Judith's bedroom. I think I'll ask the Claydens—see if they'll keep me for a bit."

"John and Judy? They're so nice. Wasn't it last summer that you stayed with them in Scotland?"

"*Two* years ago, Ammah. Yes, they paid for all my expenses. Before all the rubbish at the embassy today, they arranged to meet me during my layover at Schiphol airport next weekend. Can you believe that? They were going to drive to Amsterdam from Glasgow just to see me. I told them no, that was crazy, but John insisted. He said they'd turn it into a mini holiday. I'll have to tell them about the change of plan."

"Um. . . ." She cleared her throat and sounded uncomfortable. "About the money situation, Lally . . . unfortunately we don't have extra money for your expenses . . . not yet. You see, I'm working part-time at the tomato cannery and substitute teaching. Appah still hasn't found a job." I imagined her rubbing her nose in embarrassment. "If it won't work for you to be with the Claydens, don't worry. There are other friends you can stay with, so don't worry, girl. There's Uncle Nava in North Wales. Something will work out, so don't worry."

The more she told me not to worry, the more anxious I became. My next call was to the Claydens. My heart hammered when Judy picked up. I quickly explained the situation and asked if I could stay with them for a little while. Despite zero preparation, Judy sounded really enthusiastic. She handed the phone to John.

"Good heavens, that's a fine pickle you've got yourself into, Lally." John gave a short, humorless laugh. "There you go, that's American incompetence for you. You'd think they'd fix it up quickly because it was their fault. Hah!" he snorted. I imagined him running a hand through his jet-black hair. "And you thought *Ghanaian* bureaucracy was bad. Listen, Lally, don't worry about a thing. Once you change your flights, just call us with your flight details. We'll pick you up from Heathrow, and you're welcome to stay with us as long as it takes. We'll cover your expenses. Yes, really. We'd love to see you. It's no problem at all. And now we don't have to drive all the way to Amsterdam to see her, do we, Judy?" He chuckled. "Hold on, Lally, here's Judy again."

"Lally," Judy said breathlessly, "this is actually great timing for us. Right now we're packing up our home in Glasgow. John's just been offered a senior lecturer job at Swansea University. We've bought an old inn in a little town called Parkmill in South Wales."

"South Wales?" My heart pounded. I'd never been to South Wales.

"Yes, the Gower Peninsula is really spectacular. You're going to love it."

I wanted to cry with relief. "I really hate to impose on you when you're moving. Are you *sure* it's not a problem? There are other family friends I can ask."

"It's no problem, Lally. The inn has lots of spare rooms. Hold on, Lally, John has a question."

"Lally, when were you hoping to head out?" I imagined John indenting his chin with his index finger, his eyes scrunched up in thought.

"This Friday. Is that too soon?"

"Not at all. It's perfect. We'll be all packed up by then. Just call us with your travel details when they're finalized. We'll see you soon." His voice was tinged with excitement.

Excitement, not exasperation.

I shivered with excitement, then placed the phone on its cradle. The Claydens! They'd given me a dream holiday in Scotland two summers back. My med school wanted all first-year students to gain experience working as a nurse, so the Claydens arranged for me to volunteer at Stobhill Hospital in Glasgow. After that, we'd taken ferries to remote destinations in the Inner and Outer Hebrides and camped in places of indescribable beauty. I'd practiced my Scottish dancing skills at a ceilidh. We'd driven past countless peacock-blue lochs nestled in the beautiful rosebay willow herb–encrusted mountains. We'd even driven to Loch Ness. Once, we'd taken the ferry to Galway in Ireland. Another time we drove into Belfast when there was still a risk that the IRA might set off bombs. Thrilling times.

For months I'd felt like unwanted baggage—a burden to so many different people. Yet, John and Judy were telling me they *wanted* to see me again. They hadn't balked at making the six-hour trip from Glasgow to Heathrow to pick me up. My incomparable friends had come through just when I was in dire need of support.

Four days later, I was on a seven-hour British Airways flight to London. As the wheels left Ghana soil, the liftoff reminded me of the childhood I'd left behind. Tears rolled down my cheeks as I wondered if I'd ever come back. Not wanting to miss a second of the rolling browns and greens rapidly switching to blue ocean, I pressed my face against the window, making out the curved margin of the West Coast of Africa as we headed over the Atlantic. Finally there was turbulence, and then cotton-ball clouds obscured my view of Ghana completely.

It was probably my imagination, but when there was a break in the clouds, I thought I glimpsed land that could be America. While it was sad to leave Ghana, I couldn't hide a little stir of excitement at the mysterious, beckoning United States. I prayed that my parents were right and they'd fix up my green card soon.

In America there'd probably be huge roads and cars everywhere, and loud, brash people like the tourists who came to Ghana. They'd have rules for everything, and No Trespassing signs dotting the landscape. It wasn't England, where you could just climb over gates on walks. In fact, from what I'd learned, I'd probably get shot, because most of the land belonged to people, not the government. I'd also heard they had more guns than people but figured someone just made that up.

From the recent call with my parents, it saddened me that my dad hadn't found a job as an architect yet and that my creative mother, who'd taught all her life, was now checking tomatoes in a cannery to make ends meet. It didn't help that they'd switched continents when they were both over fifty. I was dying to hear how my three younger siblings were doing. Davis, California, was a hundred light-years away, separated from me by this blooming, endless ocean. Given this huge setback, all thoughts of becoming a doctor were a lost dream now. So much for the fortune teller's prophecy. To think I'd actually begun to believe that tale when I made it into med school in Kumasi.

Four

The Claydens

As the double thud of jet wheels hit English soil, the booming reverse thrusts of the airplane matched the roar of conflicted thoughts in my head. I was beyond excited to see John and Judy soon but wary about what would unfold in this next chapter. I pressed my face against the window to absorb every second. It was raining, of course. Gray airport buildings whipped by, their margins blurred.

If the drizzle wasn't enough, the wait in the non-British citizen's entry line at Heathrow quashed the excitement that had built up after landing. We were crammed, accordion style, into a tortuous queue of sweaty bodies, screaming children, and sleep-deprived international travelers. Just the "people" smell itself nauseated me. The grim, unsmiling Heathrow immigration officials' faces mocked the cheery WELCOME TO ENGLAND sign posted behind them on a wall next to a Union Jack.

When I'd come here last, engagement photos of Lady Di in a blue dress with Prince Charles had smiled at me from every wall. This time, there were huge, tall photos of British tourist destinations. Officials processed new arrivals, calling people up like cattle to intimidating glass shields. This made me all too aware that passport control might seek *any* excuse to kick me out of England. After the events that had transpired in the

past two weeks, I simply couldn't countenance one more rejection from a country. Hopefully, the Claydens would be in the
waiting area. I'd given them my flight arrival time yesterday. I
could hardly wait to see them. As I shuffled forward, inches at a
time, I allowed my mind to drift back to when I'd first met the
Claydens when I was seventeen.

I zipped my racket into its cover after several strenuous badminton games at the University Staff Club. It was the end of a
hot June afternoon, but it had become too dark to see the shut-
tlecock any longer. My friends milled around the courts chattering, but I followed Patricia to the gray two-story Staff Club
building for ginger ale.

"You killed me at the net." she commented.

"It's because I was playing with Mario. He's awesome." I
deflected her compliment, but the thrill of accomplishment
lingered.

"Mario's cute," she said dreamily, sighing. Soft curls framed
her face like a halo. Half English, half Ghanaian, Patricia was
a close friend.

"Yeah, but he's off-limits. He's going to marry Annie some-
day." I sighed, wishing there were someone in my life.

Upstairs, we stood in the long line that had formed in front
of the bar.

"Hey, there's JR," Patricia announced. I turned. John Russell was sauntering toward us. He'd been seated with my dad
and some other professors, drinking beer as usual. An empty
beer bottle was in his hand. As he walked to us, I noted how his
eyes lingered on young women who passed by. I thought he was
a jerk to do that because he was married.

"Hey, girls, what did I miss at badminton today?" He stood
close enough that I could smell sour beer on his breath. At
six feet four inches, a lean Peter Jennings look-alike, JR was

charismatic and told irreverent English jokes that floored us with laughter. He was English, my parents' age, but liked to hang with the teenagers. Through the gossip grapevine—the only way to know anything in Kumasi—we knew he had a wife and two kids in England. It was also common knowledge that he cheated on his wife with various local girls. One summer, when his family strolled down our street, I couldn't get over the haunted look on his wife's face. She clutched the hands of their two small sons, her eyes averted. I wondered if she knew that he was a cheat. She appeared truly miserable.

I shut my eyes to rejoin the conversation.

"You should have played with us, John," Patricia gushed. "Both courts were packed, and we had some great games. Why weren't you playing?"

"Department work," he said.

"Sure," I responded, tartly. His eyes crinkled when I pointedly stared at his loosely dangling beer bottle.

"Hey, you two, there's a new young couple you should meet: John and Judy Clayden. They've just come to Kumasi from Scotland." He pointed over to a small table where a couple sat, engrossed in a conversation. The man called John had glasses and straight, longish jet-black hair. Judy was like Yoko Ono, with circular bifocals and long, straight black hair. She wore an embroidered white shirt over a cotton peasant skirt.

Patricia, always the leader, took a few steps toward the couple. She beckoned JR. "Well, what are you waiting for, John? Introduce us. We'll get drinks later." I envied her brazen approach. I was such a timid mouse in comparison. I'd devoured Georgette Heyer historical novels about royalty and couldn't wait to find out more about mysterious, romantic Scotland.

John Russell pulled up chairs for us and performed introductions. The Claydens smiled like they'd known us a long time, and I took to them immediately. They would be stationed in

Kumasi for several years. John Clayden was lecturing in the Economics Department with JR. Judy said she hoped to teach Scottish folk dances at the Staff Club. Would there be interest among the teenagers?

"Yes, yes, yes!" I said. "I'm sure they'd *love* Scottish dance classes—as long as it's not too expensive." My heart pounded with excitement.

"Oh, there'd be no charge at all, Lally, just a commitment to show up each week," she said, smiling. She tucked stands of jet-black hair behind her ear.

"I'll be there . . . with my sister Elizabeth," Patricia announced immediately. "If you make sure it's straight after badminton, we'll get all our friends to show."

We had an excited discussion about the nuts and bolts of dance classes. JR muttered, "I've got two left legs; count me out," and stood, giving Judy a flirtatious wink as he did. I saw two pink spots on her cheeks as she turned slightly to give him a tremulous wave. John Clayden also got up. He asked what we wanted to drink, waving away the money I pulled out of my racket case. Judy told us folk dance classes would start in two weeks.

After this chance meeting, Thursday evenings became the highlight of my week for the next three years. We twirled to the strains of various jigs, reels, and other Scottish tunes, including the Gay Gordons waltz and the Dashing White Sergeant. Armenian and Greek line dances and exciting, boisterous Israeli dances were added to our repertoire. I was a consistent attendee and became Judy's right-hand person. When she was out, she gave me her tapes, and I became the assistant instructor.

The lilting melodies, camaraderie with my friends, and aerobic workout made the evenings magical. Three months later, over a dozen teenagers put on a show at the Great Hall for our parents. The matching white shirts and blue and black Ghanaian-print skirts were ordered and paid for by the Claydens.

Every Thursday, a culturally mixed assortment of teenagers bopped around to strains of the Highland Fling, while inebriated faculty peered at us from the adjoining bar. For years, the magic of dancing was always inextricably linked to the permeating stench of stale Guinness.

The Claydens were my parents' age but had no children—someone told me that they'd wanted children but couldn't conceive—but they'd loved hanging out with our teenage group and orchestrated wonderful activities for us. Along with about a half dozen teenagers, I went on a four-day safari trip to Lome, in the north of Ghana. The Claydens paid for all of our food, transport, and the entry fee to the reserve. As we piled into two jeeps for the trip, I prepared myself for the thrill of a lifetime.

At the safari compound, we lined up on the balcony of the main cabin to watch various groups of animals drinking at the watering hole at dusk and at dawn. The huge horde of majestic elephants was my favorite. A drunken German friend of the Claydens rushed down the hill to get close to them, and the stupid man was almost trampled to death. In the evenings, baboons tried to open our windows. I heard they were very good at stealing just about everything from food items to backpacks.

After dinner and into the wee hours of the night, we sat in a large circle in the main cabin. We played card games such as hearts, up and down, and rummy. We also played endless rounds of categories where we clapped our hands together and yelled out categories in turn. If you missed the beat, you were eliminated. Still later I learned a new game called lateral thinking.

The only downside was that the Claydens had also asked JR along. He showed up with a Ghanaian model named Essie in tow. Essie was not a team player. Sporting six-inch heels, hip-riding short skirts, and revealing tank tops, she would have fit in better at a nightclub than on safari. It seemed so disrespectful of his wife that he dangled his mistress in front of us in this fashion.

On the other hand, JR regaled us, night after night, with dark, Monty Python–style jokes that made me laugh till my sides hurt and tears spilled down my cheeks. Essie always hung out at the periphery, like a dark shadow, avoiding the rest of us. Each time I saw her, I couldn't help but feel sorry for JR's wife and their adorable little boys. The boys, less than age seven, had always seemed to hero-worship their dad.

"Next!" a uniformed man called out to me from his kiosk. I had reached the front of the Heathrow airport queue. As I approached, I saw graying hair and glasses on the tip of his nose—he was grandfather-like. I prayed that he'd be nice.

I extended my Sri Lankan passport through a tiny arched opening. "Guess I shouldn't go around beating people up," I joked feebly, waving my casted left arm around. Not even a vestige of a smile cracked his face as he flipped through the passport. I wondered if I'd broken some kind of unwritten rule for international visitors by trying to get him to smile.

"I don't see a visa here," he announced in a sharp tone, turning from the book to stare directly into my eyes. His gray eyes had white flecks in them. It was like looking at a kaleidoscope. If he was trying to intimidate me, it worked. "Do you have a visa, ma'am?"

I swallowed and licked my dry lips. "No, I don't. You see, it's like this, I had no time. It's complicated. I'm going to California soon. I had a problem getting there. I'm going to stay . . . going to wait here with friends," I blabbered. "I'm not staying long. Just for a bit . . . till I go to America, you see. My family's in America."

"Slow down, slow down, ma'am. You have friends here in the UK?"

"That's right. They should be here. I'm headed to California, but I'm stopping off to see them for a while. I'm on my way to the *States*." My heart whacked at my chest cage. I would have given anything for a sip of water. In fact, my mouth was so dry that I could barely get the words out. I swallowed, and it hurt. He made some notes without looking up. I figured he was probably putting down, "Moron trying to enter UK."

"Name of your friends?" he asked sharply.

"John and Judy Clayden." I spelled out their last name.

"Address?"

"Er . . . I'm not sure. I have their address in Scotland, but they told me they're moving and I . . . I don't know. . . ." Even in my state of exhaustion, I knew what a lame answer that was.

"You don't have an address?" He looked at me incredulously. "You're here to stay with friends and don't have anything more than a name? Is that what you're telling me? Do you have their telephone number?"

"Er . . . I don't have that either. You see, they're moving to Wales and. . . ."

"Ma'am," he interrupted, "that's quite enough. Please follow this officer. Someone will come to talk to you soon." He handed my passport to a sour-faced, unsmiling Asian man who had materialized behind him. From the suspicious way Sourpuss handled the document handoff, I wondered if he thought I'd grab my passport and bolt.

Welcome to England.

Sourpuss led me into the room, waved me over to a small table with two chairs, and told me to wait there. He left, shutting the door behind him. I wondered if he'd locked me in, but I didn't dare check. I tried to get comfortable on a hard wooden chair facing the door. The office was tiny with a heavily frosted window, so I couldn't see outside. The only decor was a simple black clock that hung on the wall. The room had all the personality of a slab of cement, so I amused myself for the next hour by rifling through my dog-eared diary. It was painfully empty because I'd been too stressed to write for months. Instead, I reread some letters I'd stowed inside. How stupid that I'd forgotten to ask John for their address in Wales.

After another twenty minutes, I set the diary back in my bag and gently banged the cast on the edge of the table to relieve a deep wrist itch. I traced autographs my friends had inscribed on my cast with my index finger, reliving the comments they'd made as they generated artwork or signed their names. As the clock hands continued to advance, I feared the worst, but suddenly the door opened, and there stood the Asian man. To my great relief, materializing behind him like a wizard, stood a smiling, crystal blue–eyed John Clayden.

John hadn't aged at all in the year since I'd seen him. His hair was still shoulder-length and jet black. I saw the concern in his eyes as he dropped his gaze to my dirty cast. I was so glad to see him that I could have given him a bear hug on the spot. Instead, I nodded politely and gripped his hand like my life depended on it.

The Asian man handed me the passport. "Ma'am, I spoke to Mr. Clayden here. We have issued you a one-month visitor's visa," he announced. "This means you are here as a *tourist*. You are not to start a business or seek work in Britain while you are here. If you do, you will face deportation back to Ghana. All right?"

I couldn't trust myself to speak and merely nodded.

"Mr. Clayden has confirmed his contact information and has vouched to act as your sponsor. This means that he will provide you with financial support while you are living in Britain. He has assured us that he will make sure you exit the country before your time is up in a month."

"Oh, thank you, thank you!" I gushed. I was so relieved that

I could have hugged Mr. Sourpuss. They'd only given me four weeks. I wondered if I'd have my green card by then.

After I collected my checked suitcase, John took me to an airport cafeteria and bought me a cup of heavenly coffee and the best scone I'd eaten in my life. He told me he'd expected trouble at immigration, so he'd checked in at passport control on my behalf. We laughed at how ill-prepared I'd been.

John carried my precious, beat-up Samsonite suitcase, which housed all my worldly possessions, and walked slightly ahead into the light drizzle outside. I inhaled appreciatively the cold, crisp English air, mixed with rain on asphalt. It was such a contrast from the sweltering heat assault I had left behind in Ghana. He caught me up on the immediate plans. Judy was waiting in their moving truck, and we were headed straight to their new home in Wales. Way up high in the passenger seat of a giant truck sat Judy. She smiled and waved, then descended from the truck to give me her characteristic stiff, tentative Judy-hug, raising her eyebrows at my cast. Her hair had thinned out a little, but she otherwise looked the same. As I sank back in the front seat between them, the tension of the last few months evaporated. I pushed my shoulders back and inhaled deeply. I was with my "away" family, and another adventure was about to start. My thighs trembled in excitement.

"What happened?" John asked, pointing to my dirty cast. He was half shouting because of the drizzle combined with the squelch of the huge windscreen wipers.

"Broke my third finger when I was goofing around trying to make my friends laugh and landed on my hand. The cast can come off next week. For now it comes in handy to give people the finger." I smiled, raising the cast in the air. "This is officially the craziest month I've had. Ever."

"I'm sorry, Lally," Judy said softly, in a deep, gentle tone of commiseration. I snuck a sideways glance at the long, silky black hair that framed her pale oval face, wanting to drown in the pools of concern in her dark brown eyes. Suddenly I felt a smack of homesickness as I thought about my own family, still thousands of miles away, and the hellish events of the past week.

"Yeah, there's a lot. . . ." I said, blinking ferociously to hold back a few errant tears. "It's so wonderful to see you guys. You haven't changed at all." Right then it struck me that the three of us were driving to a new home, awaiting a new life, and carrying every possession we owned.

Five

The Gower

As our enormous moving truck made its way down the M4 motorway west to the Gower Peninsula, I stepped into a dreamscape. The rain had stopped, and England showed off its freshly washed splendor. Miles of gorgeous green fields lay on either side, dotted with cows and flocks of white, brown, and gray sheep. Bright patches of lemon-yellow gorse provided bright exclamation points along the way. When we drove past the WELCOME TO WALES sign, the vegetation became even more lush.

Swansea was a bustling town, packed with cars and tall, cramped buildings, so I was relieved when we left the motorway for a gentle country road with farmland all around. It was all a far cry from the dense tropical foliage and red laterite roads I was accustomed to in Ghana. My excitement increased as unpronounceable Welsh names sprouted up on road signs, such as Cwmbwrla, Llangennith, Llanrhidian, Llanmadoc, and Penclawdd. Then there were delightfully romantic names such as Mumbles and Oxwich. I had fun practicing saying the names out loud.

"We knew you'd love it here," John said with a smile in response to my loud exclamations at each bend in the road. "I'm starting a new job as senior lecturer at Swansea University. Parkmill is about eight miles from Swansea. The house is called

New Inn Cottage. That's where we're headed." He gripped the steering wheel tightly.

"Oh, Lally, you're going to *love* the gigantic fireplace," Judy said, turning to me. "We always think about how much you loved to build fires when we camped in Scotland. Well, the inn is hundreds of years old, and John and I did some research. It used to be the village pub and was also an inn. It has two stories, and there's a terraced garden over to one side." The huge wipers squeaked loudly as fresh raindrops appeared again.

"English rain," I said, taking a deep breath. "I've missed these gentle sprinkles. The rain just hammers you in Ghana. It actually hurts your body."

"Yes, we miss those fierce Ghanaian thunderstorms. Out here, they're just passing showers. By the way, Lally," John turned to me, "Judy's assigned you the garden room, haven't you, Judy? And it's all set up, right?" He shared a conspiratorial smile with his wife. She chuckled, and her cheeks were flushed. I loved that they still adored each other.

"That's right, Lally. I put up a few hanging plants just under the skylight in your room. All the bedrooms are upstairs, and a door from your room leads out to the top of the garden terraces."

"Dreamy," I said with a sigh.

"Maybe you can help me organize the garden. I'm afraid there are a lot of weeds right now."

"I can't wait." I gripped my seat to avoid squashing Judy as we lurched around a turn in the road. "Wow, it sounds huge!"

"It's several hectares—we own part of the stream across the road from the house, and the property extends up the hill behind the house." Judy tucked a long black strand of hair behind her ears. Her face was bright with anticipation.

This sounded romantic beyond my wildest dreams. A small town bordered by farmland? A cottage that had once been a historic pub, with a giant fireplace? The fireplace was the icing on the cake. They both knew how much I loved to poke at burning logs when we went camping.

"Will you be taking tenants? You said there were several rooms."

"That's the plan, but not till we settle down, right, Judy?" He shot her a quick sideways glance.

"No, John, I'm not ready for anything like that yet. Let's wait." Her long, pale fingers picked at her pants, and then she turned to me. "So, Lally, you'll be our first tenant." The wind-shield wipers dragged, and John turned them off again.

The side windows were misted up, but Judy used a tissue to wipe her window off so I could make out the surroundings. Tiny hamlets dotted the drive. I saw stonewalled fences festooned with gorgeous flowers, and then we came upon a wild open stretch of grassland dotted with sheep.

"Almost there." Judy smoothed her white embroidered peasant shirt over her pants and reached for the jacket she had stowed by her feet.

"Ponies, wow!" A herd of a half dozen stocky white and gray ponies galloped together, not too far from us. "They aren't fenced in. Can't they get hit?"

"They're too smart for that, Lally. They're wild ponies," Judy responded. "They roam all over the Gower because this is their home. Do you see where they're headed? That's a cliff right there"—she pointed to the left—"and beyond that cliff—you can't see the ocean from here, but that's Three Cliffs Bay. It's really spectacular, you'll see."

"Three cliffs?"

"Yes. There are three jagged cliffs on one side of a huge strip of beach. Tourists drive from all over the country to see it. It's considered one of the most unspoiled beaches in Wales."

"What's more, it's only a mile from our house." John raked his fingers through his hair and flattened his fingers up against his lips. He inhaled deeply and leaned back in his seat to stretch. "You must be tired, Lally. Think I'm ready for a nap myself. Hey, Judy, could you hand Lally the Gower map in the glove compartment please?"

"Yes, John," she murmured. She rummaged around, fished out a creased map, and offered it to me. I stifled a yawn but obediently opened it up.

"Lally, take a look at where Parkmill is—can you point it out to her, Judy?" He honked at a couple of sheep that appeared to be considering whether they should make a run for it into the road. "Silly sheep! You'll see on the map that there are miles and miles of walks out here—they use green dashes for the paths—" His excitement was infectious.

"And Lally," Judy interrupted, running her finger over the coastline on the map, "this coast is riddled with limestone caves. I haven't explored them yet, but I'm sure the Swansea library will have some great guidebooks, if you're into that kind of thing."

"I'd love to check out some caves. Sounds like I'm definitely not going to be bored out here."

As we headed down an extremely narrow country road, an approaching car veered out of our way and moved onto the grassy embankment so we could pass.

"Oops!" John raised his palm to his flushed face. "I probably should have given him a little more space. Sorry!" He gave a conciliatory wave, and the man smiled and waved right back. I loved the easygoing Welsh already.

Just ahead of us, the road was completely blocked by what looked like about a hundred fat, fuzzy white sheep with black eyes. We pulled to a stop and waited a good five minutes for them to clear out of the way. I loved the loud, indignant baaing that issued from the rabble. They took their time, and I admired their majestic poise and entitlement. "This is our land," they seemed to announce, "and you'll just have to wait." I glanced sideways at John and saw a tolerant half smile on his face. They were clearly the same incredible, environmentally conscious, animal-loving friends I remembered.

I fell in love with Parkmill the moment we drove into the village. There were no more than about a dozen houses. The road was so narrow that to park at their new home, we had to drive to the center of the village and make a U-turn at a long building called the Gower Heritage Center.

"What's that?" I asked, pointing to the old gray stone building.

"Oh, that's a mill dating from the twelfth century. It's one of the oldest working mills in the country, I believe," Judy said. "You should take a tour through the center some time."

"Wow, I've never seen anything like this. You guys have landed in paradise!"

"Yes, it's pretty nice here. When you take the tour, they'll show you how wheat is turned into flour, how wool from sheared sheep is twisted into yarn—that sort of thing. There are many remote working farms in the surrounding villages."

"There's a working blacksmith there as well," John interjected. He honked as we approached a sharp turn in the road. "He's a nice chap. Maybe you can ask him to make you a horseshoe for good luck."

It was almost too much to take in, but it was clear that I was going to love living here. The road narrowed, and my heart galloped as we approached New Inn Cottage. It was a white two-story, elongated stone building, set right up against a towering green hill. The front door was barely a few feet from the main road. The home overlooked a green forest dotted with white garlic flowers. As I got out of the car, I caught a faint whiff of garlic and glimpsed a little creek winding its way into the forest. It was hard to imagine that they actually owned a portion of that lovely bubbling creek!

The Gower

Despite my weariness, I was in heaven, immersed in an idyllic setting of a childhood Enid Blyton story. As I entered the front door, I glanced to the right and, to my delight, saw an arched wrought iron entryway that led to the three-tiered, terraced garden that Judy had described.

Later that evening, I curled up in my cozy bed in the second-floor garden room. In the lamplight from my vantage on the bed, I admired dainty green ferns that Judy had hung from the angular, sloped ceiling and gazed at the whitewashed stone walls in delight. It struck me again how, despite the stress of moving from Scotland to Wales, my dear friends had made the huge detour to pick me up from Heathrow airport. Not once had they even hinted at all the extra trouble they'd taken. I resolved to repay their kindness by making myself indispensable to them in every way I could in the days ahead.

Nothing felt real anymore. In the space of a few hours, I'd gone from desolation to fairyland. It took me a good hour to calm down and fall asleep, but for the first time in many days, no tears fell.

Six

The Village
Organist

A morning routine took shape. I always woke first and rushed downstairs to bring in the bottles the milkman left on our doorstep. Sometimes the aluminum tops had been pecked off by birds eager to get the cream on top. John left early to drive to Swansea University, and Judy usually woke later and worked in the house or garden. I entertained myself by going on several-mile strolls to villages nearby, trying different trails using maps and books John thoughtfully left out for me. I explored village hamlets, then returned by bus in the midafternoon to help Judy with the evening meal.

The nightmares of the past few weeks gradually lost their punch until each blue aerogram from California delivered a fresh stab of homesickness. My brother, Vim, who was twelve, sounded very happy. He ran a paper route for extra pocket money. Nimi, three years older, was struggling to adapt to the culture shift and the established cliques at school. She said the middle school girls weren't friendly, and she wanted to return to Kumasi. Viji said it was a myth that American schools were so easy. She was working hard at community college courses.

The Village Organist

My dad had given up on his dream to secure a job as an architect. As a building projects supervisor, he lived in a drab trailer on his own in Los Angeles. As building projects shifted, he had to move sites, and he rarely returned to Davis. It saddened me that my gregarious dad was living an isolated life, four hundred miles away from the family. My mom was a teacher's aide at a middle school in Davis but still worked shifts at the cannery. It was a punch in my gut that my dainty, creative mom, who'd been a revered teacher all her life, was now staring down a fast-moving conveyor belt to sort tomatoes for hours at a time. Money was tight all around.

Thankfully, the Claydens paid for everything. I desperately wished I could work, but this was absolutely forbidden by the terms of my visitor visa. Several times, I offered to move in with friends in North Wales to lighten the financial burden, but they always brushed me off, assuring me that it was no problem at all. John joked that as my sponsor in the UK, he had to keep an eye on me to make sure that I didn't break any immigration rules.

I began to think of the Claydens as substitute parents when the three of us sat down for dinner. I'd never summoned up the courage to ask them straight out why they'd never had children but figured it simply hadn't worked out for some reason. Judy was fifteen years older than me, and John, more than twenty. They were devout animal lovers and vegetarians, so when I cooked, I learned to use TVP (textured vegetable protein) as a meat substitute. It was composed of little cubes of what looked like dehydrated dog food. When rehydrated, it had the texture of shoe leather. If slathered with tons of tomato, garlic, ginger, and onion, it became vaguely palatable. John often gave my creations high acclaim. A couple of times, Judy tightened her mouth into a straight line, as if jealous of his compliments. As my confidence grew, I increased my repertoire, experimenting with different flavors and meals and adjusting recipes as I saw fit. I also helped out with their vacuuming and laundry.

I basked in the unhurried Welsh life and enjoyed the gossip at Shepherds, the only store in the village. Despite the fact that I was the only dark-skinned person in the village, no one ever made me feel like a foreigner. The workers peppered me with questions about life in Kumasi and my upcoming move to California. In a weird way, despite my short stay in Wales, I felt less of an outsider there than in Ghana or Sri Lanka.

One morning, I handed a loaf of overpriced walnut bread to Joe, the manager of Shepherds.

"Headed to the States, then, are you? Haven't been there myself, but I've heard that those Americans say 'Hi' but don't really mean it, and it stays like that. Out here, sure we may take a while to warm up, but once we know you, we let our guard down, if you know what I mean."

"Uh-huh," I murmured, more to shut him up than anything. My family had been overwhelmingly positive about the Americans they'd met so far.

"So, with your delay and all, are you going to give up on becoming a doctor?"

I froze for a second, shrugged, and grabbed my purchase. "I suppose, yes . . . I don't know."

The blinding sunlight outside made me blink as I trudged back to the cottage mulling over Joe's comments. My former path was no longer feasible. I'd thrown away three years of medical training with nothing to show for it. I didn't even have a degree; I'd missed it by a few weeks. In California, I'd have to apply to college, get a bachelor's, then apply to med school all over again. Imagine all the wasted years.

Plus, even with an undergrad degree in my hand, I'd heard that only one out of fifty applicants were admitted into med school. I kicked a harmless pebble into the roadside vegetation with as much force as possible. It was unlikely I'd make the cut, with only foreign credentials to my name. Plus, I'd be close to thirty——ancient! I'd have to pick something science-related to do. I'd work part-time to support myself. There. It was done. I'd just made a momentous decision. In a curious way, the cage around my lungs eased.

I stopped in my tracks and shut my eyes tight until the black and red swirled, then became hazy. Contrary to the "prediction" that had been stuffed down my throat all my life, the fates had decided I wasn't doctor material. That so-called fortune teller hadn't foreseen these obstacles.

When I'd been accepted into med school three years back, the funny thing was I'd almost believed the prophecy. What a joke! A tear of self-pity snuck out, but I chastised myself for wallowing in what-might-have-beens. I was safe and in paradise for the moment. The universities *still* hadn't opened up. Thank goodness I hadn't stuck around to wait.

A whinnying sound made me open my eyes, and I stood dead still. A couple of wild ivory ponies were chomping on grass less than fifty feet away on the other side of the road. One raised his head and snorted into the air. I couldn't help but smile at his irreverent commentary and the drops of moisture that condensed around his upraised muzzle like a halo. He was so close I could see faint brown speckles on his coat. There were flies on his long silky eyelashes that I wanted to brush off and I wished I could touch his soft, wavy mane. A muddy path with hoofprint impressions took off to my right.

Why not? I squared my shoulders to face the golden sunshine and blue sky. Impulsively, I crossed the road to follow the trail to Three Cliffs Bay. The muddy path led to a beckoning, ruined stone castle. I stopped by the two-foot-thick ruined walls to face the Bristol Channel. Pennard Castle had partially crumbled away and had no roof. Grass grew on its foundations.

I'd learned that it was over eight hundred years old. What a view a king would have had from this commanding vantage point, with a spectacular view of the ocean and the ponies! The sparkling stream meandered, then widened to meet the sea at a golden sandy beach far below.

This cold, sturdy wall had held strong for eight centuries. Surely, I could hold on to my own crumbling defenses a little longer. I was safe. I was loved. I'd just captured a moment of bliss that no one could wrest from me.

"Thank you," I whispered to the majestic panorama laid out in front of me.

As the weather grew colder, I attempted to befriend the birds in the terraced garden by sitting motionless for hours, my outstretched fingers festooned with breadcrumbs. For days, I heard only the whirring of flapping wings, inches from my face, as birds approached, then panicked, too timid to take my offering. One unforgettable, frosty morning, a fat robin redbreast finally landed on my index finger. I froze and held my breath, savoring the exquisite tickle of his dainty bird feet. He delicately plucked the bread from my hand, all the while watching me suspiciously with black beady eyes. The other birds watched keenly, and soon they too followed.

In those moments of communion, I was truly at one with my environment. I understood that Bible phrase, "My cup runneth over." Over that autumn, the robins, sparrows, and chaffinches hung out in the bushes, then flew toward me as I walked to my perch. I became their best friend. Whoever coined the word "birdbrain" doesn't know that those birds learned fast and grew fat. I learned that my patience could reap incredible rewards.

Except for occasional skinny blue aerograms, contact with my family was nonexistent. Telephone calls were phenomenally expensive, so I never dared ask to place a call. Every newsy letter that came my way made me tear up. I missed them so much. My parents had restarted the green card application process. Uncle Arul, a professor of civil engineering at the University of California, Davis, said he had a friend in the biochemistry department whom I could talk to when I arrived.

Hopes for a quick fix to my visa problem faded fast. My parents had repeatedly begged the visa office to review and expedite my case, even turning to Vic Fazio, their congressman, who wrote a letter on my behalf, but the immigration office refused to budge. As weeks crawled by, it seemed that nothing could break the impasse of the slowly churning machinery stalling the green card in bureaucratic sludge.

The sloth-like process made me hate all things American. I knew it was childish to condemn the whole nation before I'd even made it out there, but in my helpless state of limbo, I was furious that there was no humanitarian gesture that would allow me to get back in school again, so I could do *something* with my life.

John Clayden was a rock throughout. He drove me to the Home Office in London to successfully extend my visitor's visa each time it was close to expiring. Knowing I was frustrated, disappointed, and likely kicking my heels for several months, John helped compose a letter to several medical schools in England. I explained that I'd completed three years of med school but was a temporary refugee/visitor. Would they consider offering me a transfer?

It was a long shot, but as I waited to hear back, I became hopeful. Was *this* the road that would fulfill the darn prophecy that I still clung to from time to time? I waited nervously but received only thin envelopes with politely worded rejections, each of which sank my withering self-esteem further into my Wellies.

About two months after I arrived in Parkmill, I made a breakfast run to Shepherds. A Mozart piano concerto tinkled out of their speakers.

"Lovely music. Know anybody who might have a piano that I could practice on?" I asked one of the clerks.

"No, I don't, dear, but the manager might know somebody. You just wait right here, dear," she announced before scurrying to the back of the store.

I rummaged through my carton of eggs to make sure they were all intact as I thought back to my early immersion in classical music. We'd always had a piano in Kumasi because my mom played. If I shut my eyes, I could recapture the delicious doggy smell of my black spaniel, Bonjo, and his reassuring warmth as I squished my slight seven-year-old body on the floor against his back while my mom played Beethoven's piano sonata in F minor. I would lie on the floor reading while the beautiful sonata filled all the empty spaces in the house. She'd committed all twenty-seven pages of the four movements to memory in preparation for her piano teaching certification exam. I had every note memorized too.

I winced when her piano teacher rapped her knuckles with a wooden ruler when she messed up. She played the adagio in such a gentle, evocative way, but my favorite was the final majestic prestissimo. I drummed my fingers along in triumph, as if I was playing along with her.

My sister Viji and I passed eight years of piano exams administered by English examiners who flew to Ghana from the prestigious Royal Schools of Music in London. I'd walk into a big scary room with a giant shiny black grand piano, wearing the best dress I owned. A male examiner dressed in an impeccable black suit and highly polished shoes would be there as well. Every examiner looked over a hundred years old, with cracks on their faces. They tried to look harmless but failed miserably.

"Play the scale of C minor, staccato, with your left hand," a disembodied voice would chant. Then there were more scales and an aural test. How I passed those tests each year is a mystery. My mother finally passed her final teaching exam and received her diploma and the title "Licentiate of the Royal Schools of Music."

The back door squeaked open as the clerk returned.

"Good news, there's an organ in Mt. Pisgah, that old chapel down the road. Hasn't been played for years because we've had no organist in Parkmill. Call Margaret, the church secretary. She'll tell you what to do." She handed me a piece of paper with a number scrawled on it.

I met Margaret outside the church the following Sunday. She had curly red hair and a bright smile that lit up her round, cheery face. She handed me a large brass key to the church.

"You can stop to play the organ whenever you like, love. In fact, if you're so inclined, maybe you'll play for our Sunday worship? We don't have an organist, and you know the Welsh, we *love* to sing."

And so it was that I was given access to the quaint old chapel whenever I wanted. It wasn't even a hundred yards from our cottage, and I'd walked past it dozens of times but had never ventured in. The very next day, I decided to check it out before my morning walk. An 1820s stone edifice, it exuded an Old World charm with a tall, imposing arched entryway.

Once inside, there was the typical chill and hazy golden light from stained glass and hushed reverence that I always associate with places of worship. I shivered as I stared at the intimate interior, with its rows of dark wood pews. The organ sat on a raised platform to the left of the pulpit, and tall organ pipes rose intimidatingly on either side. The keys were dusty, and the ivory was missing. I was too shy to try it in case someone walked by, but I resolved to return later in the evening when no one was around. I'd played the organ in Kumasi a few times when the organist was out, but it always made me nervous.

I slipped out of the house after dinner wearing several layers of clothing and thick socks. It was the first time I'd ventured down that narrow street in the dark, and my Wellies echoed loudly down the eerie, unlit street. *A perfect night for a random serial killer to snatch me up and murder me*, I thought. Large puddles decorated the street, and there was no sidewalk, but thankfully not a car drove by. The good people of Parkmill were probably safe in bed.

The chapel appeared forbidding in the twilight shadows, and its long narrow windows and doorway glared at me like a monster, as if to challenge my entry to the hallowed grounds. Before I lost my nerve, I fumbled in the near darkness to open the massive wooden side door, gritting my teeth at the horrifying grating noise the huge wooden door made as it scraped the floor. I reached for the light switch inside, slammed the door behind me, and locked myself inside, leaning back against the door and blowing out several unsteady breaths. My heart hammered in my ears, but gradually I summoned the courage to move away from the door and told myself off for being such a baby.

I dusted off the organ seat cushion and sat down to play. My fingers trembled as they hovered over the keyboard. Then I gently lowered both hands to play a C major chord on the dusty keys. With a thunderclap, the pipes beside me blasted out a sonorous, earth-shattering proclamation that sounded like all the doors to hell had been flung open at once. Every bone in my body vibrated as I leapt up from the seat.

In abject horror, I noticed that the volume pedal of the organ was pushed all the way down! Reverberations loud enough to awaken dead spirits continued up and down the tall organ pipes. I could have sworn that even the statue of Jesus across from me opened his eyes wide at the desecration caused by that roaring clamor. Frozen in place, I half expected a cadre of villagers to descend on the chapel brandishing pitchforks. When nothing happened, apart from my heart pounding out of my breastbone, I plucked up the courage to return, then tried again.

The Village Organist

The organ became my best friend over the next few weeks. For hours at a time after supper, I played scales and what I could recall of my former Mozart and Bach examination pieces. Although it improved over time, the majestic organ's growl always made me feel like a participant in my own personal horror story—you know, the part where the organ swells, the bad guy enters the chapel, and someone gets killed. . . .

I told Margaret I'd take a stab at playing for a church service as long as I knew the hymns ahead of time. The dark-haired, youthful-looking pastor was excited to meet me and gave me five songs to prepare. I explained that I was a classically trained pianist, not an organist, but I'd do my best.

"Don't worry about a thing, Lally. We're so fortunate to have you," he assured me. "*Some* accompaniment will be better than none at all. The Welsh *do* love to sing, you know."

I practiced as if my life depended on it every night that week, unsure if it were the cold, my nerves, or both that occasionally froze my fingers on the keys. I'll never forget that first Sunday worship service. The congregation was composed of only five people, with an average age of eighty. At least two of them had hearing aids, so hopefully my mistakes would get by. By the final hymn, I was actually sweating, but I had managed to avoid running out screaming with nerves. A couple of parishioners stuck around to chat. They said they really appreciated the organ, and one woman placed an outstretched hand on my shoulder.

"Just so you know, love, it made such a difference to hear that old organ going again. One thing you should know, love, is that the Welsh *do* love to sing."

The pastor wanted to pay me, but I explained that as a visitor, I was not allowed to earn wages, but that as long as I was in Parkmill I'd be happy to oblige. I skipped down the road that afternoon, thrilled that I was finally going to be put to use in the village. After Sunday, word got around the village that the chapel now had "an organist," so by the time John and Judy showed up for a service in early autumn, I'd taught myself a rudimentary way to handle the pedals, and the congregation had swelled to over twenty. In a strange way, they'd become proud parents, and I loved them for showing up even though they were Quakers.

I was delighted to finally give back to that warm, intimate Welsh village community. When village parishioners who recognized me from church nodded as they passed on the street, it gave me a little thrill. I'd already felt welcome in Parkmill, but my new role cemented me as one of *them* now.

Just before Christmas, the church committee surprised me with a lovely dinner to thank me for my volunteer work. The pastor gave a short speech of appreciation, and they presented me with a framed photograph of Three Cliffs Bay. Their kind and unexpected salute brought tears to my eyes.

And so it was that a lost twenty-two-year-old Sri Lankan girl, recently from Ghana, marooned in South Wales, a forced visitor en route to California, became the sole organist for a congregation of a couple dozen senior citizens in a 162-year-old chapel in Parkmill, South Wales.

Seven

Christmas Plans

Two weeks before Christmas, I sat at our small wooden kitchen table with John while Judy bustled around at the stove. The smell of sage was thick in the air. With oven-mitted hands, she took her famous steaming nut roast from the oven and sliced it on the wooden cutting board. I salivated when she dished out a generous helping of hazelnut and chestnut roast with gravy, wild rice, and mushrooms onto my warmed plate.

"This will be your first Christmas without your family, Lally. Would you like it if we had someone over to stay with us?" She tucked a stray strand of lank black hair behind her ear and shot a quick look at John, as if nervous that she had suggested a plan without consulting him first. He raised an eyebrow and gave a slight nod before jumping in.

"Yeah, Lally, and it's *our* first Christmas here also, isn't it, Judy?"

They both turned to me. I blinked quickly to stem the moisture in my eyes as I contemplated spending my first ever Christmas without my family. How had so many months gone by with no word on my green card approval?

"I'd love it," I said, and took a quick sip of water, "but please don't do it just for me. You've both taken so much trouble over me already."

"You keep saying you're trouble, Lally, but honestly, you're no trouble at all, as I've told you so many times." John shook his head and chomped down on an extra-large forkful of roast. I didn't understand why he was so irritated. Maybe I'd overplayed my gratitude card? The knowledge that I was a refugee with no specific departure date always hung on me like a weight around my neck. Judy reached for the nut loaf.

"Seconds, anyone?"

"I'll take some," I responded.

"John, how about asking Mike?" Judy asked. "He got along so well with Lally when she met him in Edinburgh."

"Oh, yeah, Mike! Mike's fun," I announced. My pulse picked up. Mike Downie was Scottish and a close friend of the Claydens. He'd visited them in Kumasi and attended our folk dances. We got along so well that my friends had tagged him "Lally's boyfriend, Micky Dee," even though we'd never been romantically involved.

"Mike can't make it— just got himself a new job in Edinburgh," John said, shaking his head.

"Darn, what a shame," I said. I was truly disappointed. John and Judy were old enough to be my parents, and although I really loved their company, it would have been wonderful to have someone my age come to visit.

After dessert of delicious fried bananas topped with cream, I snagged a SAVE THE WHALES tea towel and helped Judy dry the dishes that emerged from the soap suds.

"What about John Russell? Lally knows *him*," Judy suggested as she turned to face John. The dripping dinner plate wobbled in her grip. I noticed a little flush on her cheeks that John missed.

John Russell. The JR I knew had flirted with every woman he met in Kumasi. Judy had seemed a trifle breathless when she told me about his visit to Glasgow last year. I wondered if he'd made a pass at her. I wouldn't have put it past JR to be back to his old tricks again, even if he and Judy were married to other people.

As I hung up my tea towel, I thought about the way JR told stories that left me in stitches. He was their age, not mine, but if he showed up, he'd brighten up the holidays for sure.

"Called and asked him already," John said. "Said he wasn't in the mood to celebrate Christmas. He's just finalizing his divorce from Ann." John stacked placemats in a kitchen drawer and slammed it shut.

"Divorced? About time too," I observed. "She should have divorced him years back when he cheated on her with all his Ghanaian girlfriends." I rearranged the salt and pepper shakers. "By the way, whatever happened to Essie, that girlfriend who came on safari with us? Are they together now?"

"It's an on-again, off-again relationship." John laughed shortly without humor. "They get along for a bit, but then they argue, he gets tired of her and sends her back to Ghana."

Judy kept her face averted. "I'm going to sit by the fire next door," she announced. "Anyone want to join me?"

"I'll come," I said, following her out.

"I'll join you soon. Think I'll pour out some Glenfiddich. Anyone need a drink?" John headed to the adjoining larder.

"No thanks," we chorused in unison.

In the living room, Judy picked up her dog-eared Lands' End catalog and sat on the couch, while I got comfy in my customary perch on the carpet by the fireplace. I used the poker and bellows to get the fire burning brighter, then sat back on my heels to admire my handiwork as the logs sparked and crackled.

What a shame that the only two friends we had in common from Ghana, Mike Downie and JR, couldn't make it for the holidays. I'd grown up with whirlwind Christmas celebrations in Kumasi with what seemed like a huge party every night and evenings full of life and color. After five months in Wales, my social calendar was essentially nonexistent. Playing the organ for an audience of octogenarians didn't quite cut it. If only we could have a visitor . . . anybody, *anybody!* Yes, even that scoundrel, JR.

John nursed a fluted glass of amber malt whiskey when he joined Judy on the couch. He absentmindedly patted her knee, then took a deep sip before leaning back with a sigh.

"The pyromaniac is at it again," he chuckled, turning to Judy.

"That's *your* fault, John. You taught Lally how to keep it from going out." Judy smiled.

Feeling awkward in the intimacy of their moment together, I turned my back to them and did some unnecessary poking. Then I replaced the heavy iron poker in its basket before I sat cross-legged on the floor to face John.

"Hey, John, I know you said you asked John Russell and he said no, but what if *I* ask him to come over? If he's recovering from his divorce, spending time with the three of us will cheer him up. Who wouldn't fall in love with the Gower? And we could play cards, the four of us. Back in Kumasi, we played cards at my parents' house till the wee hours. What do you say? Bet I could sell the Gower to him. I've been told I have pretty good powers of persuasion, and I'm good at letter writing."

Judy lowered her catalog with an enigmatic half smile and turned to John, who appeared astonished.

"By all means, Lally." He raised his glass and took a long sip. "Go for it. Coming from you, who knows? He just might change his mind. Go ahead, see if he responds. He's teaching in Canterbury, and we're in the same field, so we'd have lots to talk about if he came over." He set his glass down. "How about it, Judy? Guess she'll have to slather on that Lally charm."

"Sure, John." Judy turned to face me. "Lally, sure, go for it. I have his address for you when you need it." She tucked her hair behind her ear. Again her cheeks were flushed—from the heat or the conversation, it was hard to tell.

That night I crafted a short persuasive letter to JR. I told him about Three Cliffs Bay and the beautiful Welsh coast. I said it would be nice to have him join us for Christmas, and we could play card games. Would he reconsider? A week later, John Clayden announced that JR had changed his mind. He'd spend two weeks with us and leave after the New Year.

I was thrilled that my letter had made a difference. He'd cheated on his wife and was quite the womanizer. On the other hand, he liked cards and had a keen sense of adventure. He'd crossed the Sahara Desert with three other men in a jeep when he left Ghana and probably had tons of stories to share. JR's tales made me laugh till my belly hurt. For my first Christmas without family, the one thing I needed more than anything was a good belly laugh.

Eight

Caving

The day JR was slated to arrive, I was chopping garlic, ginger, and onions for dinner when John Clayden's olive-green Renault cruised slowly past the kitchen window. My heart rate picked up. I'd last seen JR three years back at the Kumasi badminton courts. His visit was bound to infuse excitement into our predictable daily routine.

For some reason I felt inordinately shy when JR walked in with John. I wondered what he thought about my bold invitation. At six feet four, he stood a full head taller than my host. An errant lock of wavy golden-brown hair hung on his forehead. He wore jeans, a dark blue sweatshirt, and a voluminous gray down jacket. It was hard to believe he was forty-something—he seemed more like thirty to me. Maybe it was the jeans. The Claydens never donned jeans.

"Hullo, Lally, you look well," JR remarked as he hung up his coat. He had prominent biceps. "That jaunty brown beret looks good. Suppose it was too hot to wear a beret in Kumasi, huh, John?" He turned to John, and they snickered.

"I wear a beret all the time." Heat rose to my cheeks at his offhand compliment.

Over dinner JR caught us up on his new passion, running. He was competing in half marathons, biking, and lifting weights. No wonder he had muscles! After dinner I showed off my fire-lighting skills. JR took the armchair facing the Claydens on the couch, and I sat by the fire. The combination of my full stomach, the warmth from the fireplace, and the excitement of having a new visitor made me supremely content.

The men sipped whiskeys as JR described his Saharan adventures. He had us in stitches when he described how Tuaregs had confiscated his camera. Judy was quite different from her usual shadowy self. She giggled uncontrollably at JR's stories, even though she wasn't drinking. She'd taken extra care over her hair, which was silky and gleamed in the firelight. John sank back on the couch, his feet propped up on a small hassock. He drank a little more than usual but was comfortable yielding the floor to JR. I glanced around at the three of them having such a good time, and it struck me afresh that I'd orchestrated this lovely evening simply by writing a letter.

JR switched to talking about his new job in Canterbury and the house he'd bought.

"It's a beautiful city, Canterbury. Canterbury Cathedral's dead center, a short walk from my house." He stretched his long legs out toward the fireplace in my direction. "You'd love it there, Lally," he nodded at me. "You should all visit once I've settled in. The city center is enclosed in double-layered Roman walls."

"Sounds dreamy, but I'll be gone soon. Expect I'll have my green card any time now," I said.

John and JR started talking about their lecturing work, and I checked out of the discussion, but JR kept throwing me glances as if to include me when he could. Something about his presence made me self-conscious. Maybe it was because the Claydens were a couple, and we were a couple by default. I thought about the one time JR had asked me out to lunch in Kumasi, shortly before the med school closed down.

I was halfway through the two-mile walk home from med school when he'd pulled up to a stop beside me in his sporty red two-door Ford hatchback.

"Hi, Lally, I'm headed to Chopsticks. Want to join me for lunch?"

Chopsticks was my favorite Chinese restaurant in Kumasi. They made the best spring rolls in the world. I was flattered and shocked at the same time. Shocked more than flattered.

"No thanks," I said automatically, ignoring the plea from my growling stomach. "I'd like to, but I can't, John. What would people think if they saw us together? You're married."

"It's just *lunch*, Lally." He'd looked exasperated as he removed a hand from the wheel to brush it through his golden-brown curls. Then his hazel eyes squinted, and he shot me a mischievous smile. "Anyway, who cares what 'people' think?"

"*I* care what people think, John."

"I only asked because I enjoy your company, Lally." The smile had left his face. He stared through the windshield for a second, then turned a cold glare on me. "Fine, forget it." Clearly he was annoyed at being rebuffed. I figured women swarmed around him like bees to nectar.

After an uncomfortable silence, he sped away, leaving a dust cloud in his wake. He'd not even given me the courtesy of offering me a ride home, even though he was headed the same way, and I was drenched with sweat in the sweltering noon heat. What a jerk he was, to act like a child because I turned him down. I was glad I'd refused his offer.

Back in Parkmill, I shook off the memory and rose from my seat by the fireplace.

"Hot chocolate, anyone?" I returned from the kitchen with two steaming mugs of cocoa for Judy and me. When I handed Judy her mug, JR's eyes followed my every move, even though he continued to talk shop with John. I basked contentedly in the warmth of the crackling logs as I sipped my chocolate. Hundreds of years back, this gigantic fireplace had heated the entire inn. It was still the only heat source for the cottage. The conversation flowed around me like warm milk.

"I heard there are tons of limestone caves in the Gower," JR said, after a brief lull in the conversation. "Anyone fancy a caving expedition?" He fixed his gaze on me. "How about you, Lally?"

All three of them looked at me.

I brightened and straightened up. "Caving? Yes, sure! I've never been in a cave before, but I love to explore!" If JR had made it across the Sahara, I could probably trust him to be a good cave guide.

"Last thing *I* want is to get mucky in a muddy cave," John responded, "but I'm sure you'll enjoy it, Lally." He gave a short laugh, took a large slug of whiskey, and set his glass down a little too hard. "Judy, how about you?"

"No, sorry, count me out. I'm claustrophobic." She tucked her hair behind her ear and picked at a tassel hanging from the neckline of her shirt. "The Swansea library has many good books about the limestone caves out here. In fact, many tourists come to the Gower specifically to go spelunking."

Two days later, Judy fixed us a hearty breakfast of eggs and bacon before our first cave tour. JR had *The Caves of the Gower* in his backpack. Judy lent me her waterproof jacket, and I wore my trusty olive-green Wellies. From my perch in the back seat of John's car, I noticed fine wrinkles on JR's neck, which reminded me that he was almost twenty years older. John dropped us off at a cliff near a sea cave.

"Don't worry, I'll deliver Lally back in time for supper . . . as long as we don't both drown." JR chuckled as John waved to us before heading to the car. JR and I scrambled down the cliff to a sandy beach to search for the entrance to the sea cave. We eventually discovered a forbidding-looking black cave with a lot of frothy seawater blocking the entrance. We waited till the tide went out farther. I followed JR in with some trepidation, aware that he was a womanizer my parents' age, but I'd known him so long that I trusted him not to make a pass.

Once inside, it was thrilling to explore the glistening cave. The barnacle-encrusted walls shimmered when I shone the flashlight on them. The roar of the surf outside echoed eerily off the cave's walls, and there was a damp, salty tang in the air. I took several nervous glances as waves lapped in. Clearly, we'd be trapped in there if we stayed too long and would most certainly drown. The inherent danger of this kind of exploration gave me an intense adrenaline rush.

Shortly afterward, we left the cave and headed up to a rocky cliff overlook. We sat on a wind-sheltered outcropping of rocks, snacked on apples and crackers, and took in the booming majesty of the eternal battle between the ocean and the ledge. Surf slammed into the rock face with a sharp cracking noise, throwing water hundreds of feet into the air. It then subsided in a frothy show. I was entranced, but after a few minutes the salty ocean air made me shiver. John frowned and removed his left arm from his thick down jacket, holding it open.

"There's room in here for both of us. Want to get warm?"

After a microsecond of hesitation, with my heart beating loud enough to scare stray sheep away, it seemed like the most natural thing in the world to sit against one side of his warm body with an arm threaded into his left sleeve. I was very tense at the intimate contact but enormously relieved that it was so deliciously warm in that cocoon of jacket and body, while the icy wind whipped my hair around my face. Thankfully, he made no move toward further physical contact, so I relaxed after a few moments. We sat together for almost a half hour, just watching the magnificent spectacle in front of us. We said very little.

When the sun dipped, it became colder still, and John suggested we head back.

As I followed him into the approaching twilight, the memory of the comforting blanket of warmth from his body clung to me, and my heart felt light. John would be gone in less than two short weeks, but nothing could take away the sheer contentment of those magical moments by the ocean. With my diet of Harlequin romances, John fit the tall, dark, handsome, and most definitely the bad-boy protagonist. He was so easy to get along with, and his apparent appreciation of nature mirrored mine. I also liked that he could tolerate silence, rather than fill it with inane chatter. His quiet camaraderie had heightened the languorous splendor of the beautiful Gower coast. Peace. True peace. A welcome respite from months of angst and turmoil.

For the first time since I got to Wales, I didn't feel like a refugee.

Four days later, JR joined us for breakfast proclaiming, "Lally, we should try Tooth Cave today." His eyes sparkled, and his excitement was infectious.

"*Tooth* cave?"

"Yes, there's a stalagmite formation inside like a tooth, apparently. It's definitely not for beginners—in fact, they recommend that you join a caving club before you attempt it—but I know you can do it. She's quite the daredevil, you know." He winked at John. "The only problem is we're going to get very muddy. I looked at the cave diagram last night, and there are several wet sumps that we may have to wriggle through. What do you think? Ready for a challenge?"

"Umm . . . maybe, if you think I can handle it." My knees shook with excitement. I was thrilled that he thought I was ready for something dangerous.

"You can," he said with conviction. He helped himself to granola and milk. "I'll leave our contact information at Shepherds before we start out. That way someone can come looking for us if we aren't back at, say, four o'clock."

John Clayden's head snapped up. "John," he said, "Lally's parents have left her in our charge. Are you sure this is a good idea?"

"I'll be fine!" I interjected indignantly, bristling at John's parental tone. *I'm twenty-two!* I wanted to scream but resisted. Judy looked nervous also, but she didn't say a word.

"Don't worry, John," JR said smoothly, taking a spoonful of cereal before he continued. "I'll make sure she's safe." He turned to me. "What do you say, Lally?"

"Yup, count me in," I said. "I'll just quit if it's too difficult." I shuddered inwardly, imagining how awful it would be to drown in the sump of a cave, like a rat.

JR winked and smiled as if to congratulate me. John intercepted the wink, and I caught an irritated look on his face before he stood up with his empty cereal bowl.

"Well, Judy, since the two of them are ditching us today, fancy a walk with me to Three Cliffs?"

"Yes, John, I'd like that." Judy said. "I'll have supper made for you when you get back from the cave. Please take care."

At the entrance to Tooth Cave, my stomach lurched when I realized that, for starters, we had to navigate a fifteen-foot drop into pitch-blackness. JR shone his torch around the yawning cavernous hole and discovered a rope that dangled into it.

"I'll go down first to make sure the rope's still good, and then I'll guide you down, okay?" he said. "Can you shine your torch while I go down?"

"Of course," I murmured, thinking I was stupid to have agreed to this adventure so readily.

Caving

JR was very patient with me as I descended. I clung to the rope for dear life while I sought footholds, afraid I might crash down on the rocks below, but I was reassured by his calm voice explaining how to maneuver each foothold and handhold. Once I joined him at the bottom and stood on a flat muddy platform, I was sweating with the effort but basking in his effusive praise.

A dim, rocky passage was the only way forward. He asked me to stay put while he scouted the best way through. In some areas we had to wriggle through rocks like worms. I learned to exhale to make it through the very tight spaces. It was more than worth it; half an hour later, the rocky passage opened out into a huge stalactite-encrusted chamber, and we came up to the gleaming five-by-three-foot yellowed stalactite—like a large rotting ivory molar from a giant's mouth—that gave the cave its name.

After an hour of muddy exploration, we stopped at a place where the cave floor dipped steeply. The passage was flooded with a wall of dark water.

"Here's the first sump," JR announced. "According to the cave guide, it's in the shape of a U. There's a bit of air at the top. If we can swim through it, it opens up on the other side, and the cave passage keeps going."

"Ugh." I shivered. "Is this a place that could quickly fill up if it rains and trap us underground? I'm not going farther, John. I'll wait here, but you go ahead if you want to."

"Okay, I'm going to wade in and check it out. It may be a very short flooded section. Sit tight, okay? I'll be right back."

"Sounds crazy, John. You'd better not drown, because I'm going to need you to help me get out of this cave!" He snickered and disappeared into the black water. I heard splashing sounds, then nothing. A full five minutes went by. I was shivering and scared when he suddenly materialized again, pale and drenched but with a gleam of excitement in his hazel eyes.

"It's too deep, let's head back," he said, in response to my concerned frown. Suddenly, with no warning, he leaned toward me, held me close, and planted a cold, gentle kiss on my lips. Too shocked to pull back, I froze, thinking how incongruous it was that I had received my first romantic kiss, caked with mud in the innards of a dank cave. A strange new emotion coursed through me. I wondered if my body was shaking from the cold, or from this transition in our relationship. And just as suddenly, he pulled away from me and said with a laugh that we'd better get out before we drowned.

As we emerged from the cave for the short walk home, I remained mostly silent, unsure what to make of the whirlwind of conflicting thoughts that spiraled through my brain. There was no future with JR. He was twenty years older—almost my dad's age. He'd leave for Canterbury in a few days, and soon I'd be in California. He was a notorious womanizer who'd openly cheated on his wife. This was simply the way he operated with women. I meant nothing to him. I'd simply been available at the right place and time—a Christmas diversion.

A couple headed our way as we traipsed through a meadow on our way back home. I wondered what they made of the two of us, caked head to toe in mud, like walking brown slugs. In true British fashion, they said nothing and merely averted their gazes as they drew close.

John pointed back the way we'd come. "You might want to watch out," he warned them in a serious tone as we passed. "This path gets really muddy a little farther on."

The shocked look on their faces was priceless, and I burst out laughing when we were out of earshot.

After dinner that night, the four of us sat in the living room by the fireplace, and JR caught the Claydens up on our adventure. John gave an exaggerated yawn and said he was going to turn in shortly. He extinguished the fire by pushing aside the glowing logs. Judy remained on the couch chatting with

JR while I put the mugs away in the kitchen, wished them all goodnight, and headed for the stairwell.

I had just laid a hand on the banister when JR asked, "Hey, Lally, want to take a quick walk down the road to see if we can spot some owls?"

I hesitated and looked at the Claydens. They exchanged glances but did not say anything. John Clayden's forehead was etched with lines of concern, and Judy had spots of pink on her flushed face. She averted her face and headed to the kitchen.

"Sure, one minute, I'll get a jacket." I rushed upstairs, my heart pounding. When I came back down, pulling up the zip of the jacket, JR stood by the door. John and Judy were staring at the two of us. I sensed that they were upset at this turn of events but didn't know how to stop me from leaving.

"Goodnight," I sang out cheerily to mask the awkwardness of the moment.

Once outside, John reached for my hand as if it were the most natural thing in the world, and we slowly sauntered down the pitch-black street toward the chapel. After about fifty yards, he turned to face me.

"I have a confession. I didn't really come to see owls," he said, clutching my hand. He held on so tightly that I felt tremors in his rigid grip.

"I know," I murmured. Everything felt perfect when my tiny ninety-seven-pound frame was enveloped by over six feet of gorgeous, cave-exploring buddy. I was home. This time his mouth wasn't cold and wet from the cave. It was warm and exploring and made me tingle all over. He kissed me repeatedly, as if he couldn't get enough of me, all the while smoothing my body against his. I relaxed, feeling at one with the universe. Time stopped. Surprisingly, there was nothing awkward about the embrace. It was just right—just what my body had been yearning for as the end to a perfect day.

Suddenly, car headlights lit up the blackness of the narrow street. To my annoyance the car slowed, then stopped right beside us.

"C'mon, move along, both of you. Move along," a male voice ordered.

JR held me away from him but did not completely relinquish me, maintaining a hand around my waist.

It was a policeman!

"No romancing out in public," he said through the open car window. He kept the car idling, as if waiting for us to comply, so we turned and walked back to the house. JR gripped my hand very tightly all the way. I fumed that the dumb policeman had ruined the magic intimacy of the moment with his lousy timing.

As I snuggled under my comforter on my single bed ten minutes later, the memory of JR's warm, comforting grip and my still-racing heart told me everything I wanted to know, and also everything I didn't. Something had changed irrevocably, just as it was clear that our paths would never cross again. He was leaving in two days, and I'd fly to California the moment I got my green card. I lay awake till two in the morning with new and awakened longings for something. . . .

For something more.

Nine

An Ending

After JR left Parkmill, my restlessness became more pronounced. His absence magnified my underlying loneliness. Somehow, he'd ignited a spark in my heart with excitement this Christmas, but now I was bereft, feeling discarded and more alone than ever. I wondered if I'd subconsciously turned JR into a father figure to fill the void.

I thought about my family, and this brought a knot into my belly and a tearing sense of desolation as waves of homesickness surged. They'd left Ghana in March of 1983, and it was already January of 1984! How could ten months of turmoil and transition have sped by so fast? From their recent letters, I learned that Vimalan and Nimi had already switched grades and Viji had transferred to Sacramento State University from Sacramento City College. She'd passed me on the education train. How mortifying. They were all moving on, headed for new, exciting futures and making new friends. Meanwhile I was stagnating in Wales, unable to do anything but play the organ and help the Claydens with cooking and chores.

In short, I was becoming a true has-been.

As for the Claydens, after JR left, they appeared to expel a collective sigh of relief that their refugee was no longer in the claws of the big, bad womanizer. Judy sensed my despondency and tried to spend more time with me. Some weekends, we took drives to surrounding villages like Rhossili where we walked up to Worm's Head, a protrusion of land into the ocean. It could only be accessed for a few hours at low tide, or you'd be stuck on the head of the "worm" till the next day. Even as I yearned to be in America, I cherished those divine moments of relaxation in the splendor of the Welsh coast, grateful that fate had allowed me these unforgettable experiences.

To complicate everything, JR wrote to me almost *every single day*. It was mortifying, and I told him to stop, but he kept writing. I tried to be the first downstairs, to snag the letters before John woke up, but many times John got to them first. Although he never said a word to me, the disapproval on his face spoke volumes. He handed me the letters with a knowing look in his eye and handled the envelopes as if they were radioactive.

In the privacy of my bedroom, I devoured the long rambling letters, reading and rereading them, because they helped filter out my loneliness. He included detailed missives of his mundane daily activities and details about his ten-kilometer races. He told me I would love Canterbury and would be welcome to visit if I wanted to look around. It made me blush when he added that he missed me, and he always signed his letters, "Your John," which made me extremely apprehensive. He'd been in the Gower for only two weeks, but now he was moving way too fast. When I let him know that the Claydens were irritated by the sheer volume of letters, he told me to ignore them, that it was none of their business.

He sent me a cassette tape of Mendelssohn's *Hebrides* (*Fingal's Cave*) Overture to commemorate our caving exploits. I played it over and over, imagining our spelunking adventures as the violins captured the majesty of the ocean. He also sent me a silver Thai ankle chain that he claimed he'd picked up in an antique store. It was dainty, with wrought silver designs worked into the twisted links, and it fit perfectly around my ankle. He told me it would make him happy to imagine that I was wearing something he'd picked out specifically for me, and that each time I wore it, I was to remember that "a man" was thinking about me wearing it. That gave me goosebumps, but I fastened it around my ankle. The unaccustomed feel of cold metal against my skin reminded me of my secret, unsanctioned link with JR. I never took it off, not even in the shower.

At New Inn Cottage, things were changing rapidly in the weeks following Christmas. Judy started college courses in Bristol, so she was home only on weekends. The Claydens took on three sets of tenants: Yvonne, a psychology professor at Swansea with a blue streak in her blond hair; Chris, a PhD student who played trumpet; and Min and Dave, hippies with an adorable toddler daughter.

The tenants became my friends. I babysat for Min and Dave when I could. Chris and I tried out organ and trumpet duets at the church. Although I enjoyed their company, and the tenants were my age, I retreated to my room with a book when things got too chaotic. After months of just three of us in the inn, we now had eight people, including a two-year-old, in five rooms. It got really crazy on weekends when Judy was home, and I sensed that she was stressed with all the tenants around.

Yvonne was a hoot. She made it her mission to encourage shy, cloistered Lally to "live a little." The most liberal of the group, she tried, unsuccessfully, to get me to smoke pot. She introduced me to the Eurythmics, and we drove around in her Mini blasting her Annie Lennox tape. I shared with her how much I missed my family and also broached the JR complication.

Two months had now crawled by with no movement on my US visa. Despair weighed me down. I trudged into the kitchen one evening and interrupted an animated conversation between the Claydens. They stopped immediately, the moment they saw me, and I didn't have to be Hercule Poirot to figure out that I had featured prominently in the heated discussion. Ambushed by a frozen silence, I turned to Judy with a question in my eyes, but she refused to meet my gaze. Her face was beet red and shiny as she arranged dinner forks and knives while John drummed his fingers on the table. I'd anticipated a confrontation for weeks. They knew JR wrote to me daily, and from their nonverbal cues, they both disapproved of our alliance.

John scraped his chair back and stood up abruptly.

"Lally, we need to have a talk. Can you follow me to the garden, please?"

It was an order, not a request. I'd never seen John look this upset. His face was mottled red, purple, and white. Even the air around his face radiated heat. Without waiting for a response, he picked up his battery-powered lamp, turned on his heel, and headed upstairs to the top of the terraced garden.

I followed him meekly, with a sick feeling in my belly. My legs dragged as if I had donned iron boots, and my chest was encased in armor that stifled breathing. The frigid air outside made it even worse. Tons of questions hammered at me as we made our silent trek down the garden path to the wrought iron side gate that led to the main road. The lantern rocked in time with his stiff gait. I braced myself for a tirade that would likely feature JR. John finally stopped and turned his back to the gate to face me.

This was going to be bad.

His lamp formed a ghostly halo in the dark night. There were no streetlights, so without the lamp, it would have been pitch-black. A car drove by. After it passed, there was pin-drop silence. Even the crickets had shut up to brace themselves for what might come next. A fine mist hung in the air, and I smelled the rich, damp soil. I was freezing because I'd been too nervous to remember a jacket.

An Ending

He set the lamp on the bottom stone ledge. We were scarcely three feet apart. In the charged silence, I waited for him to begin. His face looked very serious, and he cleared his throat and shifted his stance as if he were uncomfortable.

"Lally, you've been with us almost a year."

I waited, kicking a harmless pebble with my boot.

"You're probably feeling crowded with all the tenants around. Believe me, it's a lot for me and Judy also. Maybe we shouldn't have taken on so many people here so fast." He gave a quick, humorless laugh. "Anyway . . . um, because it's so crowded, we were thinking . . ." He dropped his glance and looked away. "Listen, you've told us many times that you've got a place to stay with your uncle in North Wales, or the Asare girls in London. So, we were—we were discussing options, and . . . er . . . Judy and I think this may be a good time for you to move in with your uncle in North Wales until your visa is granted. It won't be much longer, Lally. It could come through any day now."

I said nothing, but tears rolled down my cheeks. I no longer felt cold.

"Is that it?" My tone was flat so I could hold back the sobs that threatened to explode.

"Well, actually, there's something else. Yvonne told Judy that you seem sad here. This is no life for a young person—stuck at home, unable to work or study. You've been cast adrift for so long, Lally, I'm sorry."

I hung my head. The tears chased down faster. I took a few ragged breaths and fixed my gaze on the garden path.

"And Judy's going to be back from Bristol for Easter. She's almost done with classes, so she'll be staying here permanently now." Again he shifted his posture and didn't seem to know where to look. "So, er . . . we thought maybe the timing would work out for you to . . . to maybe move out for a bit? What do you think?"

His words sputtered into silence. I hitched my fingers into my front pants pocket to brace myself, took a deep breath, and looked directly at him.

"Was there something . . . did I *do* something to upset you or Judy? Please tell me."

He shrugged. I noticed a minuscule shake of his head. He said nothing.

"Well, John, as you know, I've always had other places to stay, so it's fine. I want you to know how *grateful* I've been for . . . for *everything* you and Judy have done for me." My words were hesitant and sounded pathetic. "Is this something to do with John Russell? Ever since he came over, I've noticed that you and Judy seem angry with me for some reason."

John looked up at me with tight lips but did not respond. It was confirmation that much of this *was* all about JR.

"I'm twenty-three, John. I know you're worried, but I know what I'm doing."

Two cars drove by, their headlights lighting up the brick wall on the other side of the road.

"Do you?" He sounded furious. "Well, I'm a little concerned, Lally. I've seen how you keep sneaking off to the payphone down the road to talk to him. Judy and I wonder what your parents will think of us if this gets more serious."

"But—"

"Listen, Lally, we know John well. We've known him a lot longer than you have. When he was with Essie, he sent her packing whenever he got tired of her. Now he's writing to you every day and sending you little gift packages. He shouldn't be courting someone half his age, Lally. Not at a time when you're about to go off to America."

I saw the dark frown that spread over his face. "The two of you carrying on like this puts us in an awkward position. Your parents trusted us to watch over you, so you see—"

An Ending

I cut him off abruptly, anger replacing my sadness. "Listen, John, he's *divorced*. If I spend time talking or writing to him, that's my choice, isn't it?"

"But we feel we have to warn you—"

"I'm not stupid. I know about John. I know about Essie and how he cheated on his wife when he lived in Kumasi. We're just friends." I placed my hands defiantly on my hips.

There was silence for a few moments. The whole conversation felt unreal, as if my brain had been sucked out by a powerful vacuum. I scrunched my fingers together until they hurt.

"Okay. . . ." John turned to me. "Okay, so I'll call your uncle in North Wales to make arrangements—"

"I'll make my *own* arrangements, thank you." I mustered all the strength I had to make my voice as clinical as possible, so the hurt didn't seep out. I stared out at the dark and desolate roadway. How could he not only tell me to leave but also organize where I should go? It was insufferable to be made to feel like a recalcitrant child.

"When would you like me to move out?"

"We thought . . . um . . . *April*, maybe? How does that sound, Lally?"

Two weeks.

"Yes, yes, that's fine. I'll move out April first," I said hastily. Then all my barriers dissolved, and I broke down weeping. Huge tearing sobs wrenched through me. I'd imagined leaving the Claydens, but never, *never* like this. Images cascaded into my brain of their generosity this past year. I thought about the good times we'd had, not only in Wales, but also in Scotland and Ghana. I'd never imagined that such an incredible friendship could deteriorate like this. They'd spent thousands of pounds to cover all my expenses for so many months but never made me feel bad about it. In all the worst-case formulations, none of us could have guessed that my green card application would draw out this long. It was a perfect storm. Judy's return, the tenant stress. Now the JR piece had added yet another layer of complexity.

John took a couple of steps toward me, placed both arms around me, and held me close. He'd never hugged me before. I stood like a bedpost, completely drained and unresponsive. None of this felt real.

"Judy and I really care for you, Lally. A lot. You've been a great friend. Really."

"And I . . . I can't tell you how much . . . I'm going to miss . . . both of you." I sobbed into his chest. "You just took me in without hesitation, paid for *everything* I needed. Every single thing for almost a year! Who would do something like that? Who? Thank you so much, John. I don't know what to say or how to thank you."

He held me in that awkward bear hug, then planted a gentle kiss on my forehead, leaving his lips there for a moment. He'd never kissed me before. Given the gravity of our current discussion, it was strangely comforting. I think he was trying to say, in his own way, that he too was sorry it had to end in this fashion.

Still crying, I heard the door swing shut at the top of the garden and glanced up over his shoulder. Judy stood on the top terrace with her lantern in her hand, her hair cascading down her shoulders like an avenging angel. Despite the low light, I could tell from her posture that she was dumbfounded. I wanted to scream out to her that she was putting the wrong spin on this situation. John had never made even a shadow of a pass at me in all the months she was in Bristol.

"Jo—hn? John?" her voice trembled. There was absolute incredulity in her tone.

I pulled myself out of the embrace, and John stiffened up. The three of us were locked in a frozen tableau for a microsecond.

An Ending

"*John?*" she asked a third time, in a quavering voice. She walked unsteadily back into the house, allowing the door to bang shut after her. John picked up his lamp and stumbled up the path to follow her into the house. I was left with a tearing ache in my heart, and only the dark night sky and crickets for company.

Ten

April Fool

Two weeks later was April Fool's Day, the day I was to finally leave the Claydens. I woke up and stared at the ceiling, my body weighed down as if a dozen bowling balls had fallen on my stomach. How ironic that after years of friendship, I was leaving my beloved friends on a day reserved for jokesters. I replayed the frozen tableau when Judy saw John embracing me. She must have concluded that we'd been having an affair while she was away in Bristol. *How horrible! How mortifying!* I wanted, desperately, to correct that misapprehension, but I didn't know where to start. And if I said anything, it might make her suspicions worse. Then there was the JR complication. Judy had been so giggly and animated when he arrived at Christmas, but then he'd put me in his sights. Was she jealous that Lally, the young upstart, had stolen *both* the Johns she cared about?

As I pulled myself off the bed and shoved clothes into my open Samsonite, a kaleidoscope of images seared my brain. The many mouthwatering meals we'd had around the small kitchen table, Judy's nut roasts, her kedgeree and delicious desserts, the hours of togetherness and laughs in front of the fireplace before all the tenants showed up, the trips we'd taken together, the way John would blast out Elton John while unspeakably beautiful Scottish lochs whizzed by.

Then there were the thrilling camping trips, our walks in

the Lake District, and the many freezing ferry rides we'd taken to the outer Hebridean islands. I remembered how Judy had volunteered to teach us folk dances and how some villagers complimented me when I danced the Gay Gordons waltz at a Scottish ceilidh. The Claydens had even driven me to Galway, Ireland, and shown me such a good time. They'd taken in Lally the refugee for months at a time, asking for nothing in return. This was like losing my family all over again.

The suitcase was almost full, but as I picked up and thumbed through my diary, memories continued to flood in. I remembered the fairy tale move into this historic cottage and the painstaking way John taught me how to light a fire, until I became a pro. As I picked up a bus ticket that had dropped out, I thought about how I'd joined a busload of demonstrators to London to protest cruise missiles, with the Claydens' support. We'd taken sips of vodka from a shared bottle as we shouted, "Maggie, Maggie, Maggie! Out, out, out!" at 10 Downing Street.

I thought about the many, many times John had taken me to the Home Office in London to tirelessly fight for every British tourist visa extension, pledging financial support. I wiped my sore eyes. With virtually no sleep, I'd cried so hard that it was a miracle that more tears could still fall. With a final glance around the small room, my eyes lingered on the framed photo of Three Cliffs Bay on my nightstand, a gift from the church congregation. I gently packed the frame in a bunch of T-shirts in my suitcase. I would miss those wonderful people so much. Hopefully, they'd find a replacement organist soon.

The Claydens had become my "away" parents. How could I blame them for worrying about JR's influence on me? I loved them for their generosity. I absolutely adored them. And it hurt like crazy to leave like this. I'd romanticized multiple scenarios for the day I would finally leave, but not this. Never this. This was one huge sick joke.

The Fortune Teller's Prophecy

A loud commotion sounded from downstairs. *Now what?* Raised voices. It sounded like a big argument. I cracked open the door to eavesdrop. Yvonne was cussing out John. That much I heard. I heard her say "Lally" multiple times. Seemed like she was giving him a piece of her mind. The previous night, she'd taken me out for a goodbye drink and gone off on a long rant about the Claydens. She told me she felt they treated me like hired help and said she was glad I was leaving them. I told her she had it completely wrong and listed all the examples of their generosity for the many months I'd lived there. I told her that I'd taken on chores like laundry and cooking because it was the least I could do, as they covered all my living expenses. Yvonne would have none of it. Sounded to me like she was giving John a piece of her mind right now as well.

I sighed. The yelling continued, adding to the sick feeling in the pit of my stomach. Why had she picked this incredibly emotional moment to chastise the Claydens? What if John thought that I'd complained to Yvonne last night? No, no, no! I wanted her to stop!

Yvonne shouted out loudly, "Lally, you coming down? Hurry, or you'll miss your train! Yes, John, I'm dropping her off at the station. I'll drive right back to settle the rent. C'mon, Lally, let's go!" Her voice was more urgent now.

"Be right there!" I breathed a ragged sigh, hefted my suitcase to the ground, and took one last fond look around the quaint room with its whitewashed walls. Through my window, I treated my eyes to the tiny road outside and the beautiful bubbling creek just beyond until tears blurred the vegetation. My home away from home was home no longer. I trudged outside and shut the door one final time. The familiar click filled me with desolation because it sounded so final.

Yvonne would drop me off at the Swansea station for the train to London. I'd spend a few days with Patricia and Elizabeth

April Fool

Asare, my Kumasi friends, and then make my way to my uncle Nava's home in North Wales. Surely the darned green card would come through any day.

I dragged the suitcase down the steep stairs and into the kitchen. John sat in there, his face mottled with spots of anger. I averted my tearstained face and mumbled goodbye as I walked to the kitchen door. For the first time ever, John didn't jump up to help me or insist on loading my suitcase into Yvonne's car. Judy was nowhere to be seen. I figured she had probably gone out in the garden to avoid the drama.

"Please tell Judy bye from me. I have to go. I'm late," I told him simply. My words were flat and lifeless.

Before I stepped outside, he raised his hand, index finger extended, as if delivering a lecture.

"While you're in Britain, we're responsible for you, Lally. We'll have to know *every place* you stay once you leave, so we don't get in trouble with the Home Office. Before you leave the Asares, give me your next address as soon as you know it, okay?" His blue eyes bored into mine as he drummed his fingers on the table. I knew this was a veiled threat that I should avoid going anywhere near JR. I was furious that he was treating me like a child—worse still, a child who could no longer be trusted.

"I'll go to my uncle Nava's home next in North Wales. You have his information. Bye, John. Thank you for *everything*. Tell Judy . . ." I was too overcome with emotion to continue, and I looked away to hide my tearstained face. Shrugging my handbag higher on my shoulder, I headed through the door.

Outside, Yvonne's Mini was parked just behind the cottage.

"Get in, get in the car, Lally, let's go . . . c'mon." She gestured urgently toward her car.

I increased my pace, puzzled at the tension in her voice. She snatched my suitcase, threw it into the trunk, and jumped into the driver's seat beside me as I blindly reached for my seat belt.

"Wha—what's going on?"

"Shut the door, shut the door!" she screamed as we pulled out. I grabbed my swinging door and slammed it shut, only to be shocked by the vision of a purple-faced John Clayden blocking our path. He'd obviously raced out from the kitchen and now stood in front of the Mini in the middle of the road. Yvonne screeched her brakes to avoid hitting him, and he approached and began drumming his hands on the bonnet of the car.

"Pay the rent, pay the rent!" he chanted. He then moved over to Yvonne's side, banged on the roof of the car and yelled, "Get back inside now, Yvonne! Pay the rent! You can't leave without paying the rent, you hear me?" I could not have conjured up a more surreal scene.

"I'll drop Lally off first, so she doesn't miss her train, and then I'll come back and—"

"No, you won't! Get back in now, and *pay the fucking rent!*" He banged on the car to emphasize each word.

"Fuck you, fuck you! Lally will miss her train!" Yvonne mouthed out a string of obscenities that enraged John even further. He continued to block the car's progress and thumped some more. I was scared and confused. In all the years I'd known him, I'd never seen him act this way.

Yvonne continued swearing, but she finally stepped out, leaving the engine running, and followed John back in. She appeared oblivious to the fact that the Mini was parked in the middle of the narrow road, blocking traffic in both directions.

When she emerged a few moments later, she was alone, and her face was brick red. Her fingers shook on the wheel, but she remained silent as she drove past the house, extending her arm through her window with her middle finger raised. After we passed the house, she fiddled around blindly and pushed in her Eurythmics tape. Annie Lennox crooned, "Here comes the rain again," and somehow it was the perfect music for that hellish morning. I remained silent. My mind was a jumbled roller coaster anyway.

"I gave John and Judy a piece of my mind this morning," Yvonne remarked finally as we traveled through the green sheep-dotted moors. She ran a hand through the electric blue highlight in her short blond hair. "He's demented, he is. Get this, John thought I'd leave with you *without paying the fucking rent for April, even though it's only April first!* Fucking ridiculous! I'm a fucking professor at Swansea University! Think I'd leave my hundred-pound speakers in my room and just take off with you? He's fucking insane, he is!"

"Sorry, Yvonne," I whispered quietly, not wanting to escalate her emotions further. She turned the radio on, and her breathing gradually slowed down.

At the train station, Yvonne gave me the tightest hug ever and promised to reach out to me again in the future.

"Know what I'm going to do when I go back, Lally? After the way he yelled at me just now, I *won't* spend Easter in London. I'll stay in my room and turn up my stereo as high as it can go. I'll give them two weeks' notice and leave in May. Fuck 'em," she said with a grin. "Hey, hurry, Lally, you don't want to miss your train after all that, do you?" She was like a little pixie, with her impish grin and that bolt of electric blue in her blond hair.

"I'll miss you, Yvonne," I said simply.

I watched as that dear Mini drove away, became a speck, and was no more. My head felt as if two slabs of concrete had compressed my skull to jelly, and my eyes were ready to pop. At the platform, I sank onto a bench and squeezed my eyes tight, almost convinced that this was all just a terrible, convoluted nightmare. Surely I'd wake up in my cozy cottage bed and realize it was simply an April Fool's prank I'd dreamed up.

Except it wasn't.

Eleven

JR

Elizabeth and Patricia Asare met me at the station in London, and I stayed with them for two days. Elizabeth shoved two hundred pounds of her hard-earned McDonald's wages into my hand before I left. I tried to argue with her, but she insisted that I could settle "when you're in the States and rich." Ghana friends are a true treasure.

My next stop was with my uncle Nava in Rhosllanerchrugog (Rhos), North Wales. The plan was to stay with his family till I got my green card. It was a tight squeeze with my uncle, aunt, two teenage children, and their cousin all packed into the small tract home.

Once JR learned I had moved out, he embarrassed me by sending me letters every day, just as he'd done at the Claydens' home. I was hard put to explain his persistence and passed him off to my uncle as "an old family friend from Kumasi." Two weeks later, he invited me to visit him in Canterbury.

"I'll pay for your train ticket and pick you up from the station, Lally. Come for a short break. You won't have to worry about money or food out here," he told me. "You're going to *love* the free concerts they put on at Canterbury Cathedral every night, and you can explore the Roman wall around the center of town. What do you say?"

I was excited, but faint alarm bells sounded at his breathless description.

"Um, John, where would I sleep? I thought you said you had a tenant in your spare room. I'm not ready for . . . anything more. You know, anything more than friendship, right now." I stumbled over the words with a deep sense of discomfort in my gut. "John, I've never been with . . . you know, a guy in that sense, if you know what I mean."

"Of course, of course. You *know* you can trust me, Lally. I'm not going to pounce, if that's what you're worried about," he said with a short laugh, "at least, not unless you wanted me to." His tone was a little flirtatious now. "You'd trust me, right?"

"I guess," I said, curling the telephone cord tightly around my index finger till the tip was white.

"Good. You'll be safe, I promise. You're free to go back to your uncle's whenever you like. I thought this might be your last chance to explore Canterbury before you leave for America."

While a thrill of excitement urged me to take this adventure, a shrinking part of my brain told me it was a stupid idea. However, his persistence wore down my resistance. The new me finally threw caution to the wind. I wore a soft, figure-hugging gray sweater and tight jeans, and when I caught a look at my slim reflection in the window of the train, I thought I looked pretty cute.

When John walked down the platform to help me off the train, my heart thumped deafeningly, and my knees shook. I no longer had the Claydens as my protectors, so this was breaking scary new ground. It was reassuring to see him wearing that familiar gray down jacket he'd shared with me in Parkmill. A lock of golden-brown hair fell on his forehead, and I couldn't help but notice his athletic, handsome body, and the way he dwarfed everyone on the platform.

His eyes dropped to the silver chain around my ankle, and he shot me a warm smile of appreciation. He gripped my hand tightly as he pulled my suitcase to his car. We made small talk. I was reassured when he made no romantic overtures, as if to prove to me that he'd keep his distance, yet I was conflicted, with an unsettling blend of anticipation mixed in with paralyzing dread.

As John pointed out Canterbury's best features, I was distracted by his large hands, which dwarfed the steering wheel. The historic buildings and Roman wall that encircled the old city filled me with awe, and the glorious cathedral, all lit up at night, was truly magical. Thomas Becket, Archbishop of Canterbury, had sought sanctuary at the cathedral but was then betrayed and massacred there, hundreds of years ago, by his former "friend."

John pointed out shops set within the massive double Roman walls. Then my discomfort mounted steadily as we headed to his home.

"You'll have lots of time to wander around town while I'm working tomorrow," he promised. "My house is very small, by Ghana standards, but it's walking distance from the city center." He parked in the street in the middle of a row of two-story terraced houses. I followed him upstairs and saw the tenant's room. For some reason this comforted me. I tried to avert my eyes while he stowed my suitcase at the foot of the bed. Blood rose to my cheeks because a queen bed dwarfed the tiny room. It was neat, with sparse furnishings. A small window faced out to the road.

Dinner was green beans, chicken, and boiled rice. The only thing that spoiled the meal was when he frowned and directed me to "take small bites" when I wolfed down the food in my state of anxiety. His tone was parental, and I felt like a small child who had been told off. My nervousness was on overload as he cleaned up after dinner, so I masked it by stifling a pretend yawn. I told him I would sleep.

"It's been a long day. Go ahead, I'll put the dishes away." He gestured at the remains of dinner, looking directly at me and holding a plate covered with soap suds.

"Lally, do you mind sharing the bed? It's big, and I promise I'll keep my distance. I can always sleep downstairs on the couch if that's not okay with you. We discussed this, right? I'll assure you, I have absolutely *no intention* of pushing you into anything you're not ready for. I hope we can remain friends while you're here. Does that work?"

"Sure." I nodded, swallowing a large gulp of water. It seemed silly to make a big deal and insist he sleep on that couch. I was glad that he'd handled my anxiety head-on. It sounded like a simple, no-nonsense business arrangement.

I donned my warm pajama suit and feigned sleep when he came upstairs ten minutes later. I forced my breaths to appear regular, but my heart rocketed when he got on the bed and I felt the slight indentation in the mattress. It seemed ludicrous to trust him implicitly, but I convinced myself that it was the mature thing to do. Sleep eluded me until long after I heard deep, even breaths. I moved right to the edge of the bed, to make sure that no portion of my pajama-clad body touched his.

"Thanks for respecting my wishes last night," I told him the next morning.

"No problem," he said, and yawned as he got off on his side of the bed. "Like I said, I'd never jeopardize our relationship by doing anything that'll make you anxious or uncomfortable. Don't worry, Lally. It's going to be okay."

Several days passed in this fashion. I walked around and checked out the tiny town, the museums, and Canterbury Cathedral while John worked. He bought groceries, and I fixed dinner for the two of us. In a curious way, we felt like a married couple, albeit in a platonic relationship.

The telephone rang one morning, and I picked up, thinking it was John. It was my mother, calling from California! She'd called Uncle Nava to get John's number. My heart rate picked up when she said she'd been notified that my green card would shortly be granted. She said the entire family was ecstatic, and she'd already started preparing the house for my arrival.

I was distracted from the joy I felt at the news when she moved on to telling me how shocked she'd been to hear that I was staying with John Russell in Canterbury. She was well aware of John's bad reputation in Kumasi and the girlfriends he'd had when he cheated on his wife.

To appease her, I glossed over our sleeping arrangements and told her I was just visiting for a few days to check out the city. Without lying, I mentioned that he had a home with an extra bedroom, and another tenant was also living there. Thankfully, she asked no further questions and went back to rejoicing that my long wait would shortly be over.

When John returned that night, I told him I was thrilled to hear that my wait for the green card was over. My mother had even suggested that I might be in California within two weeks! The following evening, John returned from work with a long-stemmed white rose and a little package. Within layers of white tissue paper was an exquisite, lacy ivory silk nightdress with a matching wrap. The low neckline on it made me blush. Without specifically asking anything, he merely remarked, "I saw this and wondered how it would look on you. Want to try it on?"

After minimal hesitation I accepted it. He'd not broken my trust. He'd allowed me time to get used to the idea of taking the next step when and if I was ready. He'd given me space. The least I could do was accept his gift, I figured. I went to the bathroom to try it on. Like a nervous participant on the threshold of a brand-new adventure, I took a critical look at my reflection. The nightdress exposed way more of me than I cared to show. Taking a few gulps of air for courage, I tiptoed into the room, wondering if this was the point of no return.

John had removed his shirt and was seated on his side of the bed. The smoldering blaze of desire in his eyes when I walked in both terrified and excited me at the same moment. It stripped away our nineteen-year age difference and all the self-doubts about whether or not this was a wise move. I simply accepted the glory of feeling that a man who'd been very kind and hospitable to me for several days was finally showing that he really desired me. At the very least, I felt I owed it to him to reciprocate.

That was the night we became intimate, and my world changed irrevocably. The glory of the experience knocked me over. He had so much experience that he knew exactly how to make my body resonate. I realized what all the books and movies were blabbering about. I fell completely in love with him. Two days later, he brought home a crimson rose with a rose-colored silk negligee.

"This is to commemorate your passage from girl to woman. My woman. *My woman!*" he said later that night, crushing me beneath his body. "When you wear this in California, I want you to think about me and what we are doing right now."

John taught me to crave his touch. My traitorous body surged with passion when he walked in at the end of the day. He often directed me to focus on something else, such as the television, while he caressed me and would not let me respond until it was "allowed." I could think of nothing but when he'd hold me close next and make love to me again. His touch transported me to a different planet, where nothing existed but this unimaginable physical connection between a man and a woman.

That weekend I got the call from Uncle Nava. My green card had been granted. I could fly to California.

I couldn't stop crying as we set off on the two-hour trip to Heathrow airport. I wished for the hundredth time that I could better control my faucet of emotion. My head pounded as if it were being used as the batter head of a drum. John said nothing. His face was pale and his mouth a tense line, but I couldn't read his thoughts. There was little left to say. For the past three days, we'd gone back and forth incessantly about the insane sequence of events at his home. It wasn't clear whether we'd ever meet up again, or if this was goodbye for good. In the splendid Kent countryside, huge circular sheaves of wheat whizzed by, gleaming gold in the early morning sun. Usually they made me smile, but today, I cried even harder.

"I'm going to miss your groundnut stew," he murmured, "and all those desserts you had waiting when I got home, especially the pears in chocolate sauce." He shot me a sideways smile.

"It's been so good. Don't know where we should go with this . . . with *us*. I really don't. I'm so confused."

He adjusted the rearview mirror and gripped the wheel a little harder but didn't respond.

"I mean, what if . . . what if I missed my family so much that you just became a . . . I don't know, a *father substitute*? Is this *real* or not? I wish there was some way to tell." I blew my nose loudly, which seemed to irritate him. I searched for somewhere to dispose of the soggy tissue. Finding nothing, I hurriedly stuffed it in my jacket pocket. "I've never had a boyfriend, let alone slept with anyone, except you, and I've only been with you, for what? A few weeks . . . and you're twenty years older."

"Nineteen." He shrugged and frowned but kept looking straight ahead.

"Yeah, but you live here, and I'm settling in California." I nervously pushed my hair over my ear. He remained silent. "So, what should we *do*, John?"

"What do *you* want to do, Lally?" Again, he sounded irritated. I felt put down, like a rebuked child who'd failed him somehow. "Listen, John," I pleaded, "all these months since they screwed up my green card I've been dying—*dying* to be back with my family. I feel like a bum without a university degree. I'd like to make my own money and not be dependent on anyone. I want to start school again. Uncle Arul says some of my med school classes may transfer into UC Davis. I've heard it's a great university. Couldn't you at least say you'll come over and visit me there . . . or something?"

John reached over with a hand to squeeze my wrist. As he did, the back of his hand brushed against my breast in a calculated caress that he knew would turn me into jelly. "I don't have that kind of money yet, Lally. It's expensive to fly halfway across the world, you know. You'll have to decide what *you* want to do once you get there."

"I know. It's hard." I sniffed. Another London signpost flashed by, reminding me of the new reality I would face in another country. I gripped his hand tightly, then relinquished it. We were both silent for several minutes.

"You know," he said conversationally as he ran his fingers through his hair, "there are some women who need careers, and others are simply content staying home with a person they really care about. You'll have to find out what works for you, Lally."

"It's tough." I turned to face him. "Like . . . I could *never* tell my parents about you."

"Your *parents?*" He gave a short, humorless laugh, looking straight ahead. "You aren't a *child* anymore, Lally. Who cares what your *parents* think? This is about *us!*"

"*I* care about what my parents think, John. They had a very bad opinion of you back in Kumasi."

He honked as a car drove a little too close to ours. "Asshole!" he swore. He was quiet for a moment, then he reached out again to squeeze my clammy hand on my lap. "Okay, how about this. Just take your time. Figure it out when you get there, okay? If you choose to come back to be with me, I'll be waiting for you, okay?"

"Okay. Hmm." If he was trying to guilt me into feeling bad about choosing to be with my family to earn a college degree, it was working. I lapsed into silence and leaned back on the seat. A headache wreaked havoc in my left temple. We avoided the subject for the rest of the drive.

"I'll write to you," he said as he pulled over to the Heathrow departure terminal. He popped the trunk and pulled out my beat-up gray Samsonite suitcase. I shuffled my weight from foot to foot, unsure what to say. He cocked his head to one side and shot me that now-familiar, endearing half query, half smile, the sunlight turning his tall frame into a golden statue.

Sensing my indecision, he opened up his warm, puffy gray coat. I walked right in and was enveloped against his beating heart, fully enclosed in a supportive cocoon that shut out the cold universe. I pressed my ear against the steady, familiar thump of his heart and wrapped my hands around his back in a final tight hug. He smelled delicious, and he didn't pull away, even though his shirt was wet from my tears. As my body melted into his, the crazy whirling in my brain morphed into a dreamy tranquility. For what seemed like eternity, my world was absolutely perfect.

A loud honk from someone trying to park behind us brought me back to reality, and I pulled away sharply. John shot an angry glare at the driver behind us and flashed him the bird, which seemed a little excessive, even in my befuddled state. The enraged driver honked even louder. John walked back to the car, then turned to me to wave his final goodbye.

"I *will* write," he shouted over his shoulder. His face was red, and he slammed the door hard enough to rattle the pavement.

As I watched him pull out and drive out of my life, I felt as if my very essence had been ravaged and scooped out, leaving me an empty shell. His car weaved past other cars till I could track it no more. For several minutes I remained, rooted in place, until a passenger jostled past me.

"Bye, John, I love you so much," I whispered to the road, before trudging into the terminal.

I was a speck in the cosmos. Completely alone.

Twelve

Davis, California

"**F**light attendants, prepare yourselves. Ladies and gentlemen, we will shortly be landing at San Francisco International Airport. Welcome to California."

As the pilot's jovial announcement crackled on the intercom, my legs trembled in anxious anticipation. A sharp, stabbing jolt of excitement hit my chest so hard that I doubled over and grasped both knees for a few seconds. I pulled out my immigration and naturalization paperwork from my handbag for the tenth time, to assure myself that it had not disintegrated in transit, and caressed the shiny stamp at the top of the precious document that symbolized my passport into this new culture.

Squashing my face against the window, I tried to capture every image and sensation of this descent into my new home, America! I'd imagined tons of skyscrapers, not this blue crescent of ocean glimmering next to golden sand. A towering bridge came into view. I wondered which one it was. It looked magnificent. We got so close to the water that I could see sunlight glinting on bright blue waves.

My heart stopped when it seemed as if we were only inches from the crystal blue water. I grabbed the arm rest with all my might and flattened my nose even harder against the window. What if we crash-landed into San Francisco Bay, and I never experienced the incredible family reunion I'd replayed count-less times? I held my breath and squeezed my eyes shut until I felt the delightful double thud that heralded my connection with American soil. The roar of the engines in reverse thrust matched the pounding and clamor of my heart, which seemed to want to separate from my chest. I exhaled slowly during the giddy cabin-shaking and shuddering, consumed by a blaze of glo-rious fire that slowly spread out from my heart to every tingling extremity. After sixteen months of interminable separation, I had finally made it to my new home. Home, home, home! Tears of excitement welled and slid silently down the sides of my face.

They'll all look different, of course, I thought, as I checked the seat compartment in front of me for anything I might have left behind. I'd have to learn who they were. Now that they were Americans, *I'd* be the stranger. Oh, the stories we'd share! It would take weeks, but they'd learn about everything. Every-thing . . . except John Russell, of course. They'd be shocked that I'd slept with someone old enough to be my father! Blood rushed to my face. Oh, God, I'd die of embarrassment if they found out. I could *never, ever* tell them what happened between us. They wouldn't get it. I didn't get it either. How had things changed so dramatically in less than one month? That John box would remain sealed shut from the family. On the other hand, I wanted to conjure him up so he'd materialize beside me. He'd give my hand a reassuring squeeze, kiss my forehead gently, and tell me that everything was going to be all right.

The stocky, balding man who stamped my passport at immigra-tion gave me a wide smile as he handed the passport back to my trembling hand. "Welcome, ma'am, to the US of A," he said with a fat-fingered flourish as he waved me through to the arriv-als lounge. His booming voice was a sharp contrast to the gen-tle British reserve I'd become so accustomed to. He reminded me of the loud American tourists I'd met in Kumasi, but the enthusiastic proclamation was the perfect accompaniment for my walloping heart.

As I headed to the meeting lounge, waist-high metal railings separated new arrivals from their families. I walked blindly through a sea of passengers, desperately seeking out a familiar face. And then, my world just stopped. Everything grayed out except for the blinding vision of my beloved parents waving frantically at me. My mom had one hand clapped over her mouth, as if she couldn't believe she was really seeing me. My dad had a broad smile, and he'd worn a bright red Ghanaian-print shirt just for my benefit. It fit a little snugly around his belly. For a second, my feet refused to function. I marched toward them like a robot. The loud chatter around me muted to silence. I walked faster, then I ran as fast as my trailing Samsonite would allow and smacked into them, throwing both my arms around their necks.

Without the harsh Ghanaian sun, their faces were several shades lighter. My dad's face had filled out. They both looked so healthy and carefree that I decided instantaneously that settling here was probably the best move they'd ever made. My mom had on a flowery cotton shirt and beige pants. Her hair lay in two neat braids behind her shoulders. She looked fantastic! We hugged and cried and laughed, then cried some more. My mom exclaimed at the prominent collarbones revealed by the low neck of my white smocked shirt. She muttered something about making sure I ate better so I could gain some weight. My dad didn't smell of cigarettes, for a change. He told me he'd quit, and that it was the hardest thing he'd ever done. My mom chattered about her teaching job. I retained only portions of what they said.

I was home. I was complete.

As we drove, I gazed outside, thirsty to soak up everything, grateful that my mom had relinquished the front seat to me. Everything was massive, from the graceful buildings, clumped together in San Francisco, which towered into the sky, to giant cars that made the English ones seem like toys. I took deep lungfuls of new air, dry, crisp, and filled with promise. Dazzling sunlight lit up sprawling freeways, and the sheer array of street signs and adverts made me dizzy and giddy with excitement.

After months of wheat fields around Canterbury and Welsh country lanes littered only by cute, fluffy sheep and wild ponies, the multiple lanes of traffic and towering concrete overpasses took my breath away. Cars spun by every which way at top speed. The sky was so incredibly blue, hardly interrupted by clouds. My dad gripped the wheel very tight, casting nervous glances at the traffic. He made awkward, jerky lane changes. He spoke very little until we left San Francisco. My mother mentioned that he was still a little uncomfortable with freeway driving, as Davis was a small city, and he rarely drove to the Bay Area. I gasped as we exited the lower deck of the Bay Bridge, and I looked back in awe at those majestic, graceful silver pillars that held it up. It was the loveliest bridge I'd ever seen.

And then, just as suddenly, all the buildings and concrete gave way to giant stretches of verdant fields, some full of large gorgeous black-and-white cows. Endless vistas of grass and scrub stretched out on either side of the freeway. I gawked at the profusion of oleander from whitest white to crimson that dotted the central divide of the highway leading to Davis. Majestic hilly panoramas stretched as far as the eye could see. An advanced civilization—my new home!

I wanted to pinch myself to make sure it was real. The entire experience was a fantasy, and part of me was terrified that I might suddenly wake up and have this all stripped away. We talked the entire time, but I have no idea what my parents said. I took pains to downplay my trip to Canterbury and made it seem like it was just a brief tourist stop. There was a divine moment when my mom leaned over from the back seat to hand me a Tupperware container full of her delicious, crispy, pastry-encased Sri Lankan spicy ground beef patties. They tasted like the manna of the gods. I savored each morsel, tearing up with the incredible aroma and taste. I wished John was with me to enjoy this delicious treat.

The rhythm of their conversation lulled me into absolute contentment. I'd had only snatches of sleep on the flight, so I dozed fitfully. My heart pounded in delicious anticipation of meeting Viji, Nimi, Vim, and Rocky.

And then came the Davis turnoff. Unbelievably unique Davis. A paradise, just off the bland freeway, a small university town that stole my heart immediately. About the same size as Kumasi, it was greener, cleaner, and better laid out, with roads I felt I could lick.

My legs trembled as my dad honked loudly up the steep drive of 1118 Chestnut Lane, a corner house on a quiet cross street. By British standards, it was huge. I'd imagined this moment countless times, and the actual experience didn't let me down. The first thing I noticed was the driveway, lined with my mother's signature roses. Roses of every hue, all perfectly pruned and fertilized with love, nodded their rapturous welcome. The garage door was wide open. I jumped out of the car, giddy with excitement.

Our beloved German shepherd, Rocky, bounded out to greet me, his 115 pounds making me stagger. I clutched the side of the garage so he wouldn't knock me over and sank down, hugging him. A coating of welcome slobber told me how much he'd missed me. Seated on the garage floor, I hugged him back, welcoming his delicious doggy smell. There was also a newcomer, a timid black-and-white Australian shepherd puppy, who watched warily in the periphery, unsure if he should get in on the action. He finally succumbed. I registered floppy black satin ears and melting chocolate eyes of adoration.

Viji, Vim, and Nimi trooped into the garage also, and Vim brought my suitcase inside. They were now all giants towering over me. We collapsed in the living room, laughing and talking all at once.

I was assailed with "Lally, you'll have to . . ." and "I can't wait to show you . . ." I flopped on the floor near Rocky and stared around in contentment at my beloved, wonderful, amazing, supportive family. Exhausted, I laid my head on Rocky's shoulder, and he graciously tolerated my lying alongside him. His warmth made me think about how I'd wrapped my arms around John just last night. It seemed like I'd been back for *weeks* already.

The jet lag finally caught up with me, but I tried to keep my eyes open and stifle yawns as I drank in the enchantment of being a sister and daughter again. My refugee days were gone forever. With the family around me, I could *be* anything. I could *do* everything.

"My God, Lally, you've turned into a skeleton!" Viji remarked, staring at my legs. "What happened? Didn't the Claydens feed you?" I'd shed fifteen pounds.

"Of course they did, silly," I responded. "I've been walking around on trails everywhere, for miles most days. The British walk to everything. Guess you *Americans* drive everywhere, don't you? By the way, I love your short hair. Too cute!" She'd lost her pigtails and had soft black curls wafting around her face. A cute beige peaked hat was angled jauntily on one side of her head, making her appear very sophisticated.

"You've also picked up a strong British accent, Lally," Nimi said. Like Viji, her hair was cut very short. She wore shorts, and I noticed that she was very muscular. I heard she'd excelled in many sporting activities and was a rising badminton star. A bunch of her trophies were proudly displayed on the living room piano. Now that I could actually see my parents up close, they looked really youthful. It was probably the healthy Californian cuisine, I decided. It was as if the whole family had undergone a makeover!

The American twang, most noticeable in Vim, was a jolt, and he'd changed the most. The little boy who'd lain in bed while I read Alistair Maclean to him at night was now a self-assured, towering fourteen-year-old.

"I've got a job, Lally," he said proudly, after I finally excused myself from the family to head to bed. "Come check this out before you sleep." He walked me into his bedroom and showed me tall stacks of *The Davis Enterprise* newspapers on the floor and the bed. "I'll be delivering all these papers later on!" I was speechless with pride that my little brother actually worked! He also showed off tall, glossy posters of his sports legends covering the walls of his room: Kareem Abdul Jabbar from the LA Lakers and Joe Montana of the 49ers.

"And what's this? A computer?" I gestured to a beige keyboard and monitor on his study table.

"Saved up a long time to get it, and Ammah and Appah helped me buy it," he said proudly. "It's called an Apple IIe computer. I'll show you a cool game tomorrow, Lally. It's called *Space Invaders*. Trust me, you'll love it, and you'll get addicted if you aren't careful."

My mother ushered me into the master bedroom. "Don't argue, Lally," my mom insisted. "Appah will head off back to LA soon, and he's sleeping in Vim's room for now. I've been sleeping on the living room couch since we got here. Guess I've just grown used to it. Even if you weren't around, this is where I'd be sleeping, I promise!"

"But how about everyone else? Did someone get kicked out of this room?"

"No, no, Lally. Vim will sleep with Appah in the front room and Nimi and Viji share the back bedroom, so you can have your own room, like you did in Kumasi. When Appah visits, he sometimes sleeps in the master bedroom, but after he leaves this weekend, he won't be home for several months. We can figure out a new arrangement when he gets back. Don't argue. This has been fixed up. Go and sleep. Go!"

The room had an attached toilet and shower. As I lay in the small twin bed, eyes flickering over the shadowy, unfamiliar surroundings, my brain would not stop its search for my next steps in this new and beautiful country. I so wanted to be just the eldest child and part of the family again. I'd missed so many significant family events and all my siblings' recent achievements. Viji was already a college sophomore, so I now *trailed her* by a year. Today they'd shared their excitement about what they planned to do, leaving me very aware that I had to figure out my next steps.

Apart from my stint as church organist, I'd pretty much stagnated in Wales. I'd walked around the beautiful Gower coast, played house with the Claydens, and then done the same with John Russell. Was that all simply a huge waste of my life? Or had the fates sent me on a massive test mission? So much for "doctor of doctors"—I didn't even have an undergraduate degree to my name.

I shut my eyes tight, then stared at the sliver of light beneath my closed bedroom door. Despite all the joy in our family reunion, I felt curiously removed from my siblings. We never kept secrets from each other, but for the first time in my life, I wasn't able to share my huge dark secret of this past month with John. I turned over on my belly thinking how much I wished he were with me, so we could cuddle up together and have him turn me on. Juxtaposed on this fantasy was a conflicting wish to eradicate everything that had happened between us, so I could make a fresh start.

Viji was saying something to the family in the living room. Whatever she said was followed by a chorus of giggles, and then my mom hushing everyone so I wouldn't be disturbed. I chuckled, wishing I were there laughing along with them. Then my smile froze. If *anyone* in the family discovered my newfound relationship with John Russell, they would be beyond horrified. How could I ever explain how Lally-the-perfect-role-model-eldest-daughter had shacked up with the adulterous scoundrel from our past life in Kumasi? I wasn't sure how it had happened either. But it had.

No longer was I a naive little girl but a fully awakened woman. Just last night he'd held me close, our arms and legs tightly wrapped up together in Canterbury. Now I was a million miles away—a supposedly virginal sister and daughter again. I pulled the sheet up to my neck, sorely missing the warmth of his body. It would be morning in Canterbury now. I wondered if he missed me also, as he left our bed to get ready for work. My toes clenched with a stabbing feeling of deprivation. I snagged an extra pillow and hugged it close, but it was a poor John substitute. Despite my tiredness, sleep was a long time coming.

Thirteen

University Prospects

O ver the next few days, I struggled to adjust to the climate change. After the chilly, moist winds in Wales and Canterbury, the intense dry heat was jarring and sapped my energy. I vegetated in the house to seek refuge, guzzling up bowls of cold orange fruit cut up by my mother called cantaloupe, which tasted like a cross between papaya and watermelon. It was truly delicious.

One afternoon, I braved the heat for a quarter-mile walk to Carl's Jr. My mission was to sample an authentic American hamburger that I would order on my own. In England and Wales, someone else always accompanied me to order food and pay for it, so this was quite an adventure. I pulled open the glass door and stood just inside the restaurant, glad for the blast of cold air within. The customer in front of me was a large Hispanic man who rattled off his order quickly, so I had little time to decide what to order. He moved away with a paper cup to get himself a drink. My heart pounded as I gazed up at the dazzling menu options suspended from the ceiling. The huge list of food and drink options, together with the accompanying photos, made me dizzy and uncomfortable. A line grew behind me as I tried to digest the gazillions of choices.

"You ready?" The dark-haired lady behind the counter stared at me pointedly, her head crooked to one side. She gave out an exasperated sigh, casting a glance at the people who'd collected behind me. Flustered, I shifted my weight on my feet as I tried to absorb the different burger options. My mom had given me twenty dollars, and I wanted something relatively inexpensive.

"Er, what soft drinks do you have? I'm confused. Seems like drinks come with some of the hamburgers?" I was stalling, and she probably knew it. In Kumasi, there were limited beverage choices. You ordered soft drinks or alcoholic drinks, then accepted whatever the restaurant had.

"*Soft* drinks? I'm not sure what you mean. Our drink options are all over on this sign over here. Tell me when you're ready." She gave another exaggerated sigh and dropped her shoulders impatiently.

"Er, I need a few more minutes. Please go ahead," I said, waving at the three people behind me in line, wondering if everyone was laughing at me for dithering for so long. Ten minutes later, I left the restaurant clutching a paper bag containing a bacon cheeseburger, small fries, and a plastic cup of water. I sought out a shady tree nearby and leaned against it while I devoured the delicious thick hamburger and each crispy, flavorful fry.

By the end of the week, I'd met several of my mother's friends from the neighborhood as well as a couple of the teachers at Holmes Junior High School, where she taught special ed. The Davis residents were nothing like the brash, loudmouthed American tourists I'd met in Ghana. Most were soft-spoken and appeared genuinely interested in what my life had been like in Ghana and as a forced visitor in Britain.

The family had clearly settled in an American paradise. The green culture of recycling abounded in the town, and there was a strong focus on environmental issues rather than guns.

University Prospects

I learned that Davis was one of only three bike cities in the entire country, and only bikes could provide transport to the campus halls, not cars. The gardens were well manicured, and the streets were spotless. I spent fascinated minutes watching road sweepers and the mechanical garbage trucks with their arm extensions working their way up and down Chestnut Lane.

I also got a chuckle out of repurposed London buses, still carrying English destination signs, ferrying students. The entire bus system was run by university students, and rides were dirt cheap, so I took many a thrilling ride on the top deck of a bright red double-decker bus, just for the hell of it. The bus stopped right across from my parents' home.

One day, I walked to Longs drugstore to buy toothpaste. For months I'd shopped only at the little village store in Parkmill, which was about the size of a California living room, so when I stepped into Longs, I was dazzled by its size. The aisles extended for miles. When I finally came across the aisle stacked with toothpaste that reached the heavens, the brand names blurred and ran together as my eyes traveled from rack to rack. Whitening options, peroxide, weird additives that made toothpaste somehow better . . . I was completely overwhelmed. By the time we'd left Ghana, toothpaste was so scarce that if you were lucky enough to find Pepsodent, you'd grab as many tubes as you could afford and later share it with others who'd run out. When the tube was close to empty, I was an expert at using a wooden ruler to squeeze every last smidgen out of the tube.

As I stared at this never-ending array of brightly colored toothpastes, it struck me that I'd switched from a country where we'd made do with so little to a place with unlimited choices. Tears spilled down my cheeks as I thought about my dad's momentous decision to move here. At this very moment, my friends in Kumasi might be scouring the shelves for a single tube of Pepsodent on a nearly barren shelf, while I faced toothpaste heaven. I couldn't take it. It was too much. Way, way too much. The bright colors blurred into a mocking wall like an impressionist Monet painting. I made an about turn and walked out of Longs, empty-handed.

On Sundays, my parents and Vim shrieked at the TV as tall men outfitted like robots got clobbered playing American football. It appeared really stupid to me at first because they used their hands, not their feet, but I observed the family passion with some curiosity. One day, Vim took it upon himself to talk me through the game as it was being played. He patiently explained how scoring worked and the team's strategy. Formerly, I'd never been a sports enthusiast, but it didn't take me long to fall crazily in love with Joe Montana and the San Francisco 49ers. Each Sunday, I joined my brother and parents as we screamed at the top of our lungs, imploring them to run, run, run to score a touchdown. We got so loud that Rocky and Bonjo joined in the ruckus, barking crazily. I became the 49ers' most ardent fan, and my love fest perpetuated.

If there was a cloud, perhaps it was that finances were still very tight. My parents were still renting our three-bedroom home from their landlord, and my dad hoped to eventually buy the property. He still lived mostly in his trailer in Los Angeles and came to Davis only for sporadic visits. He'd had to shelve all architectural pursuits, and I saw the toll it took on his psyche. He said he might be offered a job any day, but his eyes were sad and his expression listless. I doubted his assertion. He'd secured a California architect's license but was already fifty-five and had no architectural experience in this country. This was a huge disappointment for my dad, who'd held exalted managerial positions and designed dozens of extraordinary buildings in Kumasi.

My mother earned a modest salary as a teacher's aide at the junior high school and continued her work in the cannery to supplement her income. Never once did she complain, but it made me sick to my stomach that she spent so much time perched in front of a conveyor belt, sorting out misshapen tomatoes, because she did not have a salary during the summer months. When they arrived, they'd not had the funds for her to get into a teacher credentialing program, so neither of my parents had benefits.

A month later, relishing my burgeoning proficiency at American freeway driving, I drove my dad's white Volkswagen rabbit to pick up my official naturalization certificate from the American Embassy in San Francisco. After the conclusion of business, I headed back to my parked car, noticing that glamorous high-rise buildings were giving rise to more seedy, dilapidated ones. I'd been too preoccupied to pay much attention to this on my way in. My heart raced as an unkempt homeless man headed straight toward me. With my diet of American crime movies, I braced myself to be jumped, mugged, or worse. When he simply asked the time, I told myself off for being so paranoid. A short distance from my car, I was much more relaxed when a well-dressed man crossed the street and headed directly to me.

"Excuse me, ma'am," he murmured politely, standing right in front of me.

"Hullo," I responded, with a smile. He'd partially blocked my progress, so I looked up at him. He was thirtysomething, a fairly well-dressed African American man.

"Could we have a quick fuck?"

"*What?* What did you say?" He'd phrased the question so politely that I thought I'd misheard. We were there in broad daylight, with people and cars all around us.

"Ma'am, just a quick fuck—how about over there, right behind that?" he pointed out a side street that was empty except for a large trash dumpster. "I'll be very quick, ma'am." His tone was more insistent this time. He kept his arm extended.

Swallowing and trying hard not to panic, I mimicked his polite tone and avoided showing fear.

"Er . . . no thanks. Thanks, but no, no thank you," I responded, equally politely, but firmly. I stepped around him and kept walking, forcing myself not to run or look around, with my pulse hammering out of my head.

To my eternal relief, he did not follow me. I accelerated my pace, jumped in the car, and locked all the doors with my head ducked. Only after a moment or two did I raise my head to cast a quick, panicked look behind. He was nowhere to be seen. It was almost as if I'd conjured him up. I laid my head on the steering wheel between my hands, shut my eyes, and waited for the shivering to resolve.

If John heard about this, he'd be *livid*. John was always so protective and controlling about everything. I felt a sudden, searing need to be enveloped by all of six-foot-four John for comfort and protection. What if *John* had materialized and propositioned me in daylight in the same fashion? After a month without sex, I knew without a shred of doubt that I'd have dashed behind that dumpster with him in a heartbeat and let him have his way.

My uncle Arul, an engineering professor at UC Davis, set up an appointment for me to meet with his colleague, a biochemistry professor, on campus. The curly brown-haired man with a smiling countenance took over a half hour to thoroughly vet my medical courses, asking me to show him which textbooks I'd used for each course. He sat back in his chair, doing some computations in silence, then turned to me.

"Lally, thanks to three years of accumulated medical school credits from Ghana," he announced, "I feel comfortable authorizing 120 transfer units into the biochemistry program at UC Davis. What do you say?"

I gawked and swallowed, but no words came out. I licked suddenly dry lips. "Really?" was all I could squeak out.

"Yes, really. It's hard not to award you a full degree. You've taken so much advanced coursework already." He raked a hand through his curls. "What's missing is a whole bunch of humanities, and a few more quarters of upper-division biochemistry. Do that, and you'll have your degree, young lady. How about that?" He beamed.

My excitement knew no bounds, and I thanked him profusely. In just a few quarters, I could complete an undergraduate degree? This was the most wonderful news, a dream come true. It was intoxicating to think that I'd managed to slide so effortlessly into university just five weeks after arriving in Davis. My brain exploded in a symphony of excitement, and I sang out loud as I biked home. I couldn't wait to share the news with my parents. I wanted to hug my uncle Arul for helping me make the connection. I wondered what John would think. Of course this was yet another barrier to us getting together in the future.

In the fall of 1984, I was admitted as a transfer student into the UC Davis biochemistry program. I signed up for social dance, badminton, American history, advanced creative writing, and a biochemistry lecture and lab. It gave me a quiet thrill to park my bike next to Olsen Hall for my first US history class. Hundreds of bikes were parked in overlapping rows, so I carefully attached my bike to the rack using my shiny silver combination lock.

Everywhere I looked, dozens of students were walking or biking. They were mostly Asians and Caucasians, with a small number of African Americans. As I wove between pedestrians and slow-moving bikes, it struck me that everyone was carrying their backpack over one shoulder. Self-consciously, I slipped one strap off to fit in. It made my back hurt more, but at least I felt like less of a geek.

I drew a deep, appreciative breath to take in the delicious smell of coffee in the cool air, as I walked up the stairs to the hall entrance. Day one, for Lally, the brand-new American college student. With all the excited, eager faces around me, I wondered what lay in stock. Was this the next stepping stone to becoming a "doctor of doctors," after my endless enforced hiatus in Britain? Was it possible to get a degree and apply to med school, as the fortune teller had predicted? Just the thought of that sent a thrill down my spine.

A sea of students carried me forward to the double-door entryway to Olsen Hall. In front of me was an extremely tall, brown-haired student. His face was averted, but I suddenly thought he could be John. A younger version of my John—my beloved, wonderful, sexy John. If only John were with me now, holding my hand. Of course, he'd gallantly insist on carrying my backpack. Then it struck me that if he were here, he'd look more like a professor than a fellow student.

If John were here in Davis, would he have my back while I completed my degree and support my dream to apply to med school? Probably not. In fact, definitely not. He'd say he couldn't afford it. He had a fixed view of a woman's place and had previously asserted that I had to choose between being a "career person" or "staying home to look after your man." Besides, if I were in college, it would remind him how much younger I was. John would be jealous of all these eager young people who might become my friends. He'd want to keep me to himself. I knew that much about him already. He was possessive, traditional, and old-fashioned.

He'd told me over and over how much he wanted to make sure that I belonged to him, just him. He'd want me home with a hot meal waiting after work. I wasn't so sure about that. Playing house might be fun, short-term, but then I'd have to sacrifice my dreams and fade into the patchwork quilt of a faithful, stay-at-home wife. I shook my head with a shudder.

A girl with a blond pigtail beside me gave me a strange look. I shot her an embarrassed smile and reached into my bag to fish out the schedule for my next class, biochemistry. The lecture and lab were disappointing. In lab I was paired with a nasty girl with coarse features and blond bangs who pointedly ignored me. She refused to collaborate on our assigned lab work, even though we'd been directed to do so.

After the warm support of my fellow students back in Kumasi, her indifference was a slap in the face. Her rejection made me feel isolated and scared as it became crystal clear that she was competitive and cared only about her own well-being. As the days progressed, her attitude, coupled with the stress of the advanced biochem lab, gave me many sleepless nights. After three weeks, I dropped the class, feeling like a terrible failure. I asked for a transfer into human physiology.

Physiology was more practical and more closely related to medicine. I was very grateful to be back in school after months cast adrift, and I actually enjoyed churning my brain circuitry at top speed again. I'd sorely missed the challenge of book learning. I got my exercise riding my bike to campus from home—a three-mile round trip.

Vim and Nimi were both excelling in their classes, and Uncle Arul had persuaded them to consider engineering degrees. I had no doubt they'd make it, because we'd all picked up great study habits back in Kumasi. I laughed when I heard Viji's story about college. She'd planned to attend Sacramento Community College, but my aunt accidentally drove her to the wrong school campus, and she signed up at Sacramento City College by mistake. It worked out later. She transferred to UC Davis for a bachelor's in international relations.

The Fortune Teller's Prophecy

Life was humming and full, and I soaked up the family togetherness, trying to make up for lost time. My cousin Siva took me
fishing nearby, and another time he drove me to mind-numb-
ingly breathtaking Lake Tahoe, set like a sapphire crystal at six
thousand feet, surrounded by towering, eight-thousand-foot
mountains. I was his talisman when he gambled at blackjack,
and he treated me to a gigantic steak dinner at Harrah's Casino
with his winnings. At the end of our meal, I leaned back in my
chair, having devoured a chocolate cake big enough to feed a
small town. With a little spark of guilt, I wondered what John
would think of me living the glitzy life out here, rather than
moping around missing him.

Slot machines clinked endlessly in the background, with
hazy smoke in the air and on my clothes. Whiffs of expensive
perfume wafted around. Waitresses hovered in low-cut black
velvet dresses that appeared painted on them, balancing shiny
trays laden with exotic alcoholic beverages. Memories of the
entire Gower Peninsula experience, the Claydens, and John
Russell were growing distant and fading fast. I'd somehow been
yanked from the lazy baaing sheep of Wales and plonked right
into a James Bond movie.

Fourteen

A Big Decision

After the sedate pace in Britain, life was now progressing at warp speed. Each day was fleshed out with schoolwork, and weekends were packed with wacky family game nights where we rolled around gasping for air as we played laughing games. My personal favorite pastime was 304, a Sri Lankan card game similar to bridge, which we played till the wee hours of the morning. It was a wild world full of action. You'd never know when a family member or friend from another county would show up for a visit. The excitement of life swirled around me constantly.

And yet, in the quiet times, when I was curled up in my small bed, something *was* missing. I missed John's presence and the way he held me and made love to me. I missed him more, rather than less, as the weather turned cooler. I missed his quick wit and worldly wise knowledge. He'd made me feel like an adult, rather than a kid at school out here, still accountable to my parents. I missed the magic of Canterbury Cathedral and the relaxed pace of life in Kent.

With the onset of our sexual relationship, I had changed irrevocably. I yearned to be enveloped in his voluminous gray coat again to shut out the world. He'd not made it easy to forget him either. Despite his promise to give me space, he assailed me with a steady barrage of letters that clogged our mailbox starting with his first letter dated Friday, July 27, 1984. As he'd done when he left Parkmill, he wrote almost every day!

The edges of my mother's lips turned down in disapproval one morning as she handed me two blue aerograms. She held the thin letters with her fingertips as if they might infect her and looked down, biting her lip. As I accepted them, I was deeply embarrassed. Of course, she knew the letters were from John. His distinctive spidery writing was sprawled all over the faded blue exterior.

"Why is that John Russell writing to you like this?" she asked in a disgusted tone, turning to face me. "This is not normal, Lally. He's disturbing your studies. Isn't he working? Doesn't he have something better to do with his time? This isn't right." She shook her head.

"He's lonely; he recently broke up with his wife, Ammah," I countered lamely, sliding them into my back pocket so I could savor them later. He always included sexual innuendos that made my heart race and my toes curl.

"Being bored, that's fine. But he's *my* age, Lally. Who writes every day like this? What is this nonsense? Tell him to stop so you can focus on school studies now, Lally. He shouldn't distract you from college." She turned on her heel and disappeared quietly into the kitchen to end the discussion. I'm sure she had tears in her eyes.

My mom was right. He was constantly writing notes that appeared calculated to make my body melt and yearn for his touch. I always grabbed the letters, ran to my room, and locked the door, then jumped up on the bed to read and reread every word. I stashed the growing pile of letters in a large brown envelope I hid under my mattress.

Typically, he provided a detailed missive of how he'd spent his day and how much he missed "my exotic Indian princess." That irritated me because I was Sri Lankan, not Indian, and it sounded corny. There was always a section in his letters that discussed how he missed "snuggling," which I knew meant sex. In one of the letters, he instructed me to spray perfume on my next note to him so he could imagine he was touching my body when he read it. He knew exactly how to turn me on, and I obediently did spray my Charlie fragrance on my next letter to him, feeling very sexy and naughty as I placed it in the mailbox.

When I didn't write for a few weeks, he sent even more letters, imploring me to write more often. "Send some fingernail clippings next time," he demanded. "I miss playing with your long fingernails." I found that absolutely disgusting and balked. Rather than defy him outright, which would probably have angered him, I told him I had short nails so I could play piano.

"I'm disappointed that you no longer have long nails I can tease," was his response.

The letters filled me with a curious mix of emotions, chief among them guilt. When I wrote long descriptions of school and the fun I was having in California, he expressed a longing to be with me that made me feel like I should be wanting to be with him, not selfishly looking at future prospects. His detailed erotic passages about wanting to recreate the intimacy of our sexual relationship turned me on and sent an answering surge of longing in my loins. He told me he hoped I was wearing his silver ankle bracelet, so he could imagine "my princess wearing it." It was clear that he wanted to stamp his seal of possession on me. Many times, I imagined being back in his arms and having him love me again. It was an unbalanced relationship. He was the puppet master pulling strings. A single word or comment in his letters could turn me to jelly, and he knew it.

In Davis, I was relishing the company of other young adults like my siblings' teenage friends. I'd missed hanging out with people my age in England, so I made up for lost time, especially during social dance class and badminton. I sampled Mexican food from Taco Bell and pizza with friends. I swooned over toasted cream cheese bagels. Game nights were a hoot with our badminton friends. To my delight, I was slipping back into the dreamy, carefree life we'd led in Kumasi. It wasn't all fun. I committed myself to studying very hard at the library to keep my good grades.

One month after I arrived, John mailed me a navy-blue sweatshirt I'd complimented him on, telling me I should "snuggle" with it to remember him. A few weeks later, I found a long narrow cylindrical package outside the front door with John's handwriting all over it. I was consumed with intense trepidation. Within it was a long-stemmed red plastic rose in a clear tube. The inscription read, "An everlasting rose, symbol of my everlasting love for you." I hid the rose under my bed with a combination of elation and dread. The accompanying letter asked if I would commit to being with him. The pressure implied by his gift made me extremely uncomfortable.

This letter was different from the others because he added a formal request and plan. How would I feel if he came to California at Christmas, married me, then took me back to Canterbury? We'd be together again. We could recreate Christmas together, the way we did when we were with the Claydens. If I went back, we'd have to stay in England only for a short while, till *his* American green card was processed.

In fact, he said he'd already made inquiries about whether he could get his own visa application to become an American resident and thought he could start the process right away "because I know how important your family is to you. I'd settle down in California and look around for a job out there while you finish school."

After the initial shock, I felt a stirring of excitement. John Russell, that gorgeous, sophisticated, sexy man, loved me so much that he was willing to fly all the way from England just to marry me, and he'd bring me back to California. He confessed intense feelings of wanting to be with me forever. Once we moved back to the States, he would give notice at his Canterbury job and lecture at a California community college.

Could I really turn him down? The rational part of me urged caution. We'd been together a grand total of seven weeks—three at the Claydens coupled with four more in Canterbury. Why the sudden pressure? Winter was almost upon us, and this gave me neither time nor space to determine what I wanted to do. Had I simply gravitated toward a father figure during my lonely wait? Would my sexual awakening fizzle out? Was this true love? How about the nineteen-year age difference? How about college? He added that his divorce paperwork was now finalized, and that he was giving his ex-wife their home in lieu of continuing support payments for her and his boys.

After a week of intense deliberation, I crafted a carefully worded response: "John, I'll have to say that I'm incredibly happy here in California, but I'm also missing you so much that it hurts at times. I'm nervous about taking such a drastic step because school has started up, and I'm loving that also. I'm still so confused because I don't know if what I'm feeling is true love or lust. Reason is, as you know, I've never been in a sexual relationship with anyone but you. Plus, we were together for such a short while. Please give me time. I'll have to think about this. If I decide for sure, I'll talk things over with my parents."

A week rolled by. I told my parents I had something serious to discuss and asked if we could walk together to Chestnut Park next door. With my parents on either side of me, we walked halfway into the park before I took a deep breath and spilled the beans. My dad stopped in his tracks and stared at me as if I had sprung blue horns from my forehead. My mother clapped a hand over her mouth, and I saw her fingers trembling.

"But you just got here! How about school, Lally? You just

got in." She had tears in her eyes. I avoided her gaze to stare at some boys playing basketball. I felt like shit.

"John Russell? He used to have beers with me at the Staff Club. He's *old*, Lally." That was my father.

"But, Appah, he looks young. No one would guess his age."

A woman walking her dog took a detour around us. She probably sensed the gravity of the conversation.

"He wants to get married to you? You really want to marry him . . . and go back to England? You just got here, Lally. We waited *so* long to see you. Can't he wait? You have just a few quarters to go, so what's the hurry? How can you leave us after just coming here?" My mother choked up in sobs, and tears came to my eyes as well.

"I know what you're saying, Ammah, but he knows that I'm determined to finish college. After we get married, I'll be gone for just a short time to England, just till he has a green card. That's why he's in a rush, so we can start the process. I won't quit school, Ammah. I really want college for myself."

"So, you got together when you were in Canterbury?" my dad asked, with a catch in his voice. I heard sadness but also resignation.

"Yes, Appah, I guess we . . . we hit it off, I guess. He's changed. He's not the person he used to be. You may not believe it, but even though I'm here with you guys, I still miss him. That's how I know this is probably the real thing. I really want to be with him again."

"But, Lally, what about all his girlfriends in Ghana? Remember, he was still married but carried on with all those girls . . . that model, remember?" My mom shook her head. Her cheeks were still wet, and there was a dazed and helpless look on her face.

"Let's sit," I suggested, pointing to a picnic table. I felt protected on the bench, with my parents on either side. "Listen, listen, he's changed, Ammah." I placed a hand on her shoulder. "He's divorced now—he's not like that anymore. He won't cheat on me. Never, ever. Please trust me. You've always trusted my judgment."

"But, Lally," my father said, leaning over with a blank look on his face, "what about his two sons? He just left them with his wife. Doesn't that bother you? What if he does the same thing when *you* have children?"

I laid a hand over my dad's hand on the table. "Appah, it bothered me too. I asked him about that. He told me that his wife made it impossible for him to have a relationship with those boys."

"How can you just drop school and then start again?" My mom frowned.

"There's something called PELP, which stands for Planned Educational Leave Program. I'll definitely come back to finish my degree. John knows I won't be happy if I'm not living near you guys. I *have* to finish school. I won't be gone long, I promise. I just love it here. America is my home now."

We talked some more. As we walked home in silence, I knew they were floored, but they also realized that my mind was made up. We maintained an uneasy truce for the next few days.

My dad was the first to give me his blessing. He perched on the edge of my bed as I sat against the headboard studying. "You know, Lally, your ammah and I also had a love marriage, right?"

I nodded, wondering where he was going with this.

"I've thought long and hard about what you told us. I know, deep down, that we brought you up to make good decisions. We've always felt that, as the oldest child, you are very mature."

I couldn't bring myself to speak. Tears dripped down my cheeks, and I used a corner of the sheet to mop them up.

"So, after thinking very hard, I want you to know that I support you, if this is *truly* your decision. Your ammah will have a harder time accepting this, but I want to give you my blessing, okay? I believe that marriage is made in heaven."

I couldn't speak but just reached out to squeeze his hand tightly.

"That fortune teller predicted you'd be a great doctor some-day, so maybe that's why I'm sad that you're interrupting your studies yet again, Lally," he said, shaking his head, his eyes downcast. "Anyway, you have my blessing, Lally." His eyes were moist and he blew his nose as he left me alone.

I'd never loved him as much as I did at that moment. He'd empowered me. A huge load fell off my back, but misgivings seeped in right afterward.

As for my mom, my dad was right. She struggled several days longer until one day when she walked over to me in the kitchen while I was washing dishes. Her eyes were red rimmed, and I noticed that both hands were shaking as she took a dry dish and stowed it in the cupboard.

"Lally, I've been thinking. What to do? It's happened now, and you've made your decision. Appah gave his permission also, so what to do? I'll support you, girl, but you have to promise me one thing. You *have* to finish your schooling. Okay? Please, Lally," she said in a broken voice. "You're only twenty-three. John is forty-two, so he's finished all his studies. Please don't give up on university, okay?"

I turned off the tap, wiped my hands on my pants, and stepped over to hold her because she was crying. Her body felt frail in my hands. "I promise, Ammah, I swear to you that I'll come back and finish, okay? He knows I want this degree. I'll come back." I hugged her very tightly and stroked her hair gently.

"It will take me some time, Lally. It's a huge shock, you know." She sniffed.

"I know, Ammah, I know." I clasped her even more tightly, hoping against hope that I would not regret my decision. The time for words was over. We'd all said everything there was to be said.

Fifteen

Tying the Knot...
around My Neck?

I wrote to John that night. "Dearest John, I've told my parents about us. Yes, they were shocked. They're also wondering why we want to get married so soon. They don't want me to quit school, but I've promised that I'll return to finish my degree. I want that for me also, by the way. Anyway, they've both come around to giving us their blessing. Finally! Guess I'm excited and nervous. Let's talk. Love you very, very much, Lally."

John was uncharacteristically silent for a few days. When I asked him why, he said he was disappointed to learn that the American visa process could not start for him until we were formally married. He also said that it could then take a year for approval. Would I live in Canterbury with him till it was granted?

I was very flustered because everything was moving way too fast. Again he suggested that we should get married at Christmas. He asked if I would work out wedding arrangements with my parents because he was facing financial problems as a result of his divorce settlement. Although they'd divorced the prior Christmas, he'd not cut all financial ties till he gave Anne their shared home in October 1984. He sounded bitter about giving up the house: "That woman gets a meal ticket for life."

He told me we'd return so I could finish my undergraduate degree at UC Davis. Although I was ridiculously nervous, he constantly reassured me that everything would work out. I blocked all my misgivings and told him that it sounded like a plan.

We had a simple wedding on December 29, 1984, at Davis Community Church. Because I'd been in America only a few months and had no close friends, I invited my parents' friends and my social dance instructor to the wedding. A handful of my dad's relatives also made the trek from Southern California. At my mother's insistence, I wore a simple white sari. Her friend, a seamstress, made me a fitted sparkly white blouse.

As I slowly walked down the aisle holding on to my dad's arm, all I could see was my handsome husband-to-be in his dark suit. His eyes were riveted on me, and I saw something like tension mixed with pride. I focused on the partial smile in his eyes because my heart was hammering.

Halfway down the aisle, one of the flower girls stepped on my long train, jerking my head back suddenly. A look of rage flashed over John's face as he scowled at the embarrassed six-year-old girl, and his mouth tightened. Something about the moment made the magic disappear for an instant. The anger in his eyes at something so trivial gave me an uneasy shiver. I chalked it up to him being overprotective and emotional.

My parents had paid for a traditional twenty-four-karat solid gold necklace that John was supposed to fasten around my neck, but it hadn't arrived from Sri Lanka in time for the wedding. In Sri Lankan culture, this necklace is fastened around the bride's neck, and the clasp is never unscrewed. The necklace is designed so you can lift it off your head without unfastening the clasp. In the old days, if your husband died, the gold from the necklace would provide you with financial security.

Disappointed that he knew about the custom but had not thought to buy me a substitute gold chain for the occasion, I instead used a chain shipped to me in a mail scam. I'd been assured that "for just one dollar," they'd mail me a "real gold" necklace. As a new immigrant, blissfully naive about such scams, I fell for it.

And so it was that John declared his undying commitment to me using a one-dollar "solid gold" chain. My parents' necklace would be delivered to me in England. John made no attempt to reimburse my parents for the necklace, the priest, the wedding expenses, or the chalet rental at Lake Tahoe for our three-day honeymoon. He said his ticket to America had been very expensive, so he was strapped for money. I was mortified and disappointed, because I'd assumed he'd help out, as it was a considerable drain on my parents' financial resources. John asked my father if we could use his car for the honeymoon so he wouldn't have to get a rental. Despite the inconvenience of being without a car for three days, my wonderful father readily acquiesced.

We had a simple wedding reception at my parents' home. My dad had tears in his eyes when he made a speech. The words that stood out were "and I believe, Lally and John, that your marriage was made in heaven." About a dozen people showed up, bringing food to share. My uncles danced around to the music, and I'd switched into a maroon dress that clung to my shapely body. I'd romanticized this day from the time I'd read Harlequin romances, but something was off for me that night. John barely looked at me, and he appeared remote and restless during the festivities. I wanted to spend a little more time with my family and the relatives who'd traveled all the way from Southern California for the occasion, but I was frustrated because John kept pushing for us to drive away to Tahoe.

We left the reception early. As we drove the two and a half hours to South Lake Tahoe, he seemed uncharacteristically remote and spoke only in monosyllables. I was frightened because he would not explain his suddenly somber mood. I attributed it to him being tired, but a disquieting feeling made my stomach churn. After all, this was our wedding day!

After we were settled in our cute chalet at Lake Tahoe, I showered and put on the lacy white nightdress from Macy's that I'd chosen with exquisite care. When I crept back to join him in the bedroom, shyly wondering what he'd think of my outfit, I found him fast asleep and snoring. He did not wake up till the next morning. None of the Harlequin romances I'd consumed as a teenager prepared me for the crushing end to what I thought would be a magical, unforgettable night. I was more than disappointed—I was totally crushed and cried myself to sleep. I'm sure he heard me sniffling, but never once did he reach out to me.

The romance I'd anticipated and built up for the honeymoon slowly seeped out, as did the gold paint on my necklace, which turned silver and then black in two days. We ate at only fast-food places like Long John Silver's. When I shyly asked on our final night if we could perhaps splurge on one fancy dinner to commemorate the occasion, he snapped that he'd paid for an expensive airline ticket to come out to California, hadn't he? Wasn't that enough?

Chastened, I let it go, hiding tears of disappointment. Not even three days after I'd walked down the aisle with him, alarm bells were blaring. The promise of his letters had evaporated. I couldn't shake the new reality that I was legally wed to a remote, unfeeling stranger, old enough to be my father, who didn't seem to understand or care about doing something special for me at such a significant time of my life.

In less than a week, I'd be leaving the warm cocoon of my

family to begin a new chapter of my life in Canterbury, thousands of miles away. I wanted to run into the snow screaming for help at the top of my lungs. I wasn't ready to go away with this stranger. Not by a long shot.

But there was no one out there who could help me, and no one to blame but myself.

Sixteen

Housewife

After the family chaos, the California sunshine, and the frantic whirlwind of college courses, I felt like a vibrant hot poker doused in a freezing pond when we returned to gray skies and drizzle in England on January 4, 1985. The brooding quiet everywhere was no longer restful. It gave me the chills. This wasn't the Gower with breathtaking walks from home to the ocean, fresh ocean breezes, and wild ponies. I missed picturesque, bike-friendly Davis. Even thinking about my family gave me a fresh stab of pain in my chest. I had to wait all over again, but this time it was for John's green card.

John began work at Canterbury College the day after we arrived. I made the best of my all-day isolation by becoming the quintessential "perfect" housewife. He walked with me to the grocery store once or twice a week to keep the fridge stocked. My loving mom had laboriously hand-copied numerous Sri Lankan recipes, and I tried many of them out, crafting dinners and desserts that were ready for John when his work was done.

Gardening became my new passion. I transformed the tiny strip of backyard into a little oasis of color, with columns of white, pink, and purple sweet peas. To be patriotic to both the US and the UK, I layered the path with a large swath of red salvia, white alyssum, and blue lobelia. My neighbor offered me horse manure, which he said was perfect for growing potatoes. I watched in delight as each potato leaf unfurled.

I wrote long newsy letters to my parents and siblings, exaggerating all the positives, so no one would know how isolated I felt. I read and reread all their letters, envious of everything I was missing. John decided to take up competitive running, so I biked alongside him as he ran his hundred-mile training runs each week. Weekends I accompanied him to his races and cheered his completed half marathons. I photographed him at every finish post and placed all his race cards chronologically in a special racing album. I also jotted down his times and how he placed in each race.

We joined a badminton group, but, unlike our outdoor courts in Kumasi, games were played in an indoor gym with people John's age. No one wanted to drink, talk, or joke around after the games, like I used to do at the Kumasi Staff Club. They simply disappeared back into their married lives. As dreary days blended into a flat plane of predictable nothingness, I yearned intensely for more activities and friends my own age, but like Rapunzel, stuck in her tower, my life revolved completely around John when he was home. He seemed to like it that way.

After dinner one evening, I told John I needed fresh air. John followed me through the kitchen door, and we stood facing the yard. The smell of freshly dug-up earth was all around us because of the soil I'd loosened up that morning. John pointed at it.

"Wow, Lally, you did a lot of digging this morning. Is this where you'll plant tomatoes?"

"Yeah." I turned away so he wouldn't see my face.

"What's the problem?" He had probably already noticed my mutinous expression. I took a deep breath and turned around to face him.

"Sometimes I feel as if you're just giving me compliments to make me happy, John. You treat me like a small child. I hate to sound ungrateful, but I need *more*. Isn't there something I can do at home? Apart from all the cooking and gardening? I'm *dying* to make friends, or find work, or go to school, or *something!* I hate to say this, but I'm bored, John. My brain cells are shriveling and dying."

Evening shadows painted the garden an ominous gray. A chaffinch fluttered away from the roof of the shed to the neighbor's tree. Its undulating wings made me yearn to fly away also.

"This is not the States, where you can just take whatever classes you want, Lally. You'll have to wait till we're back in California to complete your degree. You and your sisters and brother were pretty spoiled in Kumasi, weren't you?" He raised his hands in the air. "Your parents got you everything you wanted. You led a privileged life, with fun activities lined up all the time. Well, guess what? You're not in Ghana, and you're not a child anymore. You're twenty-four now. You're my *wife*. Isn't that enough?" The telltale flush of anger stood out high on his cheeks. He kicked a pebble so hard that it skittered against the shed.

I sniffed and wiped my cheek, hung my head, but said nothing.

"You're going to have to grow up, Lally." He moved to face me, his face a pale blur in the gloom. "You sound a little immature and ungrateful. See how hard I work all day for both of us? If this life isn't *enough*, what more do you need? You signed up for this, right? You didn't complain like this the last time you were here, did you?" He dug around another pebble with his shoe.

"That was *two weeks*, John. It's different now." A chilly wind lifted the hair from my face and gave me goosebumps.

"Well, Lally, I have news for you. This is what women *do* when they're married. They take care of their husbands. Seems like it's not enough for you. You need constant titillation. Is *that* what you need?" His words hit me like shards of ice.

"I don't, I don't!" I shook my head. "I've just run out of things to do."

"How about if I buy a secondhand piano? What do you think? Maybe you could teach piano or something?"

"Yes, yes, I'd *love* that!" My heart raced. "John, I really don't want to sound ungrateful. I really don't." I sniffed. "I just miss all the company—the life I had in Davis. The days really drag when I'm stuck at home with nothing to do, and you're not home till dark. Everything just got to me today, for some reason." I wiped the tears off my face. "Maybe I need more time to get used to this."

He squeezed my shoulder with his hand, pulled me closer, and hugged me tight. The warmth of his chest blotted out the cold night air, and his body heat magically made everything better. Too soon, he disengaged my arms, then put his forefinger up in the air, telling me to hold on.

"Wait right here, Lally. Don't come in. I'll call you in a moment." He turned on his heel and strode inside. I hugged myself because I was freezing. Scarcely three minutes later he called me. Mystified, I walked through the kitchen and into our tiny living room. He was bare chested and sat at the foot of our bed with the covers drawn. The color rose to my cheeks.

"John?" I asked in a shaky voice.

"Shhh." He silenced me with a finger on his lips. "Take all your clothes off and come here."

I walked to the light switch, but he stopped me in my tracks with a raised palm.

"No, leave the lights on this time. I want to watch my beautiful wife," he commanded.

My traitorous body succumbed to his suggestive tone, and I complied. As I peeled off my jumper, shirt, pants, and underwear, leaving them in a pool on the floor, I was acutely embarrassed and moved stiffly, hunching my shoulders as I walked to the bed. As soon as I lay down, he got off the bed and knelt on the floor beside it.

"What are you—?" I tried to sit up, but he firmly pushed me on my back on the bed.

"Shhh. Be quiet. Lie there. Close your eyes." There was excitement in his tone now. He fastened a silk tie around my wrist. My eyes jerked open, but he was partially lying across my chest now and reached over to secure my other wrist to the opposite bedpost.

"You aren't listening. I said, 'shut your eyes,'" he commanded.

"John?" There was a definite quaver in my voice now, but I complied.

"Shhh. This is how ungrateful wives get punished," he murmured. My arms were now stretched out on either side of me, and he spread my legs also, anchoring them to the bottom bedposts with cords. With yet another silk tie, I was blindfolded, and thrown into a heady mix of anticipation and fear.

When he finally joined me on the bed, he was rough and controlling.

"Is this enough for you, Lally? Am I enough for you? Am I? Am I?"

"Yes," I moaned, "yes, yes, yes!"

True to his word, John found me a slightly beat-up black Kimball piano with a warm tone. I ran my fingers over the dark wood in delight. It would be lovely to play piano again. He set me up with piano lessons from a retired concert pianist. A fifty-minute train ride through the gorgeous, rolling Kent countryside took me to her country home in Whitstable each Thursday.

Geraldine (Geri) Mason Harrison looked over one hundred years old. (I learned later that she was actually only fifty-six.)

She had gnarled, wrinkled fingers that matched her heavily creased face, but when she set her fingers down on the keys, her tone was so golden that it stole my breath away. Two grand pianos filled her front room, and I loved when we played two-piano duets together.

"How did your keyboard panel get so scratched up?" I asked, pointing to the dozens of linear tears that marred the beautiful backboard of her white Steinway.

"Pure vanity," she laughed. "I flat-out refused to cut my long painted fingernails when I practiced for my concerts. This was the result," she said with a shrug. I loved that rebellious, devil-may-care attitude.

I practiced piano six hours a day, with a half-hour lunch break. My fingers grew strong and nimble as the hours melted away, and I fell more deeply in love with Chopin's nocturnes. Geri taught me how to "love every note," and under her tutelage, I was transported away from my reality to a classical music haven.

John had set me up with lessons ostensibly to give me something to do while he was at work, but I knew he hoped that once I passed the exam and received a licentiate from the Royal Academy, I could earn back the tuition money by teaching kids piano while he worked. As I dutifully mastered my performance pieces and scales, I wondered how fulfilling my life would be if I devoted it to scribbling pencil strokes on kids' manuscripts and listening to painfully executed piano exercises five days a week.

Doctor of doctors indeed.

Seventeen

Spelunking

That summer, John announced that we'd be taking a week-long adventure caving course in the Yorkshire Dales, in northern England. The site was known for its vertical pitches or "potholes" that led to further excursions through limestone caves deep underground. I was thrilled to break the monotony of my life and meet people my own age for a change.

A lengthy train ride took us through the magnificent English countryside, dotted with sheep and cows. Picturesque villages whipped by, nestled in green fields, their brick houses gradually switching to more sturdy stone dwellings. A taxi brought us to a rustic dormitory-style building, plonked in the middle of nowhere. There was a gravel drive, grasslands all around, and a few tall trees scattered in front of the house and on the periphery.

That evening we traded life stories with ten other spelunkers over my all-time favorite, steak and Yorkshire pudding. With a full belly and a mug of warm cocoa nestled in my hand, I laughed uproariously at their Monty Python jokes. Time was drifting by too fast. I wanted to savor this break from reality; I was truly in love with this place.

The next morning, just outside our dormitory building, the organizers strung up a rope system on two tall trees about twenty feet apart. I suited up with a navy-blue wetsuit. Over this, I donned zippered, waterproof overalls and a headlamp. The instructor handed me an external body harness with all kinds of weird clinking metal clips and other gizmos attached, until I felt like a trussed-up chicken. With my first steps, I morphed into a lumbering gorilla. To my amazement, within a half hour I adjusted to the bulky getup.

In no time at all, I was dangling forty feet up in the air at the top of a tree. My harness was securely anchored to the rope. There were tree branches in my face, and I was slightly out of breath from my climb up the rope, but I cheekily took both hands off the rope to wave to John, allowing the metal harness to keep me safe. Even more exhilarating was rappelling down the rope at top speed with the wind rushing at my face. It beat any thrill ride I'd ever taken. We all took turns practicing these skills, and in the afternoon I learned to switch ropes, travel horizontally to the nearby tree, switch ropes again, then rappel down.

"You're taking to this like a natural—I'm proud of you," John remarked, snagging a photo of me in my gear before I descended. I knew from his tone that he really meant it, and my heart swelled several sizes.

On day two, we drove a few miles to a grassy area where a vertical drop led to an underground caving system. The access point was where a stream poured into a hole in the ground, forming a waterfall that cascaded and disappeared into the blackness underground. My heart stopped when I realized I'd have to rappel down the rope into pitch-black darkness. At the same time I also had to make sure I didn't drown, because a gushing waterfall cascaded only a few feet away from my face.

Once I made it to the bottom, I was transported to another world. Everywhere I looked, delicate, gleaming ivory stalactites descended gracefully from the rocky roof. Tiny drops of water made plinking sounds as they dropped from the delicate tips of these magnificent chandeliers, reminding me that the cave was still developing. I was surprised at the crisp, clean air underground, which smelled a little like the smell of rain on fresh earth. It was so humid that my breath misted. It was like landing on an exotic new planet.

The headlamps of the other spelunkers lit up the waterfall at different levels as they rappelled down, which was an incredibly beautiful sight. At the base, the waterfall became a black puddle and then turned into a meandering stream that wound through the narrow, rocky passage we would follow. The black water sparkled like dark oil as it wound its way eerily through the gloomy cave. It was an absolutely surreal experience.

Later that week, I rappelled 250 feet down a pitch-black vertical pothole and was ecstatic when I saw splendid, cathedral-like stalactites and stalagmites as soon as I hit the platform at the base. Few people in the world above would ever experience this magnificence of nature. The downside was the tortuous passages where I wriggled like a worm in a muddy tunnel, unable to completely sit or stand for what felt like hours at a time. I was festooned with mud from head to toe, like a giant mud-caked seal—definitely not a pastime for the weak of heart.

The adrenaline rush of discovery, coupled with the approval in John's eyes, gave my spirits a much-needed bounce after so many days cooped up in the house with only the piano for company. I loved the jokes and gentle banter among my fellows. The meals were wholesome, and all the spelunking gave me an appetite that shocked me. Finally, I was truly living!

Back in Canterbury, the abrupt return to isolation hit even harder. The full life I experienced during those precious five months in Davis was now just a dim memory. I yearned to be back in California but no longer dared to bring this up. It was increasingly clear that John really struggled to communicate. At times he would be solicitous, but suddenly, for no reason, he might switch to cold and unattainable, leaving me to try to figure out how I'd upset him. When I pressed him about what set off his black moods, he often brought up things I'd said or done weeks earlier. He'd marinated in the anger without saying a word at the time, so I had no chance to apologize—I had no idea he was upset in the first place! It was incredibly frustrating.

I woke up at three o'clock one morning, surprised to see him perched in an armchair in the living room reading a book.

"John, do you know what time it is?" I asked, shielding my eyes from the lamp beside him.

"Can't sleep. The sound of your snot bubbles bursting when you sleep is disgusting. You should blow your nose more," he said gruffly, returning to his book.

Humiliated, I turned away and pulled the sheets over my face. Silent, frustrated tears trickled down my cheeks, even though I knew that this might cause even more "snot bubbles." At times like these, I wondered how I could have married such a cold, unfeeling, and increasingly controlling stranger.

When I called the American Embassy for an update on John's green card application, I learned that they'd run into snags based on his prior record. John's scowl prevented me from delving further. A week later, a thick manila envelope arrived in the mail stamped with the American Embassy logo. I ripped it open at once and was shocked to discover the list of John's past transgressions that had warranted extra clearance. Aghast, I sat at the kitchen table with the documents and thumbed through the list. As a teenager he'd stolen cars and taken them on joy rides with friends, only to dump them at other sites. He'd vandalized property and damaged items at stores. I also saw that he'd married his first wife not once, but *twice!*

When John got home, I waved the stack, asking for an explanation. He studiously ignored me, but I followed him to the coat rack peppering him with questions.

"John, I thought I knew you, but some of this stuff is *horrible*. I can't believe that *anyone* could do things like this." I followed him into the kitchen and laid the papers on the table in front of him.

"Oh, I was a teenager; it was fun, Lally. Stop nagging. Who cares? It's all in the past . . . " He had a smile of reminiscence on his face. "The eggs . . . I remember that. Me and my friend would run our hands through dozens of eggs in grocery stores. Smash 'em all—it's so easy—then we'd leave the store and crack up, imagining the look on people's faces when they bought eggs." He snickered at my disgusted frown. "Got caught after doing it a few times." He helped himself to shepherd's pie and green beans.

"What about this one? Says you married Anne *twice?*"

"Yeah, after we got divorced, we tried to make it work again, but it didn't. When I split up with her, she cleaned me out at the bank. Took every penny from checking—bitch!" His face darkened as he stabbed the beans viciously.

"How about this one, John, this is recent!" I riffled through the pages. "This was back in Kumasi when you were a professor! Says, 'caught stealing a book from the library . . . placed it inside his coat.'" I looked him in the eye. "You weren't a kid then. Why, John? How could you? You made like double what my dad did in Kumasi. I just don't get it." I dropped the papers on the tables and shook my head.

He froze, holding a forkful of beans in midair. "Just leave it now. Do you have to have me explain everything?" He switched to a jeering tone. "Know what? You're such a Goody Two-shoes sometimes, going all holier than thou like you never break rules. Just leave it, okay?" His eyes narrowed, and his mouth tightened into a thin white line. He waved his fork around, but the beans held on tenaciously. "What you *should* be worrying about is whether the Americans will overlook these adolescent pranks." He munched for a moment. "If not, I guess we won't be going anywhere *near* your family, will we?" I heard a new and ugly tone in his voice now.

Afraid to say anything that might make him even more furious, I walked into the adjoining living room. I threw myself on the sofa and turned the TV on so there'd be noise to drown out the clamor in my brain. My mind was whirling. He broke eggs *for fun?* As for the theft of the book, he'd been a professor in Kumasi with lots of money. What was that about? Was it simply challenging to steal something?

Over the next few weeks, John spoke only in monosyllables, and the banter was gone from his conversations. I knew it weighed on him that the police report might sabotage his immigrant visa approval. In the past he'd often talked about the "huge sacrifice" he'd make for me to quit his job and move to America "so you can be with your family." But now, for the first time, I wondered if I'd simply been his ticket for the immigrant visa all along. Was *that* why he'd courted me so intensely and pushed marriage so fast? My stomach churned, even as I scolded myself for having such nasty thoughts about possible ulterior motives.

Imagining a future where I was perpetually stuck in England made me feel as if cold chains had tightened around my neck. I couldn't simply fly to California either. John managed all our finances. I'd never so much as written a check, so I couldn't imagine that he'd willingly pay for a plane ticket to San Francisco.

As the weeks dragged by with no updates, the nineteen-year age difference became even more pronounced. I loved hopping around to pop music from the radio when I wasn't playing piano, but as soon as John got home, the first thing he did was to switch the station to classical. I hated the implied criticism in the dreaded click that killed my bubbly spirits. After jiving around to a-ha's "Take on Me," the abrupt transition to Gregorian chants was a definite mood killer. I always tightened my lip but said nothing.

Like a bird with clipped wings, I wanted to lose myself in music. I wanted more intellectual stimulation. I wanted to be *young*, not a has-been, married woman standing silently in her husband's shadow with steadily dimming prospects of completing college. I'd never been truly free. From my parents I'd switched to the Claydens, then back to my parents, and now John was the authority figure.

To avoid wallowing in self-pity, I focused on John's caring qualities. He never let me carry anything heavy. There were times when he still called me "princess" in an endearing tone, and he oversaw all potential safety risks. He always ensured that I was dressed appropriately for the cold. At times he seemed too parental, but it was also cute. I loved how he joked around with strangers and charmed them with his quick wit. Some mornings he brought me toasted rolls and tea in bed before he left for work. Most of all, I enjoyed cuddling up with him in the armchair to watch TV. That was always reassuring, and it never grew old.

Eighteen

True Colors

E verything changed one morning in early November 1985. When I put on my bra, my breasts were tender and swollen. I did the calculation in my head with some trepidation. Eleven months . . . was I pregnant? We'd taken no precautions. I couldn't for the life of me remember when I'd last had my period.

I said nothing to John, but after he left for work, I slapped some clothes on in a state of intense excitement, skipped breakfast because I was nauseous, and walked to the nearest Boots pharmacy to buy a Clear Blue pregnancy test kit. Hurrying home, I ran to the bathroom. My fingers trembled as the dark blue stripe confirmed my pregnancy. I sat on the side of the bathtub with tears of joy streaming down my face.

I would have a multicultural half–Sri Lankan, half-English baby to fill the void while we waited for the visa. I hoped I'd deliver okay—John was over a foot taller than me, and I weighed only one hundred pounds. Would pregnancy alter our relationship? Would John still want me when my belly got huge? He was so possessive. Would he be jealous if the baby got all my attention? I gently rubbed at my still-flat belly, marveling that a little being would soon join us, if all went well. I had no work or school commitments. The timing couldn't be more perfect. I prayed for a girl.

I put together a magnificent pork chop dinner and baked a chocolate cake, then iced it with chocolate. I picked flowers from the garden and arranged them on the dining table. Shortly before John returned, I lit a candle and set it by the flowers. My entire body trembled at the click of the front door. I'd initially planned to break the news over dinner, but my excitement bubbled over, and I ran down the hallway to give him the biggest hug ever and latched my fingers together behind him.

"Whoa, what's going on?" He smiled and set down his leather briefcase, then held me at arms' length to look me in the eye.

"John, I'm . . . we're . . . we're going to have a baby! A baby! I can't believe it. I checked this morning—the test was definitely positive. I'm pregnant! I'm pregnant! It's perfect! I'm so, so *happy!*" I jumped around with such abandon that it took me several moments to register the look on his face.

He. Wasn't. Smiling.

He removed his jacket, hung it up, then turned on his heel and made his way down the hall to the kitchen. I ran after him, confused.

"John, did you hear what I said?"

He stood rigidly and avoided my eyes, even though I'd moved in front of him.

"I heard," he said curtly. His eyes flickered over the candle, the flowers, and the meal on the table, but his lips were set in a grim line. I felt waves of cold and then heat washing over me. What was the matter? This man, my husband, was an absolute stranger. I sank into my chair and bit my lip.

"Aren't you going to talk? Say something," I said quietly.

He reached for his water and took a long sip, then wiped his mouth off slowly. "What do you want me to say, Lally? You're not looking at this the right way. I'm not ready for this. We can't *afford* a child right now. No way. Can't do it." His tone was flat and brooked no argument.

"What do you mean, 'Can't do it'? You're asking me to . . . to . . . what are you saying, John?" I gripped the edge of the table to anchor my spinning universe.

He served himself pork chops, potatoes, and salad in silence. His face was pale and drawn.

"John, you, we . . . we didn't take *any precautions* all these months! You never *said* you didn't want us to have a baby. Why didn't you *say* something, John? I could have gone on the pill. You could've used condoms. You know how I feel about abortions. I was at a convent, remember? I'm not doing this. Please, John, *please?*" Right now, I despised myself for the begging tone in my voice. Tears gushed out of my eyes and dripped on my lap. He avoided meeting my gaze. "Listen, John, the timing's perfect. I'll have all the time in the world to look after a baby. It will give me something to do. *Please. . . .*" I sobbed uncontrollably, laying my head on my crossed hands on the table. In front of me lay a gaping Yorkshire pothole with only blackness below, and no exit in sight.

Surely, he didn't mean it. It would just take time for him to come around. Any moment now, his hand would snake up to stroke my hair. A minute passed, then another. My sobs got quieter, and I sat up unsteadily, using a paper napkin to wipe my eyes and blow my nose. John chewed on the pork chops and acted as if I did not exist.

Finally, he sat back and carefully patted his mouth clean. He cleared his throat. "You aren't thinking, Lally. We need to save up money for the California trip."

"But, we never discusse. . . ."

"Listen, when we decide to have a baby in the future, I want to know the *moment* I'm actually going to conceive a child, not just have you just throw it in my face like this. I'm not ready. You aren't either. Trust me. *We* aren't ready for this." His expression was closed off, sullen. The purple pansies I'd so carefully arranged on the table mocked me with their magnificent perfection.

I gave it one last shot.

"I'm alone *all day*, John. The baby would be company for me when you're gone all day. I want this baby, please . . . can you do this one thing for me, please?" I whimpered but could barely get the words out. A black fuzzy cloud obscured my vision. I knew I was groveling, but I didn't know what else to do.

"I've told you, no baby. You aren't going ahead with this—I'll find somewhere they can take care of it for us. Please stop being so . . . so dramatic and *childish*, Lally." His tone was encrusted with icicles. Each word pierced me with the horror of what he was saying. How could anyone ever know "the moment" they were about to conceive a baby? I'd always figured that people got married, then had babies. I covered my untouched food with foil and placed it in the fridge. Every sound I made appeared magnified in the deafening silence.

I trailed into the garden, banging the door shut. The setting sun faded the colors into grays and blacks that mirrored my mood. Even the moon glared at me, barely visible behind angry clouds. At the back shed, I sat on the step and focused on the individual shadows, imagining each was a leering vampire waiting to pounce.

John always made the rules, and I followed them without question, but his response was devastating. A shiver raced through me, partially because of the cold, but also because I felt small and helpless with no one to reach out to for advice about what to do. I kicked at the dirt and watched small stones skittering in front of me. For some reason, the plight of those poor, harmless stones brought tears to my eyes.

I'd always argued that abortion should be reserved for incest and rape. Years of Catholic values, instilled at the St. Louis convent in Kumasi, had cemented my position. John was forcing me to get an abortion *just because it wasn't convenient?* How could he justify termination as birth control, when we'd taken *zero precautions* over the last eleven months? How sick was that? How could I live with myself if I actually agreed?

I willed John to come out, hold me, and reassure me—to tell me he'd reconsidered. He did not. The kitchen light eventually went off. I remained frozen on the step till I could no longer bear the cold, then traipsed back in like a robot. Latching the kitchen door, I headed, fully clothed, to bed, making an exaggerated detour past John, who sat in the living room armchair reading. He did not look up. I squeezed my eyes shut in bed and caressed my belly to protect this being within me. Sleep was impossible.

John avoided coming to bed till past midnight. I begged him to reconsider. I raged, I argued, and I cried till my eyes could squeeze out no more tears. It was like talking to a cement wall. He simply turned his back to me. Shortly afterward, to my utter disgust, he started snoring.

My pillow was sodden the next morning. I remained in bed as he showered and dressed. He walked to me, fished my limp hand out from under my pillow, and squeezed it. I feigned sleep and lay there, unmoving, till the soft click of the front door latch told me he'd left. Still unable to move, I stared at the imperfections in the wall beside me, my eyes burning and sore. My brain kept replaying his hateful words. I stroked my belly for comfort.

The glare of the sun's morning rays eventually smacked me in the face. I walked downstairs but sat in the living room lacking the energy to do anything but flick my eyes to the kitchen entrance. The full reality of my existence struck me. I was a slave, tethered to mind the kitchen for John. I functioned as his chef and bedwarmer, no more. The cake I'd baked so joyfully less than twenty-four hours before mocked me now. A half-eaten piece sat on a plate beside it. As I pulled myself up out of the chair, my arm brushed against my oversensitive breast. My body had already irrevocably changed, and it would continue to do so unless I . . . unless I . . . The thought was too hard to even conceptualize.

"I'm sorry," I whispered, rubbing tenderly at my belly. "I'm sorry, I'm sorry, I'm so, so sorry. I want to, but he won't let me. He won't let me . . . I love you."

Murderer! Liar!

A wave of nausea hit, and I grabbed the back of the chair for support. I succumbed to a spate of dry heaving sobs, then I shut my eyes tight and took a long shuddering breath. John had made the decision for me. If I dared cross him, I'd face a nine-month pregnancy and all the frightening changes alone. I had not a single friend for support. Maybe he'd send me packing to America. I wished I had the spunk to stand up for myself and the little one growing inside me, but I actually couldn't. I hated myself for my weakness and dependence on John.

Never had I felt more alone.

When my brain grew weary from all the cascading thoughts, I decided to share this dreadful secret with my mom. It was four in the morning California time, but I knew she'd pick up. I held the phone with trembling fingers, trying to figure out how to phrase it. With her strong Christian faith, she was bound to be judgmental, but I didn't care. Someone in my universe had to understand the hell I was in. My mom would give me a hand out of the clouds of pea soup fog.

"Ammah?"

"Lally, is everything okay?" I heard the sleepy concern in her tone. Words I prepared refused to come out. I gripped the phone like my life depended on it.

"Lally?"

"I have to tell you something bad, Ammah. Really, really,

bad. You'll have to keep this secret. From everyone. Do you promise, Ammah?"

"Of course, Lally, you know I don't talk to anyone, girl. What is it?"

I launched in. "Ammah, I just found out that I'm . . . I'm pregnant, Ammah," I rushed along so she could not respond, "but John and I discussed it, and here's the problem. It . . . it will be too expensive for us to go forward with it right now . . . so . . . so he's . . . we've decided that we're . . . we're not going through with it. Ammah, I just wanted *you* to know. I'm not telling anyone else. We want to save up for coming to California, Ammah. . . ." I ended lamely.

I waited, with bated breath. I imagined her sadness, her crumpled face trying to come to terms with what I'd just flung at her so early in the morning. The long-distance crackle seemed to go on forever.

"Ammah? I know you're disappointed. This would have been your first grandchild . . . I'm so sorry," I spluttered. Tears plinked down on my receiver.

"Lally, Lally, it will be okay," she said. "The two of you obviously thought hard about this. You've made a tough decision. Sometimes in life you have to make hard decisions, girl. You can always have a baby when you come back to Davis. I'll help out when you're back here, Lally. Take your time. It's okay, there'll be so many other chances, girl, don't worry."

I tightened several coils of the telephone cord around my index finger till the tip turned white.

"Really, Ammah? You aren't disappointed?" I choked.

"You have to make tough decisions sometimes, Lally. If that's what the two of you decided, then that's the right decision, Lally. It's okay. Don't worry." She sounded strong, resolute.

No long lecture to fan my flames of guilt, just complete understanding and unconditional absolution. She'd crossed Sri

Lankan cultural and religious divides without a blink, despite her misgivings. The love that blossomed for my mother at that moment engulfed me like a warm tropical wave. It was so intense that words became choked in my throat. The chains weighting my heart disappeared, as if they'd morphed into a gossamer veil that lifted off me. The room, which had been blurred throughout the call, came into focus.

My God-fearing, churchgoing mother. I would never forget how she stood by me in that moment of my greatest need.

"Lally? Lally? Are you okay?" her voice crackled out, colored with anxiety.

"I'm fine. I love you so much. Thanks."

I hung up.

Nineteen

Dark Days

For the next few days I took great pains to keep as much physical space from John as possible. If his arm snaked around me in bed, I froze, unresponsive, till he backed off. I kept it civil when he was around, but we barely spoke. As if to appease me, he took on chores he usually left to me, such as washing dinner plates. Halfway through a lackluster attempt to run through my scales on the piano, I dropped my wrist to my lap and gazed blankly at the piano keys, unable to shake off dread at what lay ahead.

What if I told him no and went to California? If I flew there, the child would not know its father. I had no income, no undergraduate degree or job. Then there was the cultural issue. As the oldest, I had to showcase the "perfect union" to my siblings. Imagine showing up in Davis and having the family deal with the severe embarrassment of a pregnant daughter, separated from her husband of less than a year? They'd never live it down. I could not add myself and a small baby to my parents' home. They would welcome us without reservation, but I couldn't burden them. They'd not wanted me to marry John in the first place. I couldn't bear to tell them that they'd probably been right, after all. I felt cornered by the weight of this decision, compounded with John's absolute lack of support about going ahead.

I talked to the life within me to explain how agonized I was. I'd desperately hoped for a child one day, and John was forty-four! What if we couldn't have more? Should I stop being focused on what I wanted and think about John's needs? Was I selfish to want to keep this child for myself? Why hadn't John simply worn a condom or brought up this issue before? Why put me in this horrible position without a discussion? I was such a pathetic, weak wretch that I couldn't find it within me to throw down a challenge flag. Why? Why? *Why?*

John told me over dinner that he'd found a place where "it" would be done.

"But first, two doctors have to support this. You'll have to explain to the doctors why you want it," he murmured. He slathered butter on his dinner roll, then balanced the knife sideways on his plate. I focused on its shiny edge to avoid meeting his eyes.

"What do I say? I'd be lying."

He looked up at me briefly, as if tired of the discussion. "Say it's a financial hit or something like that."

"Whatever." I stared at the knife, imagining it cutting into me.

"It won't take long. You'll just have to stay there overnight." He drenched a wedge of potato in gravy.

I nodded as a wave of nausea hit. The food was like sandpaper, and I could barely swallow. I had become an empty, acquiescent shell.

"Small bites, take small bites," he said, waving his fork in disapproval. "Glad you've come around, Lally." He exhaled and leaned back in his chair. "One day when you're older, you'll realize that we had to go this way." He stood up and lifted his plate off the table. "Place is about an hour away by train—I'll buy the ticket."

I placed my barely touched food in the fridge. Every movement felt mechanical, pointless. Nothing mattered.

I was a zombie.

He drove me to a gray medical office building the following day.

"I'll wait out here," he said, without looking up. I was stunned that he intended to remain in the car, and anger welled up in waves. I'd obviously not seen the worst of him yet. I noticed his white knuckles on the steering wheel and wanted to tell him he was a fucking coward, but the words were stuck in my throat. I grabbed my purse, left the car, and slammed the door as hard as I could before walking away.

In the blur of white noise during my subsequent discussion with two doctors, a few phrases stood out.

"Are you *sure* this is what you want?"

Fuck no! I wanted to scream, but instead I nodded. "Yes, yes, it's what I want." Nod, nod. "We don't have enough money for a child." Nod, nod. *Liar.*

The other things they told me were terrifying: infection risk, bleeding, scarring, possible infertility, rare complications where parts might be "left behind." I wanted to vomit but somehow made it through the ordeal on autopilot.

The dilatation and curettage took place a week later. By the time the date rolled around, I wanted nothing more than to have the entire procedure behind me. Clearly "it" was still growing and developing inside me, every second altering my body as it increased its dependence on me. In med school I had learned the timeline for each organ's development. It was difficult to avoid dwelling on this as each excruciating hour passed.

John drove me to the train station. I took a taxi to a beautiful cottage surrounded by green fields. Baaing, snowy sheep dotted the landscape. I thought it was far too lovely a setting for the grisly tasks that took place inside the building. Along with five other young women, I was given a "last supper" that evening. I was somehow buoyed by the fact that we were all going through this process the following day. I would be placed under sedation. The procedure took only minutes, apparently, and I would be cleared to leave shortly after.

Afterward, I was very weak, with strong cramping sensations that made me dizzy when I attempted to walk. When I touched my belly, I had an intense feeling of loss. I wished I'd known its sex at the very least, but on the other hand I was glad I didn't know. It would have broken my heart if it were a girl. I wanted a daughter so much.

Still weak and dizzy that afternoon, I said my goodbyes, watching as each of the girls was picked up, either by her partner or her parents. I was the only one who had to make my way back home alone. It was excruciating having to call for a taxi when I worried that at any moment I might pass out. There were slivers of pain from every jolt on the taxi and train rides. Even worse than the physical pain, paralyzing guilt plagued me all the way to Canterbury.

A huge chasm opened up in our relationship after I returned. John appeared clueless and was dismissive of my psychologically fragile state. To my utter disgust, he actually dared ask me how long the doctors told me to wait for healing before resuming sexual relations. A week later, I started taking oral contraceptive pills. We never spoke of it again.

A month later, I was hunting for stationery in John's nightstand when I found four pages of scented, heavy purple paper inscribed with a girl's handwriting. For a second I contemplated putting it down, but I could not. I was insanely curious. It had been written by Essie, his long-term girlfriend, shortly before John came to California to marry me. She railed against him, saying how shocked she was, and how she'd expected him to be faithful. The entire tone of the letter was accusatory and brimmed with sheer incredulity.

My heart pounded as I read the ending: "By the way, I took

off that cheap ring you put around my finger, when you promised to be with me forever . . . I'm also glad I took care of our
baby, like you told me to." Those words made me sad. I ached
for the loss of her child, especially after what I had just gone
through. The papers burned my fingers, so I stuffed the letter
back in the drawer. I collapsed on the bed and stared at the
ceiling, taking a few shallow breaths.

When John sat in the armchair watching TV that night, I
told him I'd read her letter. He gave a dismissive shrug.

"So now you know. She didn't take it well. She thought
we'd be together after my divorce. Wouldn't have worked. We
fought all the time."

"John, these *secrets* . . . all the secrets that are coming out
are really getting to me. The police record, forcing Essie to have
an abortion . . . stuff like this that you've been hiding from me.
If we're to make this marriage work, I need to know what else
there is. Tell me. Tell me *now*. I can't handle even one more
secret. It will be over for me."

He hesitated, then turned the television off, turned to me,
and cleared his throat. I gripped my hand rest, my pulse pounding.

"Okay. There's just one last thing, that's it. I visited the
Claydens in Glasgow a few years back. John was out of town
that first night, so, er . . . Judy and I got carried away and we
slept together."

"You what? Judy?" I yelped. "*Judy Clayden? And John never
knew?*" My mouth hung half open.

"Yes, Judy." He transferred his gaze to his shoe. "Didn't think
too much of it till she called me a month later. Told me she was
pregnant, can you believe that? After just one night! Stupid girl
wasn't on birth control." His face darkened, and he picked at
the seam on his pants. "So stupid."

"I thought they couldn't have children?" I was struggling to
grasp this new revelation.

"Well, obviously *she* could."

"So, what happened . . . what happened after?"

"It would have been a disaster for her to continue the pregnancy. We were both married to other people at the time." He shook his head. "So I had to pay for the abortion. She told John she was visiting her mother in Dundee."

"Did John ever know?"

"John?" He smirked. "Nope, don't think he suspected a thing." He shot a glance at me, then raised his hands in the air. "I can see you're shocked, Lally. What was I to do? By the way, Judy's not my type . . . it was just a brief tryst. We were alone, and she came onto me that night. Didn't mean anything."

"It did to Judy," I murmured. "I saw it in her face when you came to Wales for Christmas. Now it makes sense that you took *her* side when we had that heated abortion discussion that Christmas in Wales."

"Hmm . . . don't recall. Well, that's what happened." He shrugged, appearing bored by the discussion. "Apart from that, I had a string of women in Kumasi when my wife was in England. Didn't mean anything. I was lonely." He exhaled and stretched back in his seat. "So that's it, I promise—that's my very last confession." He smiled and winked.

"That's . . . that's really awful, John, cheating on your friend with his wife." I shook my head. "Seems like it was all a game to you. *Now* I understand why she was so jealous of the attention you gave me when you visited. Wow. This is a heck of a lot to digest in one night."

"You're so high and mighty, brimming with morality lectures, Lally. That was all in the past, okay? I've changed now, I'm not cheating on you now, am I?" He had a mischievous, flirtatious tone as he walked over to pat my hand playfully. I swatted his hand away and walked into the kitchen for a drink of water.

John yawned when I walked back into the room. "Let's watch something," he remarked, picking up the remote control. A strange feeling took hold right then: stomach-turning, nauseating revulsion. I wanted so badly to walk out of the room and never return. Yet I was frozen, trapped in a deep void with no exit doors. I was now the keeper of too many of my husband's secrets—his loyal, trusted wife. As the weather forecast blared out from the telly, my brain wouldn't stop buzzing at the nonchalant way John used abortion for birth control. He refused to accept any guilt about his part in the process, instead choosing to blame the woman.

And I was married to this scoundrel.

After the loss of the pregnancy, coupled with the freeze in our relationship, I poured all my passion into the piano, sometimes playing for six or seven hours a day. When I embedded my brain in the beauty of the classical masterpieces, the music filled me with joy. I practiced scales for an hour each day. I also perfected all three examination pieces for the upcoming teaching exam. My piano teacher invited a friend over to listen to my rendition of Bach's prelude and fugue in F minor. Afterward they were both full of effusive praise. My teacher told me she thought I was prepared to take the final test.

In June 1986, I took the train to London to sit for the LRAM (Licentiate of the Royal Academy of Music) teaching examination. The venue was a very historic building, the Royal Academy of Music. Built in 1822, it was the oldest conservatory in England. My pulse raced as I headed up wide, shallow stone stairs to an arched stone entrance. Once I pushed open the massive door, my low heels echoed eerily within the cold, ecclesiastical gloom. Every hallway seemed to have a red flickering sign proclaiming, "Beyond here lies hell."

I walked down a long hallway lined with portraits. Mozart stared at me with a scowl that suggested I did not belong within those hallowed halls. My breath caught, and an uncomfortable sweat formed around my collar. I took deep lungfuls of air, but my breathing grew more labored as I walked farther into the building.

I knocked timidly at my assigned door and walked into a large examination hall. Sunlight streamed through a tall, arched window, lighting up a beautiful chestnut-brown Steinway. Three frosty, elderly examiners sat behind a long table: two men and a tall, skinny woman with glasses on her pointed nose. They sat so still that they were like cardboard cutouts. They tried so hard to look harmless, but their smiles were fake. I'd have my back to them when I played, which made my panic even worse.

I cast a despairing and helpless glance at the shut door behind me, trying to quench a desperate urge to flee. Breathing was becoming increasingly painful. I was running hot and cold at the same time. I told myself to stop being so silly. After practicing so hard for so many months, I was overprepared, not underprepared. My piano teacher had told me that.

One of the men coughed, and my heart galloped. I fiddled with my books and dropped one, so I picked it up with trembling hands, apologizing profusely throughout. I cast a nervous look behind me. The skinny woman smiled and nodded. She'd probably seen klutzes like me before. For some reason, this made me feel worse.

I somehow got through my three prepared pieces, because I was able to tune out the silent examiners. I pretended that I was home alone, playing my heart out. It was now time for my scales, my biggest strength. I'd polished every one of them.

"The scale of G minor, please. Three octaves. Both hands together, and please play it staccato," a man's voice announced. He sounded like a robot. I counted to three and began, but scarcely one octave in, my fingers became matchsticks. I aborted the scale. I was devastated, because for months on end I'd played them perfectly. Scales were my forte!

The disembodied voice of the woman behind me suggested, "Maybe your fingers are cold. Why don't you shake out your fingers and try that again?"

I shook my fingers, placed them under my thighs to warm them, and tried again, only to be hit by waves of anxiety that paralyzed me further. It was frightening to see how inexplicably incompetent I'd suddenly become. My heart hammered in my ears, and all I could hear was a roaring tearing through my brain. I shook my hands hard, placed them on the keyboard, but they simply wouldn't comply. Scale after scale had mistakes, and each mistake compounded my panic. Soon even my throat closed up. Defeated, I removed my hands from the keys, placed them on my lap, and bowed my head. Tears splashed down on my folded knuckles. It was over.

Three weeks later, I picked up the official-looking envelope from the mail and learned, to no surprise, that I'd failed the exam. If I'd been better prepared for my anxiety, I'm sure I would have made it, because I got excellent marks for my Bach prelude and fugue, the Mozart sonata, and Debussy's arabesque. None of this mattered. I'd failed. This was a first. In Ghana, I'd coasted through every piano examination despite my nerves. But not this time. Here was yet another loss, another failure.

John's face turned white when I shared the test results. Rather than console me, he threw both hands up in the air and stormed into the kitchen to get a beer.

"Well *that* was a huge waste of time," he said coldly, ignoring my tears, "after *all* that money I paid out to Mrs. Harrison!"

I felt like a squashed dog turd.

In the summer of 1986, John finally received his green card. I'd been in England for a year and a half. I could barely wait to leave. I was thrilled that I'd be back with my family. I'd make it my mission to complete my undergraduate degree in physiology. I'd had too many fits and starts. John appeared excited about the move, and he soon found a buyer for the house. Packing my paltry belongings took no time at all. My gorgeous piano had been my close companion for innumerable hours each day, and I was sorry to leave it behind. I caressed the polished satiny lid one last time before it was taken away.

"I failed you. I'm sorry I let you down. Forgive me."

As an image of that cottage in the countryside flashed into my mind, I realized that I wasn't apologizing only to the piano.

Twenty

Starting Over

B ack in beloved California, we moved in temporarily with
my parents until John could find a job. Thankfully, more
space had opened up in my parents' home because Viji had
moved out with her boyfriend while she completed her international relations degree at UC Davis. Vim and Nimi were in high
school. I started my human physiology classes.

It was incredibly satisfying to be a student again. My vibrant
zest for learning, forced underground for sixteen months, was
once more unleashed. I'd thought studying would be difficult,
after days of nothing more challenging than piano, gardening,
and cooking meals, but to my surprise and delight, my long-dor-
mant brain revved up in no time at all.

Government grants and financial aid covered university
tuition because we were so financially strapped. I reflected on
what a wonderful country this was, that it would invest in my
future in this manner. I worked extra hard, making a promise
that I'd one day give back to this amazing society that placed its
trust in this new immigrant.

To increase our cash flow, over the next three years I taught
special education as a teacher's aide at Holmes Junior High
School, a short walk from my parents' home. I also accepted a

summer job decorating ice cream cakes for Baskin-Robbins in downtown Davis.

Shortly after I was hired, we had a quiet afternoon when I could replenish our display. I decorated an ice cream clown face with blue eyes, a brown nose, a red mouth, and thick brown eyebrows, then handed it off to Bob, my manager. He piped red and green stars on a cone, placed it upside down on the face, and carefully set our creation down on the display case. As he walked around to admire it, I noticed a faraway look in his eyes.

"Something up?" I asked.

Startled, he walked back to me. "Daydreaming, I guess. Don't want to do this forever. Guess I got roped into the family business, but I've always wanted a career in . . . I don't know, science or medicine related, maybe nursing school."

"Nursing school? Sounds fun. I was in med school in Ghana, but it closed down. Political stuff. Long story." I added, to his raised eyebrows, "I had to give up on becoming a doctor."

"Sorry to hear that, Lally." He placed a large dollop of mint chocolate chip ice cream on a dark chocolate graham cracker crust, to start up a turtle pie.

"Yeah, get this, a Sri Lankan fortune teller told my dad I'd become a doctor." I squeezed out a little too much blue icing and wiped it off with a wet knife. "Can you believe that, Bob? A doctor! Actually a 'doctor of doctors,' whatever that means. Oh, well, obviously he was waaaay off. Didn't see me working here at Baskin-Robbins. I don't even have a degree, so that dream's long gone. Maybe he said, 'decorator of decorators!'"

"Er . . . your blue eye is collapsing, Lally. How about 'disaster of decorators'?" Bob smiled.

We laughed uproariously, but for a fleeing instant I yearned for that long-forgotten dream. John would never allow me anywhere near med school again. Once my undergrad degree was complete, he wanted me to find work to supplement his income, preferably as a piano teacher or something. He never failed to remind me that *he'd* supported me in England, so it was now up to me.

"You have better long-term earning potential," was his constant refrain.

John's belief that ours would be the all-American success story did not pan out. Living with my parents was an awkward chapter of our married life, but somehow it made financial sense. We helped out with the mortgage and groceries, and over the next few years John even taught my mother to drive again. (She'd not driven for years after a minor fender-bender in Kumasi when her sari got entangled in her shoe, and she hit the accelerator instead of the brake pedal.)

John took on an assortment of odd jobs. He worked a few days a week for our next-door neighbor, a contractor, and he cleaned out recently vacated apartments for a clean-up company. He also drove a school bus. At age forty-seven, with no PhD and only foreign credentials, he scored a couple of interviews, but no community college wanted to hire him. His mood grew blacker with each polite rejection letter. Our plan to "temporarily" live with my parents was becoming indefinite.

As his dreams of a lucrative job faded, John's resentment of all things American widened the chasm in our relationship. I was inordinately grateful for the opportunities our family had received. Thanks to flexible college scheduling, I was on track to earn a bachelor's of science degree. Vim and Nimi graduated from high school and both set their sights on engineering degrees. Viji graduated from UC Davis in the fall of 1987, so there was one glorious quarter in which all four of us attended UC Davis together. I took a Bach appreciation class with Nimi, and we both got A's.

Four years after we moved in with my parents, John applied for a PhD program in accounting and was accepted at Pennsylvania State University for the fall of 1988.

Rather than languish at home while John took classes, I applied to, and was subsequently accepted into, the master's program in physiology at Penn State. As part of the deal, I landed a job as molecular biology lab technician in the Animal Sciences Department. Although the reimbursement was modest, it was incredible to finally have a "real" salary for a change, which not only paid my fees but also provided a living stipend.

The work was fascinating, and Terry Etherton, the lead professor in the lab, couldn't have been a more empathic mentor. I invited his family over for dinner one night, promising a special Sri Lankan meal. He jumped at the invite and asked if he could bring along his boys, ten and twelve.

"Of course, we'd love it," I assured him. "I can't wait to meet them."

When John got home that evening, he tossed out my plan.

"No children. No way. Your boss can bring his wife to dinner, but I don't want two brats crawling around under our table, messing up this place. He has money, let him hire a babysitter."

"*Please?* I'd *like* to meet the boys, John. I'll clean up whatever mess they make."

"No. I said *no*. Tell your boss, no kids. If they come, the dinner's off."

I bit my lip, wondered if I should argue more, but I gave up when I saw the red blotches on his face and his angry frown. He'd thwart any challenge and would likely sabotage the whole dinner experience.

I was consumed with resentment but gave in. John had trained me well. My colleagues at the lab warned me that I should try to get out because the relationship seemed toxic, but I could always come up with reasons to explain away his behavior. This time I figured that Terry's boys were roughly the same age as John's when he'd lost contact with them. Maybe if he saw young boys, he'd feel guilty that he hadn't kept in touch with his own. He always went into silent mode if I asked about his boys, so I'd learned to never go there.

It broke my heart to see Terry's crestfallen expression when I told him John didn't want him to bring his beloved sons.

"Not a problem, Lally, we'll get a babysitter."

I wanted the ground to open up beneath my feet and swallow me whole.

Although the lab work was intellectually stimulating, sacrificing research animals was the downside. We had to attend pig slaughters to obtain fresh liver samples for DNA research. I'd injected those pigs with growth hormone for our research, but now it was time to harvest their livers. At my uncle's farm in Sri Lanka, the cows, goats, and chickens were kept for milk and eggs, but they were family. They had names, and we never killed them.

For the first harvest session, we gathered in the abattoir where the slaughter took place armed with labeled Ziplock bags for liver samples. We would chill the livers on dry ice so we could rapidly extract the DNA before the specimens decayed. I steeled myself to be strong.

I'm doing this for the good of humanity. Yeah, right.

The entire process was nauseating. The terrified screams the pigs made as they were herded into a compound before they were sacrificed sent sick shivers down my spine. They knew what was going to happen. They knew. They were smart. They'd heard the sounds their companions made before they got the stun gun. They were freaked out because they knew they were next.

I wished to the depths of my soul that I could run away from this and end their slaughter. I thought of those magnificent large animals being killed so we could snag tiny chunks of liver, kidney, and brain. Excusing myself from the other lab workers, I fled the building, gasping for air. I clutched my labeled Ziplock bags, trying not to gag on the sickeningly sweet smell of pig blood. Humming loudly, I squeezed both hands over my ears to drown out their bone-chilling squeals of impending death, but this only slightly muted those screams. They kept playing in my ears long after it was over.

"I'm sorry, piggies. I'm so sorry. I loved being with you and feeding you. I can't stop this massacre," I babbled as I sobbed. I knew one thing for sure. I could never become a researcher if it involved killing animals on a regular basis.

By the time I returned to the harvest area, a row of pink decapitated pig corpses moved along slowly, strung upside down, on a raised conveyor belt. They'd trusted me as I'd walked into their pens. They'd squealed with delight that they had company. I'd touched their pink snouts as I fed them during the year. Now I was part of their slaughter machinery. I'd violated their trust. I absolutely hated myself.

My other lab colleagues calmly bagged specimens, showing no outward discomfort as I sheepishly helped out, looking down at the specimens to hide my red eyes. I was such an incredible hypocrite. If I really cared for the well-being of animals, I'd become a vegetarian or quit research altogether. Millions of animals were slaughtered daily for food, of course, but this was different. I had played with each of those cute pigs. Their distressed, high-pitched screams played in my memory for months to come.

Our multicultural lab "family" became close friends. They were closer to my age than John and his friends. We had a Chinese girl, an Indian man in his forties, a Finnish girl, my boss, and a Texan.

I noticed that a bunch of films had accumulated on the Indian postdoc's workspace one afternoon shortly after the pig slaughter.

"Hey, why haven't you developed those films?" I asked him curiously. He was usually on top of all his work.

"It's that bitch downstairs," the Finnish girl interjected, waving her pipette in the air. "I've put off developing mine too, see?" She pointed at her collection of films. "Lally, we all *hate* going downstairs. She makes it such a pain for us."

"She's racist," the Indian man muttered under his breath. "Something about the way she talks to me, I feel like dirt." He shrugged as he filled a large flask with an amber reagent.

"Yes, she's racist *and* rude," the Finnish girl added. "Nasty to *everyone*. *I'm* not brown, but every time I'm down there, she finds some way to humiliate me."

"What? Accepting films for developing is such a brainless thing to do. That's ridiculous!" I shook my head, feeling anger twisting my innards. How could one person instill such fear in my awesome coworkers? I felt especially bad about the gentle, quiet Indian man, who could have been my uncle.

"Go see for yourself, Lally. How about you take my films down and check her out, huh?" the Finnish girl suggested.

"Absolutely! I'll take *everyone's* films. In fact, I'm going down there right now. I'm not taking shit from some petty worker downstairs. Let her try to boss *me* around." I pushed my test tube rack to the back of my workspace. "Everyone, give me your films. I'm off to meet the dragon."

In the bustling office downstairs, I waited at the counter. A blond skeleton of a woman, with a face that looked like it hadn't seen the sun in months, stood in a far corner of the office. She glanced at me and the half dozen people in the line that had formed behind me, but then looked away as if I were invisible. A few other clerks worked at their desks, but I figured she was the dragon. After being ignored for several more minutes, I cleared my throat and addressed her quietly. "Hello, I'm here to drop off films."

She stayed put at the far reaches of the room, making no attempt to come forward, then glared as if I were presumptuous

to intrude on her love affair with a file cabinet. In a voice dripping with ice particles, she snapped, "Speak up, can't hear you."

I probably looked like a quiet, diminutive Asian who'd be
easy to boss around. I'd never address a dog, let alone a human
being, in such an insulting tone. Rage rose from my chest, choking me. My fingertips tingled. With all the power I could muster,
I took a deep breath and yelled, "*I said I'm here to drop off some
films!*" There was a hushed, shocked silence, as everyone in the
office froze. Out of the corner of my eye, I noticed that the lady
behind me in line had clapped her hand over her mouth. The
looks I got from other workers were priceless. Best of all, Dragon
Lady's jaw actually dropped. Mortified with embarrassment, she
scuttled up to the counter with cherry-red cheeks to help me.

From that day on, I was feted by my coworkers and became
the official lab film courier. My burgeoning self-confidence got
a huge boost, and the dragon lady never gave me grief again.
Although I embraced this ferocious new Lally, it was a marked
contrast to the shadowy wife I had become at home.

The fall I turned twenty-nine, John and I went on a visit to California. Viji cornered me in my bedroom one afternoon. I was
reading, with a pillow propped against the headboard, when she
marched in, looking lean and muscular in her badminton clothes.

"I was wondering, Lally," she said, with one hand on her
hip, "you've been married, what, for six years, but you don't
have children." Her halo of dark curls hugged her head.

"So? So what?" I injected a don't-you-dare-go-there tone
and glowered at her. Despite the five years since my abortion,
it ached deep inside when the subject was broached in any
context. Viji, of course, knew nothing about it. In a very delib-
erate fashion, I turned a page and pretended to read, hoping she
would lay off. Instead, she looked me straight in the eye.

"So I asked John about it before he left for work today."

"Oh, and what did John say?" I forced myself to maintain a disinterested tone. My insides were churning.

"That's why I wanted to talk to you, Lally. He said I should ask *you*, because the only reason you don't have kids is because *you* don't want any. He told me that he *does* want a child, Lally."

"He told you that?" I all but shrieked.

"I know I shouldn't butt in, Lally, but why are you holding off on having a baby? Don't you think you should give John a chance to—"

"Get out, Viji." My tone was flat and ferocious now. "*Get out right now! Get out of here!*"

After she shut the door, tears flowed down my cheeks. I clapped my hand over my mouth to stifle a huge sob. The sun had fashioned a tangled pattern of shadows on the wall opposite my bed from the creeper outside. My thoughts were also in a deep tangle. The long-suppressed raw guilt and loss rushed back in, accompanied by a white-hot rage directed at John for lying to my sister.

I ran outside as soon as John returned from the grocery store a half hour later. Barely allowing him to shut the car door, I stood in front of him, hands on my hips.

"How dare you lie to Viji about *me* holding *you* back from having children, John. How dare you, after forcing me to have an abortion I didn't want?"

He dropped his eyes to avoid my gaze. "Well, I'm thinking . . . I think, maybe it's time."

"Time? You think it's time? Then why didn't you tell me that, John? Why lie to Viji? Why?"

"I don't know." He shrugged. "I guess I was planning to talk about it," he said, lifting the grocery bags out of the car. "Well, that's what I'm telling you. I think it's time for us."

The very next day, six years after I'd first started using birth control, I went off the pill.

Two months later I was pregnant.

Twenty-One

Discord

I was now twenty-nine years old and pregnant. This time around, John did a 180 and was extremely solicitous as I progressed, even offering me tea and a sourdough roll in bed before he left for work every morning. *What to Expect When You're Expecting* became my bible. It helped me navigate the new and frightening nausea, heartburn, and later on, my waddling gait. We decided not to determine the baby's gender. I did weekly folk dancing classes on campus and played competitive volleyball at Penn State, all the way up to my fifth month. I only made it to 115 pounds, but I was assured that everything was going well.

When I was eight months pregnant, I flew to Wyoming to present my master's research findings to several hundred scientists at their national animal science meeting. Petrified about speaking to such a learned audience, I practiced my speech repeatedly to my lab partners, the living room wall, and the kitchen table, until I had every word memorized, including the transition statements between slides. Several scientists complimented me at the podium after the presentation. One even told me I was a "born speaker." Thankfully, he had no idea how many hours I'd sweated to make it flawless! Buoyed by the positive feedback, I entered my research poster into a competition and won a $400 prize. The fates had told me to believe in myself, and I was now daring to listen to them.

The cold October morning when we drove our gorgeous newborn daughter, Shermila, to our grad student house was one of the happiest moments of my life. During the ten-minute ride, I sat beside her in the back, unable to stop marveling at this contented Russian doll with pale pink skin, much closer to John's coloring than mine. She had silky dark brown hair and long-lashed eyes that constantly checked out her glorious new world. John parked on the street and retrieved the bulky baby bag from the trunk. I struggled with the buckle for her infant seat until I was able to retrieve her. I inhaled her new baby-powder smell and snuggled her warm body against mine. She gurgled contentedly, fluttering her long, dark eyelashes at me. Inches from me, we locked gazes.

"We're home," I whispered.

She was so perfect that it was hard to believe she was a real person. I heard footsteps, and John materialized. He was shouting at me at the top of his voice, destroying the intimacy of the moment.

"You've taken it apart, Lally! You've dismantled the whole bloody buckle." He snaked an arm past me into the car to fiddle with the seat belt buckle. "How stupid you are! All you had to do was to unlock it like this. Like this! See? *This way!* You're so dumb! You should have waited and let me do it! Let *me* take Shermila."

Without waiting for a response, he dropped the diaper bag by the car, plucked Shermila out of my arms, and stormed off to the house, leaving me dumbfounded. I held on to the open car door, astounded by the violence and anger in his tone. We'd been together seven years, but I had not faced this repulsive and unsettling facet of his personality so intensely. He'd been so caring all these months, but suddenly he'd morphed into a malevolent stranger once again.

He'd flipped out about a belt buckle!

How ridiculous. I wondered if he was simply jealous of our moment of shared intimacy. Ever the optimist, I'd dared to hope that as he adjusted to fatherhood, his behavior to me would improve. I'd hoped that with Shermila home, it would herald a brand-new beginning in our relationship.

How wrong I was.

After three days of the emotional roller coaster of first-time motherhood, a deluge of shocked tears poured down my cheeks. Shivering in the cold October breeze, stripped of the joy of escorting the baby inside, I slammed the car door so hard I was surprised it didn't fall off. I left the baby bag next to the car for John to retrieve and stumbled blindly into the house. John was bent over the bassinet in the front room, tenderly adjusting the pink baby blanket around Shermila's face and shoulders. He didn't look at me as I walked in. His studied avoidance appeared designed to keep me out, which hurt as if he'd driven a shard of glass into my heart. As a vehicle, I guess I'd served my purpose, and was now . . . unwanted baggage.

"Baby bag's on the street," I muttered tonelessly, as I walked past them and into the bedroom. I collapsed, face down, on the bed. I thought I'd known what alone was in this relationship, but what had just happened was worse than alone. It was like he'd flung raw sewage at me on one of the happiest days of my life.

Matters only grew worse. From the moment Shermila came home, John controlled every facet of her upbringing. At first, I chalked his behavior up to anxiety, but it rapidly became obvious that he was completely obsessed with her. I'd worried that he would ignore her, the way he'd ignored his two sons, but I couldn't have been further off course.

Discord

We had long and furious arguments about everything. We fought about sleep and feeding schedules. John insisted on maintaining absolute silence at her bedtime. If she made the slightest sound during the night, he rushed in to comfort her and sometimes fell asleep in her room. One morning, I recoiled when I touched her. Every inch of her body was slathered in sticky layers of Vaseline; her arms, face, feet, and even her thighs were wet and sticky.

"John?" I carried the slippery one-year-old into the kitchen, where he was fixing a bowl of cereal. "What happened last night? You've slathered her with Vaseline. Look!" I showed him her wet chest. He shrugged and looked away, but not before I caught a strange look that sent shivers through me. He looked . . . guilty. I tried to convince myself I was overreacting but was left with a feeling of unease and disquiet deep within.

My sister Viji made a trip to meet the family's first grandchild. She'd almost completed her PhD in education at UCLA. Nimi, I heard, had landed a state job at the California Water Resources Department in Sacramento as a civil engineer, and Vimalan was an electrical engineer but had chosen a job in computer consultancy at UCLA.

The day Viji arrived, dressed to the nines as usual with her black shirt and casually draped silk scarf, she sat with me in the living room while I folded baby clothes into neat piles. Shermila was at her daycare, and I had two precious hours to catch up.

"Let's grab croissants. C'mon, Lally, is there a good bakery?"

"I . . . er . . . we don't usually do things like that." I avoided her eyes and carried a pile of socks to the changing table.

"You don't eat out? That's crazy!"

"We do for birthdays and wedding anniversaries. We have a joint account, but John handles our finances. When he and Anne split up, he said she cleaned out all the money. Guess he likes to be in control. It's fine because I don't have to pay bills or think about money," I said hastily as I folded some bibs and towels. "It's not a problem because we're together all the time."

"Wow, so what if he isn't around? Credit card?"

"We shop together, but he writes the checks." I shrugged. "It's simpler that way." Even to my ears this sounded like bullshit.

"My God." She shook her head, then reached for her jacket and purse. "Don't worry about it, silly, it's my treat, let's go!"

Let's go! I thought how heavenly it would be to take a break from mom chores with a walk to the bakery.

"Is med school in the cards?" she asked over tea and pastries. "You know, the whole 'doctor of doctors' thing?" She elevated her eyebrows and raised her hands in an exaggerated double take.

I bit off a piece of almond croissant and chewed on it thoughtfully. "Med school? I asked John once, but he scoffed at the idea. He said I would be 'playing at' being a doctor instead of being a mother. He's very old-school about 'woman stays home, watches baby,' that sort of thing. Think he'd be fine if I stayed home and taught piano lessons or something. Plus," I patted the crumbs off my cheek with a napkin, "I'm too old anyway. I'm almost thirty-two, Viji. That 'doctor of doctors' was a load of rubbish. I don't think I ever *truly* believed it—not even in Ghana." I stabbed viciously at the chopped strawberries with my fork.

"How are things with you guys? John seems very good with Shermila."

"He gives her everything she wants. He's going absolutely nuts about her. If he spoils her like this, I'm terrified that she'll turn into a brat. Remember how Ammah and Appah set limits with us? I feel like I'm watching helplessly from the sidelines."

"Aw, give him a break, Lally, he's a new parent."

"Whatever. We're always arguing. He keeps blaming me for the move to America. He's resentful of what he calls the 'capitalist pigs,' the 'fat cats' of society, and how they're screwing the workers."

Discord

"But, that's because of his background in economics, right?" It irked me that Viji often found a way to take John's side.

"Whatever." I stood up abruptly. "It just gets to me because I *love* it here. There are jerks in every country—I mean look at us, we came here, didn't we? I really hate it when he goes on and on about all the bad he sees here. I'm going for my citizenship test next month. John's not thrilled about that, but I told him it's what *I* want. He can't stop me. Hope I pass."

"It's easy, Lally, just be sure you know the three branches of government and can recite the last five presidents in order. I'm so glad you're getting your citizenship, Lally. We've all become citizens, and then you can vote! Moving here from Ghana was definitely the best thing Appah did for us. Imagine if we'd stayed behind in Kumasi? We'd all be bagging groceries or something." She threw her head back and laughed, her dark curls dancing around her face.

I giggled along with her, wishing she didn't have to leave so soon. She'd brought rays of California sunshine and her youthful perspective into my life. Maybe she was right to side with John. Maybe I should ignore my reservations about his behavior and simply try harder. Or something. . . .

One afternoon shortly after Viji left, my Finnish lab colleague, Taru, made her first visit to our grad student home to meet Shermila. Her boyfriend, Lucas, came along too—a tall, skinny Pennsylvanian boy with corn-blond hair and a sweet smile. They sat in the living room and watched Shermila show off her culinary prowess with her play cooker. The visit was a special treat because the only people we hosted were John's work friends, all old enough to be my parents. I'd baked shortbread cookies for the occasion.

As I prepared tea and arranged the cookies on a tray, the front door banged shut. Raised voices issued from the living room. Clearly John was home and some kind of altercation was already in progress. I hurried into the living room with my tray. How could John screw everything up in less than ten minutes?

Lucas was perched on the edge of his seat, with a flushed face, engaged in some sort of face-off with John. John hadn't even removed his coat, but he had his back to me and appeared to be trying to intimidate Lucas with his six-foot-four frame. He had both hands on his hips and their faces were only about two feet apart. Shermila was next to her cooker with an alarmed look on her face and her eyes fixed on John. My heart skipped around. I wondered how the tranquil scene I'd left moments ago could have transformed into this tense standoff. Out of the corner of my eye, I noted that Taru was also poised to get up from her seat.

"So, you're an *American*, huh?" John jeered at Lucas. "I'd say 99.9 percent of the Americans I know are assholes."

There was a shocked silence. Taru looked at me and shook her head infinitesimally. She was very pale. Words would not come out of my mouth. I set the tray down on an end table with shaky hands, deeply mortified that John was bullying someone half his age whom he'd just met. Shermila turned her back to the commotion and twiddled with the cooker controls, mumbling barely perceptible baby talk.

Lucas locked eyes with John. "If you hate Americans so much, why did you come here?" He had a facade of bravado, but his prominent Adam's apple bobbed as he swallowed.

The back of John's neck grew redder still. He moved a half step closer to Lucas and brandished his middle finger. "So English people can't come here and criticize this country? What about free speech, huh? Isn't that what you Americans are all about, free speech? Huh?"

"John, John . . . stop, stop it, please!" I could not stomach his reprehensible behavior.

Lucas stood. "Let's get out of here, Taru."

"You haven't even had your tea—" I interjected weakly, pointing at the tray.

"Another time, Lally. We're leaving." Taru shot me a quick, apologetic sideways glance.

"Oh? So, you're too scared to stay here and discuss this?" John ridiculed. "You coward." He looked scornfully at Lucas. "Why not stay—let's fight it out." He rolled up his sleeves and balled his fists. "How about we sort this out right now?"

"We're leaving now, Lally," Taru repeated. She looked like a ghost. She reached for Lucas's hand, stepped around John, and the two of them left without a backward look. I wanted to scream and rail at John for totally ruining the visit, but I didn't want a scene in front of Shermila.

John slammed the door shut behind them, hung up his jacket, and crouched beside Shermila's cooker, avoiding my furious gaze.

"Hello, Shermila," he said in his most charming voice, "what are you going to cook for Daddy today?"

When I walked into her lab the next day, Taru was pipetting a clear solution into a rack of test tubes. I pulled my backpack off one shoulder and stood beside her, stammering out an apology.

"Lally, *he* should be here apologizing, not you. I know he's your husband, but what he said was not acceptable. Lucas was shocked. He doesn't even know your husband."

"Yeah, I know," I stammered. "He's . . . he's under a lot of stress." I placed my backpack on the floor. "He's been applying for jobs but hasn't had any offers yet. He's almost fifty, Taru." I shook my head.

"Stop making excuses, Lally. He's a grown man. Know what *I* think?"

I shook my head.

"It was nothing to do with Lucas, Lally. He's controlling *you*. When he insults your friends, he's isolating you by making sure people your age leave you. *That's* what he's doing. Something about him scares me." She put her pipette down and turned to face me. "Think about it! We had fun till he showed up yesterday. As a friend, I have to tell you something, okay? I really, *really* suggest that you leave him. His behavior was crazy. He wasn't joking—he really wanted to start a fight! It was horrible. I'm worried about you." There was warm concern in her hazel eyes.

"You didn't even try my cookies." I used humor to deflect the uneasy feeling that was taking hold. "I don't know what to do, Taru, or how to stop this. And there's Shermila to consider. Anyway, please tell Lucas I'm sorry, okay?"

She shrugged and returned to pipetting.

I cycled home from work that evening with a vice squeezing my chest. The closer I got, the tighter the vice became. Even the thought of scooping Shermila up in my arms couldn't take away the black cloud of dread. My breathing was labored as I thought about what Taru had said. I didn't want to go home.

Home had become a battleground. Any chance he could, John criticized my parenting. What made this intolerable was that he played dirty and swore at me around Shermila, even though I asked him to leave the room or wait till she was asleep if he wanted to argue. Rancor and abusive expletives had become the new norm. If I remained mute or refused to respond to his barbs, his insults escalated.

"Stupid cow, bitch, fucking bitch," he called, right in front of Shermila. I either ignored him or walked away so it wouldn't impact her. At the same time, I hated that she witnessed the verbal abuse, and I didn't like the flash of anxiety I saw in her face each time it happened. She might grow up thinking it was normal for a man to insult a woman in such a hateful way.

Discord

One Saturday afternoon, I walked with John and Shermila to the grad student children's playground right across from our house. John was nursing a bottle of beer on a park bench. It was his second since lunch. I watched Shermila climb laboriously up a short ladder to reach the slide. A little boy, no more than three years old, clambered up past her. In his haste, he accidentally stepped on her hand. Shermila put her hand in the air and turned to John wailing, "Daddy, Daddy!" She waved her hand around. It looked fine to me.

"Asshole!" John screamed at the little boy. Beer in hand, he stomped over to the little boy who'd just slid down the slide. "Be careful! Wait your turn, asshole!" he snarled. The boy took one terrified look at John's face and ran, crying, to his mother.

"Shermila, come here, let me look." John picked her off the ladder with one hand and cuddled her. I walked over also. Not even a bruise was visible, but she sobbed unconsolably into his shoulder, clearly milking the situation. The boy's mother walked up to us stiffly with her son in her arms. His terrified eyes were fixed on John's, and he'd grasped his mother's neck and shoulder tight enough to make little indentations in her skin.

"This is a children's playground. You should never use this kind of filthy language in front of small children. I'm calling the police. Come on, Jason, let's go." She pulled the toddler's chubby fingers from her neck and adjusted the squirming boy in her grasp.

"I'm so . . . so sorry," I stammered out to their departing backs. John set Shermila down then gestured violently at the retreating woman with his beer bottle. A little beer sloshed out as he called out, "Go ahead, be my guest, call the cops. Your son injured my daughter's hand. What do you think the cops will do, huh?" His tone was goading. I desperately craved a "vanish" button.

The woman momentarily stopped in her tracks, turned partially as if to respond, but then walked rapidly away.

Stunned, I wanted to confront him, but not in front of Shermila. I collapsed on the nearest park bench, a haze of frustration blurring my vision. Thanks to John's overprotective behavior, we were rearing a budding monster. Shermila produced severe meltdowns and tantrums at any provocation, so that precious Daddy would gallantly rush to her rescue.

My parents had always avoided becoming overly involved when we had issues with other children, telling us to brush off small incidents like this. As John fawned over Shermila, the acrid taste of acid burned the back of my throat. I should *say* something. I should *do* something. He shouldn't get away with this. Half-formed sentences came to mind, but, to my shame, the words all froze.

It was fast becoming intolerable to be repeatedly placed in situations like this, and I was furious at myself for my inability to stand up to John. Should I leave him, as Taru suggested, or just "deal" a little longer, as Viji implied? Leaving seemed pretty drastic. As the oldest, I'd always had to set an example for the younger siblings. Our Sri Lankan culture of marriage lasting forever had been pressed down on me from the moment I understood what marriage meant. My own parents had remained married, even though I'd seen my mother repeatedly scrunch her face and straighten her mouth into a tight, thin, hard line when my father spoke to her, as if something between them had turned sour. I sure didn't want *my* marriage to become years of tightly harnessed frustration.

I looked up at them. Shermila chortled in excitement as John pushed her even higher on the toddler swing. Clearly, she'd exaggerated her finger pain, because she had a look of sheer delight when the swing became so high that it dropped before it swung back. Their eyes were locked in a bubble of happiness. I was very much the outsider. Was I evil to consider breaking up this relationship? It was all so damned complicated. . . .

Discord

A car slowed down, and my pulse hammered as a campus police car pulled into the parking lot. I hurriedly snatched the beer bottle off the bench and dumped it in the trash. John lifted Shermila off the swing, then he sauntered over to stand next to me, striking an insolent pose, with his other hand on his hip.

A young campus cop, possibly in his mid-twenties, strode over to the playground. He consulted a notebook.

"Sir, I'm here to check out a dispute. Lady described you, said you used vulgar language in front of her toddler?"

"Yeah? Really?" John pranced around like a clown, taunting the cop. "Vulgar language, huh? Where's your proof? What're you going to do about that, huh? Arrest me? Huh?" He gestured with his hands. "This is a free country. You should be doing something better with your time," he snorted.

The cop's eyes widened, and his jaw dropped as John paraded around disrespectfully, as if trying to rile the young officer. He seemed taken aback by John's boorish taunts, but rather than escalate the situation, he backed off, muttering, "Well, sir, this is your first warning. Don't do it again." He put his notebook away and drove off without issuing a citation. John smirked and waved at him cheekily. I wanted the ground to open up and swallow me whole.

Over the next few weeks, our relationship became more frayed and tense. Shermila woke up every single night, screaming, and John always went to her cot and stayed for a long time.

One evening, I was at his friend Shawn's home, reading *Clifford the Big Red Dog* to Shermila, when I overheard him launching into his usual rant about "fat cats of capitalism." "Americans are like contented cows. Maybe this country needs random acts of urban violence. That'll wake up those capitalist pigs." John snickered to Shawn, who laughed.

"I hate it when you bring America down all the time," I ventured, lowering the book I was reading.

They looked up at me, startled that I'd intruded.

"Don't you guys know how much this country has done for me? For my family? It's a dream to me. I love it here. And I'll be a citizen in two months if I pass the test. There are weirdos everywhere, guys. When you talk about random violence, I know you're joking, but you sound like terrorists!"

John flashed me a broad, condescending smile and leaned back to face Shawn. "Lally doesn't get it," he said, smirking. "Her background is science—she's never taken sociology or economics." The men returned to their discussion. I continued reading to Shermila, but a pulse pounded in my forehead as I dwelled on the fact that I'd finally said something for a change. As usual, John's dismissal was demeaning, yet tonight, for the first time ever, I'd decided not to zip my lip and blend into the room decor.

Something new was stirring within me—a strange discontent. It was exciting, but at the same time, scary as hell!

Twenty-Two

Citizenship

Shermila had turned two when I flew back to Davis for Easter break in 1993. Visits home were increasingly a point of refuge so I could bathe in the warm essence of my family's overwhelming support. I cherished those long, lazy, sunny California days filled with unrestrained laughter and fun activities, such as a trip to Los Angeles to hang out at Santa Monica beach. Life there contrasted sharply with the brooding dissonance of State College, where the cold froze my smile half the year, and I was saddled with this equally frigid, boorish stranger called my husband.

John met us at the Harrisburg airport terminal when we returned. He pointedly ignored me, stooped to hug Shermila, then walked away with her in his arms. I followed, dragging my suitcase, feeling doused in excrement after two weeks of pure bliss. Perhaps he wanted to punish me for leaving him behind. As I trailed them, walking about twenty feet behind along the void of the frigid terminal, it seemed impossible that I could handle this state of affairs much longer.

As the date for my citizenship ceremony grew closer that summer, John continued to mock my decision to become an American. Not only did he refuse to drive me the two hundred miles to the appointment in Philadelphia, but he also said I'd have to take Shermila with me. He said he was working and flat-out refused to make arrangements to drop her off or pick her up from daycare, since that was my duty.

In desperation, I asked if anyone at the lab could help and was thrilled when my amazing next-door lab buddy, Vikki, came through for me.

"No problem, Lally, but we'll need to leave around six in the morning." She smiled, her red curls like a halo around her cheery face.

"And can you look after Shermila while I'm in?"

"With pleasure; she's a doll. The parking there's terrible. I'll just drive her around Philly if she's antsy. Don't worry, Lally." I wanted to kiss her.

We left State College when only a tiny pink horizon showed in the black sky. I consulted my bulging folder of notes to cram in last-minute information about the branches of government and the presidents. We arrived in Philadelphia an hour early. I'd always wanted to see the Liberty Bell, and Vikki humored my wish to drive there first. She warned that there was usually a long line, but Shermila was asleep, so I told her I'd run over for a quick peek if I could. People emerged from a door, and I dashed through it.

Within minutes I was face-to-face with that magical, burnished copper bell. It was smaller than I'd imagined, standing only a little over four feet. I marveled at the huge crack that ran through it. As my eyes caressed the inscribed words, "Proclaim LIBERTY throughout all the land," I had an indescribable, almost supernatural moment of communion with that bell. It symbolized independence and freedom from oppression. Like me, the bell had become cracked over time, but there it stood, broadcasting its message of hope and endless possibilities. . . .

"It's worth it," it whispered. I shivered.

"Ma'am, you came in through the exit door." A uniformed

male usher startled me and pointed to where I'd walked in. Mortified, I realized that there were hundreds of people patiently lined up to see the bell, but I'd apparently accidentally jumped the line. I apologized and rushed back outside.

As we drove away, I turned my head to look back at the building. A new restlessness was raging in my brain. That old bell had rustled up a fight deep within my heart.

I want to be free. . . .

We drove deep into the heart of Philadelphia to a simple white building where I would take my test. My heart hammered as I sat across the table from a white-haired judge, who relaxed me with a smile. He asked me to name the three branches of government, chatted for a moment about my studies and family in California, then he scribbled something down. I stared at his pen for one heart-stopping moment. He glanced up at my misty eyes, smiled, and told me I'd passed. Doves fluttered out from my body in ecstatic flight. I had just erased my last barrier to American citizenship.

Still awash with the profound emotion that had consumed me when I saw the Liberty Bell, I waited in a long, polished hallway, knees knocking together, with dozens of other nervous applicants. Their faces ranged in hue from the palest white to ebony black. After what seemed like an eternity, a uniformed bailiff opened a door to usher us into a courtroom. An elderly black-frocked Caucasian judge with a deadpan expression presided behind a raised podium. The early-morning light shone through tall windows and skipping dust particles to illuminate a magnificent American flag that stood beside him. The oak trees outside were decked in their brightest green finery for the occasion. Leaves danced in exultation, mirroring the skipping rhythm of my own heart.

We shuffled around, a few nervous coughs and muffled whispers contributing to the tension. I caught a whiff of Old Spice.

Beside me, an older Hispanic man with weathered hands fiddled with the top button of his impeccable navy blue suit. Cracked, blackened fingernails occasionally reached up to brush tears off the side of his face, which made tears rise in my own eyes.

I looked away, guilty that I'd intruded on his emotional journey but fully embracing the camaraderie with a stranger whose nervous exultation seemed to match my own. *What is his story?* I wondered. *Might it be as meandering as mine?* When the bailiff shut the door and moved to stand beside the judge, it became eerily quiet. In this hush of anticipation, my palms began to sweat. The momentous nature of the step I was about to take made my temples pound to match the erratic rhythm of my heart.

I was overcome with gratitude. Gratitude for all the blessings this wonderful country had already showered on me. In just a few moments I would join my siblings and parents in our commitment to this land that had become our home. The oak leaves still swayed outside in delight. I imagined palm fronds waving at me from Sri Lanka and saw the majestic lion on the flag turning his head sideways to face me as he raised his sword in a triumphant salute. I conjured up a delicate shower of fragrant pink-and-white frangipani blossoms falling on my shoulders from the tree outside our home in Kumasi to herald this final step.

How far away those countries were now! Tears pricked at my eyes. What I'd absorbed from both countries would always be an integral part of who I was, but America had captured my soul. Standing in those shafts of slanted sunlight, we faced the glorious flag, placed our hands on our hearts, and recited the Pledge of Allegiance. My heart threatened to burst out of my body, and I wanted to shout out in sheer exultation. I imagined the Liberty Bell triumphantly pealing out to proclaim to the world that a new American citizen had joined its ranks.

Citizenship

And just as suddenly, that glimmer of uncertainty I'd experienced earlier flowered within me, seeming to come out of thin air and turn into a conviction. It reverberated within my body, growing my heart a few sizes. This time, I was shocked with its intensity.

I want to be free.

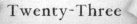

Twenty-Three

Shanthi

After the ceremony, my ugly marriage felt even worse. I felt like a chastised child because I'd become a citizen against his wishes. When John ignored me or spoke coldly, I was better able to steel myself to ignore him and not let it drag me down. It dawned on me that I no longer sought or needed John's blessing for decision-making, and this empowered me. Citizenship had become my badge that John could never strip away.

Sex was no longer pleasurable and down to once per month, if that. I had become a passive participant, too afraid to repel him if he reached out to me. After one such encounter, he turned over and promptly fell asleep. I lay awake, feeling like scum, and mulled over a battle plan to escape this relationship. Being with John no longer brought me any happiness. I could only crack a smile at Shermila's toddler antics. She was excelling at her daycare, and I was told she was exceptionally gifted. It wasn't a surprise, because she'd spoken twenty words by age one—I'd written them all down in her baby book.

Divorce was a four-letter word. At our wedding reception, I would never forget the pride on my dad's face as he stood by the piano and proudly raised his brandy glass aloft. "Marriages," he proclaimed, staring right at me, "are made in heaven. Cheers!" People in Sri Lanka pretty much *dealt* with loveless marriages. It was culturally sound to remain together in a resentful union for child-rearing. If I left John, I'd have to admit that I'd decided to give up on something, and that my parents and the Claydens had been right all along. How mortifying, and what a blow to my pride! Perhaps I hadn't tried hard enough to find a way to make things work out. And then, there was Shermila . . . I should stick it out for her sake, right?

Yet, should I? I punched at my pillow. I wanted fresh pastures for exploration and growth. Here I was, trapped in a marriage cocoon with an angry old boor who seemed to put me down any chance he got. I ached to be blanketed with love by someone who supported me, rather than face John's daily assaultive barrage of criticism. I stared at the shadows on the ceiling, too drained to turn over. My nocturnal gymnastics always had the power to paralyze me into a state of resentment and powerlessness. Even when we didn't fight, a deep-seated disquiet was always within me, like the fluttering of a butterfly's wings against a rusty wire cage.

"I'm pregnant again," I announced to John at breakfast in September 1993. His head jerked up, the spoon poised in midair. Blood left his cheeks. Afraid of what I might see next, I turned my gaze to Shermila, now almost two, who was blithely ignorant of the tension in my voice. She was intent on tracking errant Cheerios around her bowl with plump fingers. I swallowed an extra-large helping of porridge, which burned my tongue, then snuck a quick glance at him. From the frown that spread across his countenance, it was easy to see that he was furious. He averted his eyes and chomped down on his cereal without responding.

I was conflicted also. This was probably the worst possible time to add a gigantic stressor to our crumbling pretense of a marriage. Communication had become so strained that we'd never actually broached this possibility. John knew I wasn't on birth control, and he didn't use condoms. We should have discussed this right after Shermila quit nursing, a year back. Our almost nonexistent sex life was clearly still capable of creating a new being.

Any time I'd thought about becoming pregnant, I'd assumed that John might simply accept it this time around. I'd even wondered if it might draw us together somehow. Matters between us certainly couldn't get any worse. The bright blue positive pregnancy test had sparkled like a fresh blue sky that might replace the gray our lives had become.

John patted his mouth deliberately with a napkin. "I'm not ready for another one," he announced flatly, without looking at me. He clattered his spoon into the empty cereal bowl. "Things aren't the greatest between us. We didn't plan on this. We can't afford it. Forget it." Arctic air blew my way and my breath caught.

"Forget it?" I spluttered. "What are you talking about? Yes, things *are* terrible. But guess what? We did nothing to prevent this, did we?" My voice was shrill, and Shermila looked up at me, one fat fist raised in alarm. I took a deep breath and patted her arm, pushing more Cheerios her way.

"I'm not ready." John shook his head, avoiding my quick sideways glance at Shermila. He ignored the index finger on my mouth that tried to shush him. Threatening hazel eyes bored into mine. "No more babies. You'll have to get an abortion. I'm not going through this again." His chair grated loudly as he pushed it back and stood up.

I choked on my porridge, and Shermila looked up at me in alarm. "So that's it, huh? Simple . . . just terminate, like I did in England? I can't believe you. Actually, I can." I took a sip of coffee. "I honestly don't know who you are any longer."

He soaped off his cereal bowl at the sink. "There's nothing between us anymore, Lally. *Nothing.* I warn you, if you go ahead with this, I promise I won't spend a penny of my money on you—or the child." He brandished his spoon, his face contorted into an ugly, mottled pink-and-white mask.

"Daddy?" Shermila turned to him in alarm, her mouth festooned with Cheerios fragments. He walked to her highchair and tenderly spooned off the debris from her face, wearing a manufactured smile.

I was speechless and repulsed by this ugly old man. Then cold fury exploded. The old, scared, naive me of many moons back was no more. I morphed into a seething dragon.

"I will have this child whether you want it or not," I muttered in a low, tense voice to avoid alarming Shermila. I shouldn't have worried. She was sucking on her spoon. "And you know what?" I gripped the edge of the table and leaned forward. "We're still married, and I expect you to support me right through this pregnancy."

He tried to interrupt, but I talked louder. "I'm *not* telling Shermila she could have had a sister or brother in the future, except you didn't think the timing was perfect. I'm not a stupid, clueless girl. You can't force me to have another abortion, okay? We simply don't communicate. Never again. I've changed, John. This time, I'll do what's right for me *and* for Shermila."

I took a long sip of coffee, trying unsuccessfully to blink away the tears that had collected. John shot me a disgusted look, as if the sight of my tears revolted him. He snatched up Shermila's bowl and dropped it into the sink with a loud clatter.

"You're not thinking this through," he said through clenched teeth. He released Shermila from her seat and placed her on the floor, his face still flushed with anger.

"I'm thinking *very* clearly," I said. "How dare you tell me you won't spend *your* money on our baby? It's *our* money, not *yours*. If you didn't want me to get pregnant, you should have worn a condom, or we should have quit having sex. It's too late now." I stormed out of the kitchen to the bedroom, slammed the door, and threw myself on the bed. Given the venom in his voice, I was fearful that he might follow me and actually hit me this time, although he'd never raised a hand to me before. Then again, I'd never dared cross him so defiantly. I was shocked at my courage.

Instead I heard him walk Shermila to the living room play area. "Here you go, Shermila. Daddy has to go to work now, so maybe your mother will come out and play." He spat out "mother" like an expletive. Of course he knew I could hear him. The front door slammed so hard that the photograph frames rattled. When Shermila ran to the bedroom door calling out for me, I opened the door and hugged her tight. As we rocked together, it wasn't clear who was doing the comforting.

Twenty-Four

Witch Way Forward?

We never discussed the pregnancy again. John became even more remote as my abdomen protruded. Meanwhile, job rejections piled up in the mailbox. As I fought the early-morning nausea and breast tenderness, his verbal assaults became a constant refrain. I cringed as he crumpled up the rejection letters and tossed them in the trash.

"You think you know it all, you stupid cow, you stupid witch, what a fucking piece of work. I sacrificed my job in England to come here so you'd be closer to your family but look where we are. I don't even know if I'll get a job after I graduate in a few months. And now you're going ahead with this baby. I did everything for you. Stupid. We should never have come to America."

His self-pity made me sick. I could have reminded him that he had unrealistic job expectations, given his age and lack of a PhD when we came here. I could have brought up how much pressure he'd put on us to marry quickly so he could get a visa and how he'd feared that his past rap sheet transgressions might have denied him an American green card. I could have said a lot of things, but I said nothing, knowing he might explode. I told myself he was stressed, he had no job, and his PhD was imminent. Things would improve when he found work . . . that is, *if* he found work. Maybe the second child might help in some fashion? How could things get any worse?

Then things got worse. John seemed to take a perverse pleasure in belittling me in front of Shermila. She now understood our words more clearly, and he knew I would not fight back in front of her, so it was an easy, one-sided fight. Later that month I sat by Shermila's highchair, watching her eat her rice, chicken, and vegetables. After a couple of anemic bites, she pushed her plate away.

"Cookie!" she demanded imperiously.

"You aren't done," I said, shaking my head. "I said you'll get a cookie after you finish. Come on, a few more bites."

"Cookie!" She tossed the spoon onto the floor, pounded on the tray, and screamed. John walked in from the living room and stroked her head. Shermila sobbed and wailed with crocodile tears streaming down her face.

"Mommy say cookie. Want cookie!" she yowled.

"Lally? You're reneging on your promise? You told Shermila she could have a cookie?"

"Yes, after she eats all her food. She's barely touched it."

"That's stupid, Lally, she's eaten some of her food. C'mon Shermila, *I'll* get you a cookie."

He placed her barely touched bowl of food in the sink, picked her up out of the highchair, and hoisted her to the cupboard to pick out a cookie. As if that weren't bad enough, it stabbed me in the heart when she raised the cookie with a victorious smile and waved it at me, hoisted on her gallant father's arm.

"Mommy toopid," she proclaimed, as he whisked her away.

Four months later, in February 1994, I was reading Shermila her favorite book, *Go, Dog, Go*, on the living room couch. To ease the discomfort of my nearly seven-month protuberant belly, I was half sitting, half lying, and Shermila was in the crook of my arm. Moments like these were time capsules of pure magic. They more than made up for all the sleepless nights and the endless cycle of feeding, diapers, and washing clothes, coupled with John's simmering hatred that encapsulated my waking world.

John walked in from the bedroom and glowered at us, as if the image of the two of us bonding irritated him. "Lally, let's finish our discussion about how we are going to agree to put Shermila to bed. We didn't finish talking. You took off."

"You lost your temper. I didn't want another fight, John. Not now, I'm reading to Shermila. We'll talk later," I said quietly, turning a page.

John did not like being ignored. He walked over, grabbed Shermila off my arm, and knocked the book to the floor. With Shermila in his arms, her eyes wide and staring at me uncertainly, he snatched up the large circular bundle of house and car keys and shook them around.

"Know something, Shermila?" he jeered. "Your mother doesn't want to talk to me now. She's a witch, that's what she is, a *witch*!" His face was mottled red and purple, and the rancor in his eyes turned my stomach.

Fear spread over Shermila's face as she stared from him to me and back.

"Bitch!" he jeered, flinging the heavy bunch of keys across the room. They struck the center of my belly. Tears of pain trickled out. I winced and clutched at my abdomen. Even more painful was the horrified look on Shermila's face. John snatched both his jacket and her coat from the rack and walked jerkily to the door with her in his arms. "Let's get away from that witch, Shermila," he said curtly.

I read shock and confusion on the tiny face that stared at me over his shoulder, as he whisked her outside. The slam of the door made me jump. I sat there in shock, rubbing my belly, till his footsteps faded. For a moment, I simply stared at the door, feeling nothing at all. The pain was diminishing, but I was terrified that the innocent baby inside might have been hurt by the heavy keys. In the ten years we'd been married, he'd never done anything like this. This was new. And he'd done it in front of Shermila, who knew what a witch was.

This changed everything. As tears rolled down my cheeks, I contemplated my options. If I did nothing, John could become even more physically assaultive. If he actually hurt the new baby at this critical stage of pregnancy, life would be terrifying. What if he hurt me badly next time? I set my lips and wiped all the tears away. There would never be a next time. Over my dead body. Shermila should never have observed what she did. It could destroy her.

I had to do something, but what? My thoughts scattered. I needed space to think. I picked up the Dr. Seuss book from the floor, the one that exhorted me to "Go, Dog, Go!" A sign from the gods—it was time to leave. I picked up the keys from the ground. John had literally thrown me my escape route. Rushing into the bedroom, I grabbed a backpack into which I threw my pajamas, purse, and two changes of clothing, as well as toiletries.

One moment Shermila had been warm and secure, snuggled up in my arms, having her favorite story read to her, and the next, her father had snatched her up, called me a witch, and hurled keys at my belly. Shermila knew a baby sister or brother was inside. She knew that witches were evil. I couldn't even contemplate the psychological toll on my adorable, impressionable girl. Fresh tears blurred my view, and I played back her stricken look as John carted her away from me.

"Over my dead body!" I swore out loud. "My *fucking dead body*! You hear me, John? You'll never hurt me again, you sick fuck!"

Yelling gave me a much-needed boost of courage. With a huge lungful of air, I hoisted the backpack on my back, wrapped a coat around my shoulders, and drove away like a woman fleeing a burning building. I drove blindly out of town for ten minutes, with no specific destination in mind. The green pastures of the countryside normally soothed me, but long shadows of the impending night gave them a menacing look. Half blinded with tears, I pulled over to the side of the road, facing rolling gray hills. My breathing was still ragged, and sodden tissues were balled up on the seat beside me.

What now? I rubbed the tender spot on my belly. John had actually hurt me without provocation. I'd always found ways to excuse his behavior. Not this time. I could call the police, but of course, he'd deny everything. The keys hadn't left a bruise. I remembered the irreverent way he'd jeered at the playground cop. Plus, if they came and did nothing, Shermila might freak out, and he'd be furious. He'd never get a job with a fresh police report on file. It would end our marriage.

But wasn't our marriage over anyway? Could I complete my pregnancy in California? I'd take Shermila, of course. She couldn't stay with that unstable, angry jerk. What about my plane ticket? He controlled our finances.

I didn't have Vikki's address, so I drove to Shawn and Sue's place instead, even though they were John's friends, not mine. When I sobbed out what happened, Sue hugged me, let me cry, and made me a cup of tea. They congratulated me for taking a firm stance and leaving. They fussed over me and fixed me dinner then held a prolonged whispered consultation in the kitchen. Sue returned to the dining table and put her hand on my shoulder.

"Lally, we both think it'll be best for you to go back home, not stay here. Of course, you're welcome if you like, but we think you should go back." Together they ran through a whole bunch of reasons why I should return. John's nerves were on edge because he had no job offers. He'd lost it in the heat of the moment, but of course they knew him well. He'd never try anything like that again. It was the first time ever, right? The fact that I left him would make a statement that I would never again tolerate such behavior. I should call the police if there was a next time. John would be distraught if he thought I'd left for good. He couldn't drop Shermila off at daycare without a car. What about Shermila?

What about Shermila? *What about Shermila?*

My fighting spirit evaporated. More than anything else, I worried about Shermila. I'd never skipped kissing her good-night. The image of her wide, scared eyes flashed back. How would she process what happened if I wasn't there when they got back home? What would he say about *that witch*? Was she crying? The last thing she'd seen was keys hurled at me. I had to return. For Shermila's sake. I set my mouth in the same straight line of determination I'd seen many a time on my mom's face and gripped my mug until it shook in my grasp. I was tough. I was strong. I could do this. He'd never touch me again. Never.

It was almost ten thirty when I took the turn to our darkened home on campus. The gravel crunched under the light coating of snow, despite my attempt to drive as quietly as I could. I sat in the car outside with the engine turned off for several minutes, trying to summon the courage to get out. Light snowflakes landed gently on the windshield, as if to soothe my frazzled nerves. The front door was unlocked when I cautiously turned the handle. Shermila must be asleep. I crept to her door and placed my ear against her door, relieved to hear light breaths. John had retired to our bedroom. If he'd heard me walk in, he hadn't come out.

I lay on the living room couch, too exhausted to even shrug out of my backpack. A nagging, thumping headache was now my only companion, while a kaleidoscope of questions swirled around my tired brain. I was so exhausted that I dozed off till just after three. My back hurt due to the awkward angle and my huge belly. Even though it was the last place I wanted to go, the only available bed was in our shared bedroom. I crept into bed and lay as far away from John as I could without falling off.

He left for work before I awoke later that morning. There was no note of apology. It was as if I'd dreamed the entire incident. The phone rang around nine o'clock. Long distance. My mom was calling from California.

"Lally? Lally? Are you okay? Is everything okay with you and John?" She spoke fast, with an urgent tone and a catch in her breath.

"Everything's fine, Ammah," I lied, trying my best to sound reassuring. "Why, what's up?"

"John called me last night."

"He did?" My ears perked up. I held the phone receiver with my shoulder and picked up Shermila's Slinky toy from the nightstand, pushing the accordion folds together and apart. I was truly flabbergasted that John had brought my mom into our issue.

"He told me you went away, or something. He asked if he could drop Shermila off in California to stay with us for a while, because he has work. I told him, of course—"

"He said *what?*" I screeched, gripping the receiver so hard it shook in my grasp. "He said he'd fly out with Shermila?"

"He said he didn't know where you were, Lally. I told him of course she could stay here with us as long as he wanted. What's happening, Lally? Are you okay? Where did you go?"

"I'm fine, Ammah," I snapped. "We argued. I took off and spent some time with friends. I can't . . . I still can't believe he dragged you into our private argument. That's ridiculous! He's so childish. I'm so sorry he bothered you, Ammah."

"It's no bother, Lally."

"Ammah, no one's taking Shermila anywhere! We'll come

in the summer for a visit after the baby's born. It's all sorted out," I lied, twisting the cords around my index finger.

"But if there's anything—" I imagined her tiny body all tense and the anguished look on her face. My beloved mom. Of course nothing was ever a problem for her. I loved her intensely in that moment.

"I know, I know, Ammah. Thanks so much. I'll talk another time. Have to take Shermila to daycare now. We're late. It's all good. Thanks for calling. Bye."

I slammed the phone down with shaking fingers and stared blankly out through the window. True to form, John had thought only about himself when he thought I'd left for good. Shermila's amazing knight in armor, her own father, simply planned to dump her in California with her grandparents when things didn't go according to plan. He could have located a babysitter for her while he worked but had taken zero responsibility. Obviously, he hadn't even considered the impact on our impressionable little girl if she were suddenly snatched away from both parents and sent to live thousands of miles away.

I'd thought that nothing John did could shock me, or drop him lower in my esteem, but I'd been wrong.

Charming man.

John and my mother attended the birth of my second daughter on May 4, 1994. We called her Shanthi, which means *peace*. My mom received the singular honor of cutting the umbilical cord. I'd hoped against hope for another girl and was delighted when my wish came true. She was incredibly fair with skin like porcelain, and she had a mop of jet-black hair even darker than Shermila's. Everyone had told me that Shermila was unusually attractive, and here was another gorgeous girl who would compete.

From the start, she had a sunny disposition with an insatiable appetite for breastfeeding, and she snuggled close to me every chance she got. I loved the dreamy look in her eyes when she tightly clasped my pinky with long, dainty fingers and latched on to my breast. I felt sick that John had sought to erase this perfect girl simply as a convenience.

As expected, he distanced himself from Shanthi right from the start. Once, I caught him glaring at her, as if he couldn't bear to look at her, even as he hugged Shermila close.

The day she came home, Shermila walked up to Shanthi's bassinet and tentatively reached out a finger. Shanthi clasped it, and the sisters gazed in wonderment at each other. It was as if a lifetime of bonding took root from that moment. Something twisted within me as I lifted Shanthi out and hugged them both close to my heart on the bed. True peace and an all-encompassing happiness blanketed the three of us in an unforgettable outpouring wave of delight.

"You've no idea how much I love both of you. You're my world," I told them softly, feeling answering thumps of their heartbeats against my chest. I inhaled that delicious new baby smell, thankful for that moment of magic that no discord with John could ever erase.

A month later, I was halfway through Shanthi's diaper change when John sauntered in with an opened envelope in his hand.

"Flying to Southampton for an accounting conference in July." He waved a sheet of typed paper animatedly. "Haven't been to the Old Country for a while. I'll be gone a couple weeks."

Shermila, now a precocious two and a half years old, solemnly handed me a baby wipe. John went behind her and tried to hug her, but she squirmed out of his grasp and waved the wipes to let him know that she was on an important mission. Shanthi cooed and blew bubbles at him. Again I noticed that he averted his gaze.

"Southampton, England?" I asked as I bagged the soiled diaper and launched it into the diaper pail.

"I go, Daddy," Shermila announced as she handed me a fresh diaper.

"Sorry, Shermila, it's for grown-ups, not children." He spun her around to plant a kiss on her head and held her to his chest while he stroked her back. "Daddy will be gone for two weeks. Lally, maybe, it's a good time for you to take the girls to Davis. Your mom can help with Shanthi. You should go." He released his grasp on Shermila and turned to me.

"Okay, it will be good to have some help." I moved the blankets around the bassinet to hide my expression. Excitement coursed through me when I thought about how wonderful it would be to leave. "I'd like to stay at least four weeks if I'm flying there. My work contract ends in June."

"Sure, why not?" He shrugged. I noticed prominent gray hairs in his sideburns. His voice was cold. A pang of sadness hit when I remembered that we'd actually been friends in the past. Those days were long gone. We hadn't been affectionate or intimate in months. Come to think of it, we hadn't communicated at all about his key throwing, my brief escape from home, or even our future. In two short months he'd graduate but without a job in hand. As usual, all important discussions had been swept under the rug.

He ruffled Shermila's hair. "Still don't have a job offer. The whole job thing worked out just great in your wonderful country, didn't it?"

The cold, biting sarcasm made my stomach plummet.

He released Shermila and turned away. "I'll take a look at flight dates."

"We're flying to California—to California!" I whispered to the two girls after he left the room. I picked Shanthi out of the bassinet and clambered onto the bed with both girls. "Oh, you girls are going to just love it there. You wait! Shermila, are you ready for a big, big adventure? With Grandma and Grandpa . . . and your aunties and uncle?"

She nodded vehemently, her bright brown eyes sparkling. I jiggled Shanthi's arms out by her side and blew on her belly. Her smile lit up the room.

Twenty-Five

The Call

I'd dreaded the long flight to Sacramento, but Shanthi slept right through, and Shermila entertained me by asking incessant questions about every unusual sight or sound and providing a running commentary, much to the amusement of the adults nearby. As she jabbered on, it struck me afresh how nice it would be to rid myself of the constant refrain of John's demeaning comments.

Once in California, my parents would undoubtedly fawn over the antics of the first two grandkids in the family. Vim and Viji were both working at UCLA. Nimi was home with my parents and would be a doting auntie. Viji had apparently set up a weekend trip to Santa Monica, where the girls could see the ocean for the first time. The ocean . . . I hadn't smelled that incredible salty sea breeze for over a year.

"Mummy, mummy, green light, green light!" Shermila chirped excitedly, pointing to the seat belt lights overhead. As I released the buckle, I thought about how John had yelled at me when I first brought her home.

Enough! Put him out of your mind!

I'd be in the California sun in two hours and fifty-nine minutes. I yawned, stretched out my arms, and let out a huge sigh of relief. I'd been given the green light for sure.

The Call

A week later, I was in my parents' TV room in Davis with both girls as we settled into to our bedtime wind-down. The smell of the roast chicken we'd had for dinner was still heavy in the room. Nimi had vanished into her bedroom with a book, and my dad was asleep. My mom buzzed like a bee, flitting around in the kitchen at her usual frenetic pace, clearing dinner dishes. She'd shooed away my offer of help.

Shermila stretched her feet out on the sofa. She solemnly turned the pages of *Clifford the Big Red Dog* and mouthed silent words she had memorized for each page. Shanthi lay on her back on a colorful padded quilt on the carpet, contemplating the mysteries of her toes. She was on a mission to collectively stuff them into her mouth. Her chortle, coupled with a wide, toothless grin, portrayed her delight at her gymnastic contortions.

Curled up with *What to Expect in the First Year* on my parents' easy chair, I frequently lowered the book to bestow sneaky glances of adoration at their antics. In no time at all, we'd settled into a beautiful clockwork schedule for bedtime. I already dreaded that in just three short weeks, we'd leave this heavenly existence to return to John. My stomach cramped up just contemplating it. I returned to my book to distract myself.

The strident ring of the phone stabbed the peaceful nothingness of the evening. My mom was nowhere to be seen, so I rushed over to the phone.

"Lally?" John's voice, and I heard the long-distance crackle.

I tensed up immediately and twisted the cord around my index finger several times. "Yes, aren't you at your conference in England?"

"Yeah, still here in Southampton." There was a thread of animation in his voice that made me wary.

"Everything okay?" I asked. "You sound . . . weird. Isn't this early in the morning for you?" I engaged more fingers in the cord, waiting for a response.

"Yes. Everything's fine. . . ." His voice trailed off. My fingers were so ensnared in the cord that the tips had become white. I released them and shook out my hand, grasping for inspiration to fill the void. This roadblocked conversation reminded me precisely why I dreaded a return to the mechanical, strained way we interacted. In the week we'd been apart, I'd missed him about as much as I'd miss an unanesthetized root canal.

"Didn't expect to hear from you so soon," I finally ventured.

"I know."

"So, how'd it go?" I wondered if he could tell I was filling space and honestly didn't care.

All I got was the long-distance hum.

"John? Still there?" I tried not to speak too loudly to avoid disturbing the girls. "Hullo? John?" I hoped he'd disconnected.

"Southampton offered me a job." His words came out in a rush.

"They what?"

"They offered me a *job*—"

"And?" I was incredulous; my mind spun in crazy circles.

"And I accepted it."

His tone was a study in nonchalance. I couldn't believe how casually he was relating something so earth-shattering.

"You *what?*" I shrieked.

Shermila looked up at me from her book with a concerned look but returned to reading when I waved her off. My mother stepped out of the kitchen with eyebrows raised. She hovered for a moment but disappeared when I gestured that I was fine. I clapped my hand over my free ear to hear him better.

"They offered me a job, senior lecturer, University of Southampton. I said yes. I'm sick of all the rejections. As you know, I'm not getting any younger."

My brain pitched as I attempted to comprehend. I gripped the phone even tighter with shaking fingers.

The Call

"John, they offered you a *job*—in Southampton, England? And you're telling me you just went ahead and accepted it?" Disbelief choked my voice. "That's why you called? To tell me that?" Shermila lowered her feet to get off the couch so she could walk over to me, but I gestured that she should stay where she was. She seemed to have deciphered my shock and anger. A white mist swirled around the room as my thoughts ran amok.

"Yes." His tone was cold. He could have been talking about the weather.

"Did you even consider what *I'd* think? We didn't have a discussion, and you're suddenly saying we're moving, and the girls will have to grow up *in England?*"

I tried hard to stay calm, but my voice cracked at the end. The back of my neck felt as if a cold wave had suddenly smacked into it.

"I've thought about it. You'll stay in California for now with the girls. Once I have a place set up, you can bring the girls over. That's what I thought would be the best plan."

"You thought? You *thought?*" I stammered, totally helpless. Molten steel poured over me with each word he uttered. The room, my girls all disappeared. The only thing that felt real was this tenuous connection to the telephone and John's shocking disclosure. The whirling turned into cold emptiness and in my chest, I experienced a terrifying, pervasive dread.

No, no, no, no, noooo! my brain shrieked, but I was numb.

"Lally? Hear me out. They have a competitive sala—"

I slammed the phone on the cradle with hot tears trickling out of my eyes. Tremors rippled through me, and I had to open and shut my eyes a couple of times till the room gradually came back into focus. Walking like a robot, I headed over to Shermila, placed her on my lap, and gave her a reassuring hug, more for my own benefit than hers.

The phone shrilled out again. Shermila pointed at it, but

I shook my head with a finger on my lips. My mom rushed in and made as if to pick up the phone, but I held my palm up to stop her. I glared at the phone, wanting it to vaporize. After five rings, blissful silence reigned. Shanthi, completely unaware of the gravity of the situation, was still in toe heaven.

I could hardly digest what John had said. At a conference halfway across the world, he'd accepted the Southampton offer, without checking with me! Did he think I'd simply succumb, in the Sri Lankan, submissive-wife, you-command-I-follow way? He'd pulled the same stunt in Kumasi, left his wife and children in England, and they'd visited for summer holidays at his bidding. Was my opinion so inconsequential to our future family plans? Obviously.

In essence, he was telling me that when he was "ready" for us, I had to pack up the girls and end our lives in America. By moving thousands of miles away, I'd sever the critical psychological support of my family. No longer would we have family visits at Christmas, Easter, and during the summer. When given the summons, I was directed to fly out to be with His Highness. He'd decided this with zero discussion. This was intolerable!

Shermila let out a faint squawk because I'd squished her too tight. I apologized, picked up her book, and sat with her, barely registering her words, but her painstaking rendition calmed my irregular breaths.

John never cared about anyone but himself. I was stupid to think otherwise.

"Mommy, see? Big dog." Shermila pointed to her book.

"Yes, Shermila, nice dog," I responded mechanically, absently ruffling her hair.

My mother walked in with a full laundry basket partly balanced on her hip. Her short-sleeved shirt had cooking stains, and flour had tracked all over her black pants. Her smile vanished when she saw my tearstained face. She set down the basket.

"What's the matter, Lally?"

Her tone, full of honey and warmth, was my undoing. My face crumpled, and my tears fell faster. "Ammah, can you please watch the girls for ten minutes? I have to get outside." I wiped the tears off my face.

"Of course. Shermila will help me fold these clothes, right, Shermila?"

As she approached, her shiny black braids bobbing, I felt a welling of love for her I'll-drop-everything-for-you attitude. She asked nothing further, but I wanted to drown in the concern in her warm brown eyes.

I walked out to the front garden, inhaling the heady scent of roses. A white car was stopped right in front of the stop sign outside the house. I watched as it pulled away and disappeared into the gloom. I, too, was paused at a stop sign. I could plow straight into the dissonance and chaos headed my way or make a sharp turn. Our marriage was a sham.

So much for being bathed in a culture that expected marriage to last "for life." I'd been on autopilot too long, too afraid to view other options. How could I uproot my girls to a place so removed from all family support? And from this country I had grown to love? The moon peered out of a bunch of clouds, cloaking the rose bushes in an eerie gray-white coat. I wished I'd worn a jacket. The chill reminded me of English weather, English weather and John—a bone-chilling thought.

My predicament was becoming crystal clear. I'd teetered too long on the high wire, refusing to accept the reality of our miserable existence. I'd experienced John's dark, brooding side for the past four months, after his eruption with the keys. If I meekly followed him to a place with no one to turn to, what if things got worse? He'd undoubtedly belittle me in front of the girls. They'd think that's how women should be treated. Our marriage lacked substance and warmth. It lacked consideration, empathy, and understanding. It lacked communication, as his call just demonstrated.

Our marriage just blooming *lacked*!

And, right there and then, as I stared at that fateful intersection outside my parents' home, I decided it was time to switch myself off autopilot and turn down a new path. My place was *not* in England with John. The violence of his call had desecrated that beautiful moment of peace with Shermila and Shanthi, like a neon sign blaring out danger. I wanted to generate more enchanting moments for our growing family, not have them witness a mother constantly put down, operating in a constant state of nervous tension.

Damn it, I was now an American citizen. I was done being the staunch puppy dog follower, done playing second fiddle, done making sacrifices to the Lord and Master of the Universe. Done, done, *done*! As if on cue, the moon ducked behind the clouds again, and it became pitch dark.

Leave him, the dark sky shouted to me. *This darkness is what your life could become. Leave now, while you still can!*

A large white owl took flight from the tree across the street. As I watched its graceful wings flapping, a strange feeling of exultation and resolve grew deep within my chest. An elixir of power burgeoned, surging over me, warming my core and speeding up my pulse. I became that stately owl. I imagined how, perched on the tallest tree in the forest, I was afforded an unimpeded view of the jungle in which I'd been trapped for ten years.

Shanthi fussed a little in the house but stopped almost immediately. My incredible supermom had no doubt intervened. In just a week, both girls had blossomed like sunflowers in the California sun. Shermila had transformed from a bratty toddler with multiple tantrums a day to a girl who giggled with delight at her baby sister's antics. In Pennsylvania, she always woke us up screaming in the middle of the night, but from the day we'd arrived in Davis, she'd slept soundly through the night. That alone was telling me something.

If my girls grew up here, they'd have unimaginable opportunities to thrive in the magical multicultural mix of Sri Lankan, American, Ghanaian, and English values. The world awaited their first trembling steps of exploration and discovery. They'd depend on me to chart the right course for their lives. I'd help them become strong, wild young ladies with an awesome role model for a mother, not a doormat.

I threw my hands up in the air, extending my fingers to the sky in a triumphant salute. I was no longer the naive, clueless twenty-three-year-old bookworm John had snatched up a decade before. Oh no, I was the lion on the Sri Lankan flag, wielding the sword with grim determination. I was the central black star of the Ghanaian flag, symbolizing emancipation from John's brand of colonialism. I was a bell ringer poised to deafen the world with the chimes of the Liberty Bell. Undoubtedly that bell would peal out thunderous approval of my decision tonight. I twirled in the darkness, making two full circles, to fully absorb the glory of the moment. The electricity exploding from my chest could have powered a football stadium.

John was unaware that, with a simple call from a different continent thousands of miles away, he'd pushed me to make a life-altering decision. Without such an ultimatum, tossed out of the blue, the passive old Lally might have been content to tag along and live unhappily ever after. . . .

Twenty-Six

Separation

The days that followed my epiphany were rocky. Shermila occasionally asked when Daddy was coming back. Some of my exuberance leaked out, and I guiltily wondered if I'd been too hasty to make the decision. Sleepless nights and headaches became the new norm as I struggled with the mental tussle of how separation might negatively impact the girls. Through it all, my dad's words, "marriage is made in heaven," echoed in my ears. I simply couldn't break this to my parents. As the eldest, I'd accepted the cultural shackle of role model to my siblings that I could hold my marriage together. They had absolutely no idea of the rancor we'd developed in our relationship.

Consumed with guilt about the family reaction, rather than come clean about my decision, I chickened out. John, I told my family, had a job lined up at Southampton University. Once he settled down, I added, the three of us would head out to England to join him. It was only a half lie, I reasoned. There was still an infinitesimal chance that we might actually do that. My parents registered some shock, but to my relief, they didn't ask too many questions.

And that was that.

John had probably returned to Pennsylvania, so I couldn't

procrastinate for long about my decision to remain with the girls in California. A week before our scheduled departure, I found the perfect time one afternoon. Shanthi was asleep and Shermila was in the back garden with my mom, watering plants. I ducked into my bedroom to place the call.

"John?" I cleared my throat.

"Yes?" His tone was encrusted with ice particles.

"You didn't call after you got back, so I . . . er . . . wanted to check in. Figured you'd be home now," I babbled.

"You're the one who hung up, remember? I called back and you didn't pick up. You didn't seem overjoyed or even supportive about my job." He sounded aggrieved, like a petulant child.

I lay back against my pillows, my pulse hammering. Across from me hung two watercolor murals Shermila had created. My eyes caressed the colorful smudges. I took a deep breath. "It was a shock, John. A huge shock. I'm still struggling . . . I still don't know what to say, actually."

The silence became more uncomfortable. I wanted to scream at him to say anything to decipher his thought process, but he remained obstinately silent. I fingered the tiny gold gondola pendant around my neck—a present from my maternal grandmother when I turned sixteen. Touching that memento always gave me a connection with her. Her lean, kindly face with gray hair tied back in a ponytail came to mind. I wished I could draw on her wisdom. I shut my eyes and inhaled deeply.

"Okay, so I've been thinking about everything, John, you, me, the girls . . . the whole deal." I slid the pendant from side to side on the chain. "First . . . er . . . congratulations on your job." I tried to sound happy, but the words were flat. I grasped the phone tightly, but he remained silent, so I hurried on.

"So, here's my problem. You took the job without asking what I wanted. We didn't discuss the best option for our family.

I guess my opinion just doesn't count anymore. You simply decided your future lies in England . . . and then you told me what you envisage for the future for us—for our family."

He didn't respond. I imagined him staring out the window of our home wearing that shuttered gaze that hid what he was thinking. He'd always earned an F in communications.

"But, guess what, John?" I warmed up. "I'm not ready to just pick up and leave. Things are different between us now. I don't like how you speak to me anymore." I shook my head. My fingers trembled with the intensity of my grip on the phone. The artwork caught my eye again. If Shermila only knew what this conversation might mean to her future life.

"You forget, Lally, that I'm the one who made the sacrifice to come here to America for you, didn't I?" His voice held an ugly and accusatory tone now. "It's your turn now to—"

"I know . . . I know," I interrupted, "but John, we hardly even talk or communicate anymore. I'm settling down here in California. I'm so happy. So are the girls. I love it here. I'm an American citizen. I'm not ready to leave, okay? The atmosphere here is so different from Pennsylvania." I hated the pleading tone that had crept into my voice.

"There you go again, thinking only about yourself as usual," he cut me off impatiently. I imagined his eyes narrowing and squinting as he turned into the cold, emotionally distant John I'd come to know. "Lally wants this, Lally wants that—" His sneering tone left me rigid. "Most men I know get support from their wives. Not from you, it seems. Grow up, Lally. You're a child who wants to live with Mummy and Daddy again." The jeering, belittling tone reminded me of why I wanted out. I imagined he was pacing furiously now, his cheeks red, his mouth a tight grim line.

I glanced at a tiny photo on my nightstand from shortly after our marriage. John and me at the peak of a mountain. We looked so happy. It was so different back then. If he'd turned on that old charm, he might have actually sucked me into acquiescence. I remembered the teasing look the old John had. He'd have pulled me into his grasp, told me he loved me, blotted out the universe, and I would have followed him wherever he went.

Today, his curt tone and the distance of a few thousand miles helped avert that quagmire. I stood up and drew the curtains closed. Cutting out the external world helped me focus. I shut my eyes tight and opened them.

"Our communication's shot, John. We don't know how to talk to each other anymore. I'm sick of arguing about Shermila. Out here, she's sleeping through the night. She's happy, and her tantrums are almost gone. Can you believe it? It's wonderful."

"But—" He tried to interrupt, but I was on a roll.

"And you know what gets to me the most? Your negativity about America. That gets to me every single day, John. I love this country so much. I just *love* it here. There are so many possibilities, not just for me but for the girls also."

"For *you*, not for *me*." His voice was bitter. "I had zero job offers from your precious country. Do you want me to drive a school bus again? Huh? Is that it?"

"Of course not, John. You've changed, I've changed. I'm an American now, John. I'm not going back to England with you. We argue all the time, you beat up on me in front of the girls, and you don't communicate. I'm like a shell of a person when you're around. Living here in Davis . . . it's different . . . it's so peaceful. The girls are thriving."

"Sure," he sneered, "of course you don't have the guts to stick with your aging husband. Classic. After all I've done for you." I imagined him raking a hand through his hair. "Now that I finally have a decent job, you're digging in your heels." I could almost see the splotches of red in his face as his anger built up. "You know what? Go ahead and do your own thing, Lally, and try to grow up. Maybe one day you'll understand how much you've just thrown away."

When he threw in the age factor, he always made me feel guilty. He sure knew how to push the right buttons. The silence stretched out again, the long-distance crackle the only sound. I dug the edge of the gondola pendant into my thumb until it made an indentation.

"Okay, John, and just so you know, I'm not planning to fly back next week. By the way, I'll never try to stop the girls from seeing you, you know."

"Fine. Just fine." His voice was hard now, indifferent. "Yes, go ahead. Stay there. We'll save the airfare. I'll box up your stuff and mail it. Southampton starts in January, so I'll pack up the house and leave soon. Go ahead—enjoy your life." The biting, angry, sarcastic tone was back. This time *he* hung up.

Tears flowed down my cheeks as I heard loud beeps of disconnection. A loud conversation was taking place outside my window, and I drew back the curtains. Two young junior high girls cycled by, chattering and giggling. Those could be my girls in the future, on their way to the school just a block up the street. I smiled through my tears. Behind them lay a bright green lawn decked with white flowers that hinted at new possibilities.

My eyes dropped back to that small silver-framed photo of the two of us on the pinnacle of Mount Thielsen in Oregon. John knelt by the cairn, and I stood behind him with an ecstatic glow on my face. My hand was on his shoulder. He was young, muscular, and handsome, and we both looked like we didn't have a care in the world. A lock of golden-brown hair curled on his forehead, begging to be tucked away. I ran my hand over the photo, remembering. . . .

I'd been so proud to climb that nine-thousand-foot mountain, especially the two-hundred-foot rocky scramble up boulders to the summit. During the arduous ascent, I was thrilled that

I hadn't given up, even though that thought had crossed my mind repeatedly.

"Look down at your feet. Baby steps," he'd directed. "Don't look up at how much farther we have to climb." Under his tutelage, I'd done it! I'd conquered that scary mountain peak.

How could such a wonderful relationship have turned this bleak? My stomach twisted with a deep sense of loss. I picked up the photograph and turned it over. Not satisfied, I snatched it up and threw it into my nightstand drawer face down. I placed a small book on top of it to obscure the entire frame.

Baby steps, John. I'm taking baby steps like you taught me, but this time I'll do it solo.

One month later, I stood in the garage unpacking seven thigh-high plywood containers of possessions from Pennsylvania. Thrown in with Shermila's teddy bear was a package containing all the handmade cards and poems I'd created for John's birthdays and our anniversaries over the years.

I turned them over, rereading foreign-sounding verses of adoration from a loving wife I could barely envision now. Acid rose up in my throat. I set them aside and continued unpacking, but a leaden feeling hit my stomach. John could simply have thrown out all his cards. Instead, he'd deliberately sent them back to me after holding on to them for years. Clearly he wanted to inflict as much hurt as possible and show me that leaving him was a big mistake.

I put the cards away, face down on a table. Later I'd slip them into the large beat-up manila envelope where I'd stored every letter he'd ever sent me from the time I lived with the Claydens back in South Wales. His symbolic gesture had cemented the death of our ten-year relationship like nothing else could.

I didn't want to feel anything. Didn't want to give a shit. Fought the feeling . . . fought it . . . fought it. . . . Didn't want to give him the satisfaction of wounding me, punishing me for leaving.

But later that night, as I added the cards to the stash of letters he'd written to me, I sobbed for what was no more.

Twenty-Seven

Welfare

Because I'd planned to be in California only a few weeks, the cash I'd brought dried up fast. John provided no further financial support, and I had no access to our bank account in Pennsylvania. I begged John for money, but he did not respond. I tried to be understanding at first. He was preparing for the move to England, so it would be a financial hit. However, as weeks became months without any support, my patience transformed to anger. My parents, with so little to their name, were now supporting the three of us, despite the fact that John had a regular paycheck as a university professor. He knew I was not working, but apart from one or two pitiful deposits into an account I set up in Davis, my emails pleading for support were ignored.

The final straw was his callous move to withdraw $100 from a special account we'd set up for Shermila—money my parents had sent for her birthday. I was shocked that he could simply wipe us off his slate as punishment for not agreeing to follow him to England. Thankfully, my siblings sent clothing and gifts for the children, and Shanthi could wear Shermila's hand-me-downs.

One Sunday morning, after the sun had toasted away the morning chill, I took both girls to the park just down the road. Shermila's laughter pealed out as she showed off her athletic prowess on the structures. Shanthi cooed from her stroller as she watched her sister with adoration. The girls' uncomplicated and unfettered love of the world made something catch in my throat, as I reminded myself that I was no longer going to be embarrassed by an errant husband screaming at other kids and enraging their parents.

It surprised me that Shermila asked where Daddy was only a couple of times in the first few weeks, then completely stopped asking about him. She seemed content with my explanation that he had flown in a plane to work somewhere, and since he never called to speak to her, it was probably easier for her to move on. These days when she had skirmishes with other children, they sorted it out without adult intervention, just as I had done as a child. I remembered how Shermila used to throw herself to the ground, all her limbs flailing, screaming as if she were being murdered to get her father's "gallant" intervention. It was all simply like a bad dream.

I continued to beg John for money. Occasionally, if I begged hard enough, he wired a meager amount that ran out in a few weeks. I think he enjoyed making me grovel. One day, for no reason that I could fathom, he cut support and communication completely.

When the realization dawned that I was now the girls' sole provider, I threw all my efforts into digging us out of our plight. I filled out reams of forms to get us on welfare, stood in long lines for food stamps and financial assistance, and accepted every handout from Women, Infants, and Children (WIC) and MediCAL. I was embarrassed to be on the receiving end of the welfare state but overwhelmed with gratitude for the empathy of the smiling workers who assisted me. The medical and food benefits were a true godsend, and I was humbled by the incredibly generous support from the state at our time of greatest need. The city of Davis provided daycare for my girls so I could job-hunt.

Welfare

When I stammered my thanks to Lynne, the kind city worker assigned to my case, she gave me a warm smile.

"We're here to help you on your job search, Lally." Her brown bangs danced as she nodded. "That's why we've released these funds. Go out there and make us proud."

I shut the door and stumbled to my car, overwhelmed by her warmth. It was staggering and humbling to think about how many hundreds of dollars they were investing in our futures. It was so difficult to accept all this charity. I laid my head on the steering wheel, feeling ashamed. On the other hand, it boosted my confidence immeasurably that they believed I'd find a job and step out of welfare eventually. As I wiped my wet cheeks with my hands, I promised myself that one day I'd show them that they hadn't misplaced their trust. I'd make them more than proud. This was my safety net, and I swore that one day I'd cheerfully pay right back into this amazing system with my income tax from a future job.

Grocery store lines were tough. Many times, I ushered customers to go ahead of me so they wouldn't see the shameful orange food stamps that branded me a freeloader. I didn't want anyone's pity, or worse still, disgust. One afternoon, I brought home a large French roll from a free food giveaway to needy people from the Upper Crust Bakery. Salivating over what it might taste like smothered in butter, I cut myself a thick slice from the edge. When I turned it over, with the loaded butter knife in my hand, a long, wide band of green mold ran all the way down the other side. Cringing, I threw it back on the counter and used the tip of the knife to steer it into the garbage can. I stared at it in horror, as if it might wriggle back out to contaminate me. Tears of shame spattered the lid of the trash bin.

Doctor of doctors indeed. . . .

The classified section of the newspaper became bedtime reading. I carefully highlighted promising job announcements in Davis and the surrounding towns. My sense of accomplishment increased as the pile of newspaper clippings grew on my nightstand. I printed a dozen copies of my resume on regal ivory parchment paper that Viji bought for me. Surely, there was a job out there with my name on it—I now held both bachelor's and master's degrees in human physiology.

Rejections also piled up. The one that stung the hardest was the rejection from a Woodland seed company—a minimum-wage position counting seeds. After the in-person interview I figured I was a shoo-in for the job, but perhaps the employers were wary I'd use them as a stepping-stone for a higher-paying one. It wasn't too far from the truth. If something more lucrative or challenging showed up, I'd have jumped ship for sure.

I learned how to navigate the online UC Davis job site and applied for a multitude of lab assistant jobs. After two months of searching, in November 1994, I was offered a position as lab assistant II at the UC Davis Nutrition Department. When I brought the girls home from daycare that afternoon, Shermila and I plonked Shanthi in the center of the living room, and we danced around like demented beings, shouting out, "Ring around the Rosie!" at the top of our voices.

Twenty-Eight

The Lab Assistant

At age thirty-three, I finally had a real job, with a salary plus benefits. For the first time in my life, I could accumulate vacation pay and sick leave and fund a retirement account. I was now able to contribute to daycare expenses for the girls. Before this, my only other income had come from a grad student stipend in Pennsylvania, the summer Baskin-Robbins ice cream cake-decorating job, and a part-time teaching job at Holmes Junior High School Learning Center during my undergraduate years.

It was glorious to be in the workforce earning $2,100 a month. I set up my first bank account at a local Davis credit union and skipped out, humming, as the glass doors swung behind me. I didn't own a car, but luckily work was only a twenty-minute cycle ride to campus. So drunk was I with the giddy feeling of managing my own money that I spent half my salary to rent the three-bedroom house across from my parents to salvage a modicum of independence. The week after work began, both daughters came down with chicken pox, but thankfully, I could use two weeks of sick time to care for them.

The first day I got the house keys, I left the girls with my parents, raced across the street, and slammed the front door shut behind me, panting so hard I thought I'd have a heart attack.

I then raced around to all the rooms in the house in turn, and also to the backyard, shrieking like a little child let loose in Disneyland for the first time.

"I worked for this!" I addressed the house in a crazy loud voice. "I did this. No one can take this away from me!"

After several garage sales and a few donated chairs from my kindly landlord, we finally had a motley collection of mismatched furniture, but it did the job. One of the perks of living so close to my parents was that the baby monitor worked from across the road, so I could drop Shermila and the baby monitor off at my parents' house, leaving Shanthi sleeping at our home when I grabbed groceries from Albertsons down the road.

At work, I learned that one of my duties would be to prepare rat kibble, so I sculpted myself into a master rat food chef to prove my worth. The research lab was intriguing, and I enjoyed meeting other students my age. A researcher in the next-door lab, also a single mother with a daughter Shermila's age, became my close friend and confidante. After years of relative social isolation, it was refreshing to have a good friend. For the first time ever, I was free. Free to be me. Free of the Claydens, free of John, free of my parents. Free!

The Liberty Bell clanged out its joyous endorsement.

Within two months, the novelty of ministering to thousands of rats wore off. To make rat fodder, I stood alone in a cold basement, fifteen feet above a giant mixing vat, and measured out grains into a vast metal container beneath me. One afternoon, I stared for several minutes through the hazy mist of chopped grains at the hypnotic, churning steel blades grinding beneath. The smell of wheat and fresh-cut grass filled the air. A disturbing thought struck, that if I leaned over too far, I'd fall into the vat and be turned into rat chowder. Worse still, because I worked alone, no one would know . . . except for a few discerning rats.

The Lab Assistant

I thought I'd miss John tremendously, but to my relief, every time I walked past the wedding photo still prominently mounted on my parents' front room wall, my chest constricted in dread. I felt not a twinge of sadness. Guilt remained my cross to bear because of all the years I'd invested in the relationship. There were still times when I questioned if I should have stuck it out a little longer.

The job came with mental health benefits, so with some trepidation I impulsively made an appointment to see a counselor through the Academic and Staff Assistance Program. It would be good to hear what a professional in that field thought about my separation and tentative plan to seek a divorce.

The counselor had long, dark hair, with eyes like shimmering gray pools that invited you in. The little African violets on her table and the view of the garden through her window calmed my hammering, anxious thoughts. I also sniffed appreciatively at the delicate smell of lavender from a tiny candle on her desk. I admired the dainty floral skirt that draped so elegantly over her knees, feeling like a tramp in my jeans, T-shirt, and battered sneakers. Making myself comfortable in an overstuffed leather chair, I shared with her the travails of my last few months.

At first, I was hesitant. I'd barely shared details of John's behaviors with anyone but my friend Tammy, but as the therapist sat there, nodding, I dissolved in those all-seeing gray eyes. The words flew out of my mouth, like a hose with a kink that initially sputtered, then gushed out at full throttle. It was profoundly relieving to unload my experiences on someone who appeared fascinated by my tale. She acted as if she had all the time in the world to hear me out, like a kindred spirit figuratively holding my hand. A hasty glance at my watch showed that my consultation time was running out.

"And so," I said, leaning back, "I want to hear what *you* think. That's why I came today. Do *you* think that maybe I should have tried a little harder? He said I was selfish to refuse to join him in England. Do I sound selfish? Please tell me—I can take it." I scanned her expression for a response, unable to read her thoughts.

She exhaled deeply and twirled a pen in her fingers, saying nothing for a moment. Finally, she leaned forward, laid her pen on the notepad, and looked me in the eye. "Lally," she said quietly, "I am absolutely shocked that you're asking me a question like that. Truly shocked." She shook her head.

"What do you mean?" I stiffened and looked at her in bewilderment.

"Your husband, John, sounds like a control freak," she announced, "and yet, you stuck it out for ten years." She shook her head and threw her fingers up in the air. "You took on so much, Lally. Of course, you're making the right decision. You should absolutely file for divorce, so the judge can order him to make payments. He's working as a professor, you say, yet not supporting you or the children? That's inexcusable."

I exhaled as a huge weight of guilt lifted off my chest. She supported me! She hadn't gently suggested that I reconsider. She didn't think I was a gutless coward for refusing to follow him.

"Really?" I asked.

"Unconditionally. Absolutely." She leaned forward with her chin on upraised hands placed on the table between us. "The sooner you file for divorce, the quicker child support payments will come in."

"I see." I looked down and picked at a thread in the knee of my jeans. I'd never thought it through like that before. "I don't . . . I don't know the first thing about how to get a divorce. Sounds scary. Never thought I'd be stuck in a place like this."

"Few do, but something like fifty percent of marriages end up this way these days. And since you're on welfare, I imagine you'll qualify for a public defender. Think he'll fight for custody?"

"Nope. No way. He's cut all contact with them. He had two sons before he hooked up with me, and he didn't stay in touch with those boys either. I begged him, several times, to connect with them, but he refused."

I stood up and hoisted my backpack on my back. "Thank you. You've been incredibly helpful. More than you can know. Thank you very much!" My eyes were moist.

"I'm glad you found this helpful, Lally. You're making the right decision. Please schedule another appointment if you need to talk some more." She ushered me outside into the blinding sunlight.

As I half walked and half skipped to the parking lot, I hummed the lyrics from Helen Reddy's "I Am Woman." But that's when the oddest thing happened. As I sat in the driver's seat, I turned on the car radio. My hands froze on the steering wheel to the lyrics of Roxette blaring out, ". . . listen to your heart, before you tell him goodbye." My fingers literally shook on the wheel, and tears oozed out of my eyes. Of all the shitty times to hear these lyrics. I snapped the music off, heaved a bunch of shaky breaths, and drove home as if the entire Davis police force were on my tail.

A few months later, I met with a public defender at the Woodland Courthouse—a freckled, earnest-looking young Caucasian man with a prominent Adam's apple. He seemed passionate about his work, although he probably earned just about nothing, representing people like me with no money. I liked him immediately.

His office was not much bigger than a closet, and there were binders and folders and stacks of papers everywhere. He sat across from me at his no-nonsense wooden desk and pushed over what seemed like an encyclopedia of forms to fill out.

"It's all pretty basic. Let me know if you need my help. Should be straightforward because you've got no assets—no home or property to fight over. You have an email, but you don't even have his physical address in England. Is that right?"

"That's right."

"You've requested one hundred percent custody of your daughters. Any chance he'll challenge this?"

"Nope. He's not going to question it, trust me. If he wants visitation rights, that's fine with me."

"The judge will make a determination about that, and also set alimony," he said.

"Alimony? Support for me?" I leaned forward, gripping the desk tight.

"Yes, ma'am. That decision is based on—"

"I don't want alimony—just support for the girls." I shook my head vehemently.

He looked up sharply from his paperwork, pen poised in midair.

"I'm not sure you understand. If he's a professor, he probably makes ten times your salary. By California law, he should make alimony payments." His eyebrows migrated almost into his curly brown hairline.

"I can't explain, but I don't want his money. I want to make it on my own." I dropped my eyes.

It was hard to explain, even to myself. If he gave me money, I'd feel as if I "owed him." It would be infinitely more meaningful to the glowing she-wolf I'd recently become to steer my future without being shackled to him.

"As you wish," he said, straightening the papers, "but I strongly encourage you to reconsider before we finalize the paperwork."

"I won't change my mind, but thanks for your advice." I loaded the large stack of papers into my backpack.

"Well, Lally, it was good to meet you. Let me know if you have any questions when you're filling out those forms." A radiant smile transformed his face, making him appear handsome. I had the sudden urge to straighten his chestnut locks and bestow a gentle kiss on his hair because he was so adorably cute and earnest. I blushed, thankful that my dark complexion hid the coloration on my cheeks. Phew. John hadn't killed every spark of romance in my body. I could still take a healthy interest in another man.

I walked slowly to the car, glad that yet another person had endorsed my decision. Head bent against the blistering heat, I went back over our entire conversation. We'd cold-bloodedly discussed the termination of a ten-year marriage. I replayed tender moments John had shared with Shermila. He'd given her a saucepan of raw rice and several plastic cups, and they'd made an unholy rice mess all over the carpet. When I walked in on the mountains of rice strewn everywhere, he'd thrown me a guilty smile like a child caught doing something wrong.

There'd been those times when he'd patiently spooned cereal into Shermila's mouth, never seeming to care that it was smeared into her hair and all over the highchair. Once, on a stroll after a blizzard, he'd laid Shermila face up on a four-foot snowbank. She shrieked out in delight as she waved the arms of her robin's-egg-blue snowsuit to fashion a snow angel. He wore a bright cherry-red snowsuit, and something caught in my chest at the way they smiled at each other, the vibrant colors of their jackets showcased against the glistening white snow.

Now the ugly word "divorce" was poised to banish moments like these forever. Dark, tangled feelings clashed with the brilliant sunlight outside. I reassured myself that this was a rational choice, making a mental note of all the reasons for my decision.

Back in the car, I turned on the radio, then gripped the steering wheel in horror, as the very same fucking song played. That bitch, Roxette, once again exhorted me to *think before I told him goodbye!* What a horrible coincidence! I smacked the radio knob like it was an advancing monster. After a few heaving breaths, I took a sideways glance at the thick sheaf of divorce papers sticking out of the backpack beside me. They gave me a reproachful pout: *Are you sure you want to do this?*

I placed my forehead on the steering wheel and sobbed uncontrollably till the sobs turned to hiccups. Then I drove home in silence.

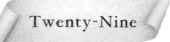

Twenty-Nine

The Donated
Body Program

S ix months into my job, I averted my face past the rat cages to avoid the mute appeal in those pink eyes that implored me to set them free. The knowledge that I was part of the machinery that would lead to them being experimented on and then sacrificed ratcheted my guilt. I had to quit.

Within a week of job searching, I was hired by the UC Davis Medical School's Anatomy Department as their director of the Donated Body Program. It came with a salary hike, but the catch was that I'd be working solo, embalming human bodies for medical student dissection and harvesting human body parts for medical research. Just lovely. The difference with *this* job was that the human donors had gifted their bodies, unlike those hapless lab rats.

Given that I'd spend all day with only dead humans for company, holed up in a basement office, I wondered if the salary increase would be worth the horrors of the job. I'd been assured that someone would teach me how to embalm bodies at UC San Francisco (UCSF). With no prior embalming experience and only a few months of cadaver dissection during medical school in Ghana, I didn't know if I possessed the psychological toughness to stick it out any longer than the rat job.

On the first day, I cycled to Tupper Hall, an ugly gray three-story building, much like a concrete tomb. My supervisor, Dr. Kumari, took me down the elevator to my cramped office in the basement. The back door of the office led to a huge med student dissection hall, illuminated by blinding fluorescent lights. From there, we turned right to traverse a dark, foreboding cadaver storage room that reeked of formaldehyde mixed with death, until we made it to our final destination, the blindingly white-walled morgue.

Yellowing bottles of chemicals were scrunched up together on a long shelf on my left, beside a stainless-steel embalming table and pump apparatus. The right side of the room held two refrigerated shelves in one corner. I shuddered at the gleaming silver vertical latches.

"I believe there are bodies waiting in both coolers, so you'll have to decide what you'd like to do with them." Dr. Kumari waved at the doors airily, as if commenting on the weather. My heart skipped a beat when I realized that death lurked close behind the closed doors. To my immense relief, she didn't pull them open.

"Uh-huh," I responded nonchalantly, trying not to gag on the unfamiliar, nauseatingly sweet odors. I felt an involuntary shudder when I glanced at a collection of evil-looking silver instruments tossed on a gurney beside us. What they were used for I couldn't imagine, and frankly, I really didn't want to know. The queasy feeling in my stomach remained long after we closed the door to the morgue and walked out together in silence.

Doctor of doctors indeed . . . this was Welcome to Hell.

I learned the fine art of dead body preservation from Dr. Patterson, a charming white-haired UCSF doctor who'd previously worked my job for over a decade at UC Davis. With his deep, booming laugh, affable engagement, and dedication to showing me the ropes, it was no surprise that he'd earned many teaching awards. Nothing from our first meeting gave me a clue that nine years later his body would be discovered hanging from an oak tree on the university campus near my work site with a crumpled note in his pocket citing job stress.

Death and decay became my new norm. When I checked the two refrigerated morgue shelves for bodies first thing every morning, I always sent out a silent prayer that they'd be empty. Unfortunately, the fates wore earplugs most of the time. Once a body was delivered, it was up to me to decide whether to embalm it or harvest body parts for research.

With four students sharing a cadaver and approximately one hundred students per year, we needed twenty-five to thirty embalmed cadavers for our first-year medical students. The other "fresh" donated bodies were dismembered and frozen, as body parts were in high demand, both for our own UC Davis surgeons and other researchers.

About a month after I began embalming on my own, I woke up sweating from a nightmare. I was embalming my sister, Nimi, when she sat up on the embalming table, yanked the cannulas out of her neck, and told me she'd changed her mind. The embalming fluid spurted all around the room, and dark blood ran in rivulets from the hole I'd made in her neck.

"Nimi, I'm sorry, it's . . . it's irreversible. I can't stop it," I tried to explain. A few days later, I dreamt I was pumping embalming fluid into my parents' beloved black spaniel. His gorgeous hazel eyes dulled as his body became lifeless. What hurt the most was the wisdom in his eyes and the trusting paw he raised up on my knee, as if he forgave me for what I was doing to him.

Bands of daylight peeked through the blinds as I peeled off my sweaty T-shirt the next morning. I sat up against the headboard and hugged my knees. If I quit, I'd be doing so before my first paycheck. If I held on a little longer, I could probably support the three of us fairly well. Plus—and this was the kicker—I hate to give up on anything. Ever. On the other hand, the nightmares were like blinking warning lights. Surely there were other jobs out there that didn't involve caged rats or cadavers.

I would quit, I decided. Today, before I could change my mind. In my office extra early that morning, I took a deep breath and called Dr. Kumari to tender my resignation.

"Lally, Lally," her voice crackled urgently, "wait, please wait. Let's talk. Now. Let me buy you coffee, okay? Meet you in the café in ten minutes."

Filled with misgivings, I dragged my feet all the way to the bustling med school café, resolved that I would not back down from my decision to quit, no matter how persuasive she became. The aroma of fresh-roasted coffee was a welcome respite from my usual bouquet of formaldehyde-laced decaying humans.

After trading a few niceties about the coffee and pastries, Dr. Kumari launched in, her dark eyes focused on mine. "Please, Lally, please reconsider. You're doing a great job. Several faculty members have commented about your great organizational skills. The med students appreciate your help on the cadaver dissections. We need you, Lally," she begged. Her prominent South Indian accent made me feel that if I walked away, I'd let down the entire Asian race. Something about the slant of her face reminded me of my aunt in Sri Lanka.

I told her about my nightmares.

"But, Lally, *anyone* would have nightmares at the start of a job like this!" She raised her coffee and took a long sip, her eyes still fixed on mine. "Who faces death every single morning? Of course this is tough, Lally. How about this, Lally—just give it two months. *Two months*—that's it. It'll get better, I promise. You *will* adjust."

"You don't understand, Dr. Kumari. It's not just nightmares. The worst thing is chopping off a person's head. I'm doing it all alone and it's . . . it's too much. I can't do this anymore, I just can't." Tears blurred her face. I swallowed coffee too fast and it burned my tongue.

"Then how can we support you? What will make you stay with us, Lally?" She leaned forward and placed her hand on my wrist.

I tried to imagine a change that might make the job vaguely palatable.

"Would the department hire someone to help me out?" I hated that I sounded like a whining wretch.

She bit into her cookie and chewed thoughtfully for a moment, saying nothing. I wondered if she was shocked at the temerity of the new hire.

"I'll look into it and let you know," she responded.

To my astonishment, she called me a week later to inform me that the powers that be had given me permission to hunt for an assistant. It would be a minimum-wage job, and the person would work directly under me. I was thrilled at the rapid response but at the same time beat up on myself for succumbing so quickly.

At the bustling Davis farmers market that Saturday, I bumped into Bob Eernissee, my previous manager. I'd decorated ice cream cakes for the Baskin-Robbins family franchise ten years earlier. He said they'd sold the franchise. His goal was to get into nursing school, preferably UC Davis.

I told him I was hunting for an assistant, but the job was minimum wage. Bob's family had paid me seventeen dollars an hour to decorate cakes, so it appeared insulting to offer my prior manager five dollars an hour to dismember human bodies! To my amazement, he jumped at the suggestion. He would *love* to work for the medical school. We had worked together well before, hadn't we? The experience would pad his resume and improve his chances of getting into nursing school. When could he start?

Within two weeks, two people who'd previously collaborated to design clown cones and ice cream cakes had switched managerial roles and worked side by side to carve up and embalm refrigerated humans. Go figure.

I'd been working at the job for over a year when I received an unusual call during my lunch break.

"Donated Body Program, can I help you?"

As I parroted my habitual response, my eyes rested on a portrait of swirling red, yellow, and brown paint taped to my office wall. Shanthi had inscribed her name to her masterpiece with the trademark S pointing the wrong way, as usual.

"Hullo? This is the Donated Body Program," I repeated.

"Er . . . this is Mike." He had an educated, soft, hesitant voice. "I'd like . . . I'd like to donate my body to your, er . . . program."

"Sure, there's a process, and—"

"I'm forty, is that okay?" he interrupted, his words tripping over each other.

"We take ages eighteen and over. There are forms you'll have to fill out." I twirled the phone cord around several fingers.

"But I have to do it now! Can you make an exception for just this one time?"

He had been an adventurous outdoors enthusiast but turned paraplegic after a diving accident. ". . . so I'm sick of being a burden on my parents. Will you accept my body donation by phone? Please?" He was crying now.

It was clear to me that he planned to kill himself. He didn't say how, but his desperation told me it was imminent. I'd never had training in how to handle suicidal people. A pulse pounded above my ear, but I tried to stay calm. From the dim recesses of my mind, I remembered that you're supposed to keep them talking while you alert the authorities. Despite trying every trick in the book, he stubbornly refused to divulge any identifying information.

I plugged one ear and forced the phone against my other ear to listen closely. If these truly were the last moments of this poor man's life, I wanted to remain as close to him as possible. When there was a lull in his impassioned diatribe, I explained that I was sorry, but we never accepted body donation by phone. I told him how beautiful it was to be alive and how sad his parents would be without him. I explained that my cadavers were like empty shells of the vibrant people they once had been. I talked poor Mike's head off for forty minutes. He listened politely till I ran out of ideas to keep him engaged.

"You're a good person," he murmured. "Thanks. I hope you have a good life." Click.

Frozen, I sat with the phone still in my hand, staring at Shanthi's artwork until loud beeps started. Warm, fat tears dripped down my chin and onto my lap. If only I'd had some kind of mental health training. . . . I gently replaced the phone, unsure if my argument had made the slightest difference to his plan to kill himself. I would never know.

After lunch, there was a cadaver to embalm. Downing the remnants of my ham sandwich, I stepped into a white zippered coverall and booties outside my office, then donned purple nitrile gloves and baby-blue shoe covers. I lumbered to the morgue much like a half-deflated Pillsbury Doughboy with my respirator in my hand.

Bob, similarly decked out, had just pulled out a bagged knee from the freezer and added it to other bagged specimens in a white polystyrene box. Smoke from the dry ice formed a mist around his short brown hair. It felt as if I'd stepped into a grisly music video. He closed the polystyrene box with a loud squeak that set my teeth on edge.

"Hey!" He nodded at me, and his bright blue eyes creased into a smile. He used his chin to indicate the morgue coolers. "Big guy in there. Definitely a two-person gig."

"Yup." After I set my respirator down and picked up a face shield from a cupboard, we both walked over. Bob opened the top latch, and a huge body wrapped in white linen glided out soundlessly on the long rails. Under the cover, an obese Caucasian man, likely in his seventies, spilled out over the sides of the rack. He had a balding head and bushy gray eyebrows and looked so peaceful that I could almost imagine that his eyes might flick open if I said hi. He had to be over three hundred pounds, almost three times my weight.

Bob placed a heavy iron chain near the man's head, and together we lifted the man's shoulders and slid the chain under his back and around his armpits. Sweat broke out on my forehead within minutes. We placed a second chain under his buttocks.

Dangling from a rail system in the ceiling above us was a large iron hook. I maneuvered the hook till it dangled directly above the man, then lifted the four ends of the chains into the hook. Utilizing a winch contraption, I hoisted the naked body up until it dangled six feet in the air. Like a wizard commanding a levitated body to move forward, I steered the cadaver fifteen feet till it hovered right above the gleaming stainless-steel embalming tray, much like a giant basting pan. One leg drifted toward Bob's head, and he carefully steered it away. Bob stepped up beside me as we slowly lowered the man, making sure he was perfectly aligned on the raised central platform, and then we unhooked and removed the chains.

"Thanks, I'll take it from here," I said.

The Donated Body Program

Bob gave the thumbs-up signal and turned around to complete the label on the knee package.

I discarded my face mask, replacing it with the bulky respirator. It was a tight fit, but thankfully, it cut out the pervasive smell of formaldehyde. From the cabinet beside me, I pulled out a pair of shiny metal cannulas and attached them to tubing from the pump. Turning the man's limp head sideways, I made a quarter-inch nick into the carotid artery. A tiny trickle of dark crimson blood oozed out, and I fastened the cannula in the artery with twine. This port would infuse the sanitizing formaldehyde cocktail.

As I severed the femoral vein in the thigh so blood could drain out during the process, I marveled that his beautiful arterial distribution system would allow me to replace his blood with preserving chemicals over the next two hours. I turned a tap, and low-speed jets of water flowed underneath the body to remove spills. At the head of the embalming table, I flipped a switch and the pump emitted a soothing humming sound as embalming fluid flowed into the body. I watched the wrinkles magically vanish from his face, one by one, transforming him into a more youthful version of himself. I imagined him flashing me a faint smile of gratitude for the cosmetic enhancements. "You're welcome," I mouthed silently, so Bob wouldn't hear me.

Once he was completely embalmed, I'd double-bag him and transfer him to the storage room next door to join dozens of other embalmed comrades. And there he would lie, like a fine wine, for months, prepped for a future medical student's dissection.

And I'd thought feeding rats was bad. . . .

Thirty

The Suggestion

I could barely believe I'd held on to this horrible job for almost two years already. With the extra income I bought my girls better clothing and saved up money for a used car. To make the job more palatable, I ordered a new body parts freezer to replace our rusted, decrepit one, discarded some ancient bottles of fluid that looked like toxic waste from my predecessors, and threw out old equipment that looked as if it had languished since dinosaurs roamed the Earth.

Once the morgue sparkled, I compiled a bunch of tasteful photographs of the facility into a PowerPoint presentation I could use to educate people about how important body donation was, both for medical student education and research facilities. I set up tours for students from elementary school to high school who visited the facility. They learned about the program and viewed the cadavers and our human body part library or pro-sections. The refined presentation became the cornerstone of a talk I provided to our entering medical students before they started anatomy, as well as hundreds of pre-med students from all over the country, affiliated with the National Youth Leadership Forum.

They sat glued to their seats in the large lecture hall as I explained, "So, as you can see, the person may have passed away, but their body may continue to teach student doctors for thirty years or more after death. We are so grateful for our wonderful donors."

I always ended the presentation with a quote from Ian Fleming's *You Only Live Twice*. "'You only live twice. Once when you are born, and once when you look death in the face.' I think Fleming meant you live again when you're staring down the muzzle of a gun, but I've been given the privilege here of really looking death in the face. I hope you'll leave with a fresh appreciation of how short and beautiful life actually is."

The students' rapt attention and applause gave me a warm feeling of accomplishment and even exhilaration. In teaching them appreciation for the donors and the process, I turned the finality of death into something positive and motivating. Inspiring those thirsty young minds was way more fulfilling than steeping in death and dismemberment down in my basement!

It was not all for the sake of those young minds. As I marinated in a life infused with death all day, I found that I'd paradoxically acquired a new slant on how precious and mysterious the whole gift of life was. All vitality had left those lifeless human shells called cadavers. Perhaps the universe had directed this job opportunity my way to stop me from taking life for granted. My epiphany affected my sleep patterns. I stayed up till around midnight and was up by six in the morning. With death skulking around the corner in plain sight, it was incumbent on me to extend my living, waking hours!

Two years into the job, I happened to take the elevator up to the third floor with a middle-aged Caucasian businessman. The old Lally would have shyly avoided his gaze and focused on the buttons on the control panel, but the new eyes-opened-by-death me dared strike up a conversation. He was headed for a meeting. At the end of the day, I met him again. He was going down this time.

"You again?" he said with a smile. "What a coincidence. Like one?" He lifted the lid of a pink box in his arms, and my eyes feasted on rows of assorted doughnuts. As I walked to my office with a half-eaten cake doughnut, I decided the universe had rewarded me for daring to embrace my burgeoning self-confidence. I'd forged a connection with a total stranger in an elevator. Had we traveled up in total silence that morning, I wouldn't be on this glorious sugar high.

I wiped doughnut crumbs off the desk and picked up a list of body parts needed for the first-year students' upcoming anatomy quiz, then donned a lab coat to select suitable specimens. In the murky lighting from the cavernous, formaldehyde-infused storage room were triple-layered, gleaming aluminum racks reaching to the ceiling that housed the embalmed cadavers, all engaged in a macabre sleepover. Although we'd worked out a mutual respect for each other over the past two years, I always had a prickly feeling when I turned my back on them to load body parts on my gurney. As fast as I could, I selected a dozen specimens and wheeled them into the blinding fluorescent light–illuminated dissection room. Then I began tagging the nerve and muscle specimens.

The door to the dissection hall swung open suddenly. My forceps dropped with a clatter on the silver gurney as I instinctively shielded the prosection samples from view. Medical students were strictly forbidden from entering the hall until they took the quiz. I straightened up and relaxed when I recognized the athletic figure of Dr. Doug Gross, one of the anatomy instructors. He had curly dark brown hair and a mischievous smile that transformed him into a kid.

"Hi, Lally, looks like you've started up. I'm here to help tag specimens, okay?"

"Please be my guest." I waved generously at the gurney loaded with body parts.

The Suggestion

He gloved up and used forceps to inspect my tags. "Nice job, Lally, as always." He turned around with a broad nod and wiped his forceps on blue paper napkins. "You've been with us for what . . . two, three years?"

I beamed at his compliment, then watched him clear fat globules to better expose a brachial plexus specimen.

"Almost two, but it feels like ten sometimes. Know something, Doug? When I was in med school in Ghana, they tagged the upper limb just like this for our anatomy quizzes." For some unknown reason, tears welled in my eyes, and I blinked them away, looking down quickly so he would not see them.

He straightened to face me, forceps in hand. "That's right, Lally, you said you were in med school in Ghana . . . and that was when, again?"

"Um, let me see. . . ." I did the calculation. "That was a whopping sixteen years ago, Doug. Wow."

He continued tagging for a few minutes, then laid down his forceps and swiveled on his stool to face me.

"Is this really what you want to do for the rest of your life, Lally?"

I choked up. Afraid he might see my misty eyes, or worse still, that tears would fall, I turned my back to him and pulled out an elbow prosection. I laid it on a table.

No way in hell, I wanted to respond. *I'd quit tomorrow if I could make this salary doing something else.* But instead, I took a quick breath and resorted to my favorite defense, humor.

"You telling me this is a dead-end job, huh, Doug?" I gave a fake snicker. He didn't take the bait.

"No, Lally, I'm asking in all seriousness. You got into med school. That's quite an accomplishment."

"I guess." I wiped my forceps off on a paper towel. "I was halfway through when the school closed down, and then I had a visa snafu and . . . anyway, it's a long story." I shrugged. "But that was, you know, my other life. So much for the fortune teller who told my dad I'd become a doctor one day . . . I was a baby when he made that prediction. Look at me now. He was waaaay off course."

"Hmm. . . ." He placed a tag on the clavicle of an upright skeleton. "Ever think of applying again?"

I shook my head numbly. "Never in a thousand years. That dream's long gone now. Maybe I don't look it, but I'm thirty-five, Doug. Ancient." My forceps dropped on the table with a clatter. I retrieved them and cleared off some fascia to better expose the ulnar nerve. "Plus, I wouldn't stand a chance."

"Why do you say that?" He wiped a lock of dark hair off his forehead with the inside of his elbow. His gloved fingers were brown with body juices. "Did you know that Davis admits more mature candidates than most other medical schools? Plus, you have all this experience now." He waved at all the specimens and looked right at me. "You did your bachelor's here at Davis, right?"

"Yes, human physiology. I have a master's in physiology also, from Penn State." My forceps shook. His words had released disquieting glimmerings of hope that I thought I'd left buried over a decade back.

"There you go, you'd be a competitive candidate." He was back to looking me straight in the eye now. I was hard put to break eye contact without appearing rude.

"But . . . as you know, I've got two little girls," I stammered. Before I began at the morgue, Doug was our pediatrician—the only pediatrician in Davis who accepted MediCAL patients.

"Lally, I have *three* daughters. How old are yours now?" He bent over one of the specimens with his forceps.

"Shermila's five, and Shanthi's almost three." I hovered with a hand on the gurney.

"Well, you're working here full-time now, aren't you? How

would it be different if you got into med school? If I recall correctly, your parents help with childcare, right?"

"They do . . . but . . ." The whole anatomy room vanished, and nothing was real but Doug's piercing dark brown eyes. My heart was beating erratically and pounding in my ears.

"There you go . . . well, why don't you think about it, Lally. I think you'd be a great addition to our school." He peeled off his gloves and threw them in the trash from a distance, as if he were shooting a basketball into a net. "And if you decide to apply," he straightened and looked directly at me, "I'll write you a letter of recommendation."

I gripped the gurney handle as if it were a life raft. His words had opened up a hornets' nest of possibilities.

"You will? Really?" I mumbled. "That's . . . that's so nice. Thank you, Doug," I stammered, my innards heaving with a quagmire of unsettled anxiety. "I . . . I guess I *will* think about it, and I'm . . . er . . . so flattered that you'd write me a letter. That means a lot. Thank you." As he left the hall, I stumbled to the solitude of my office and collapsed in my chair, my head buzzing with released hornets.

Thirty-One

New Possibilities

T hat evening, after the girls were asleep, I took my favorite perch with my back against a pillow on the headboard of my bed, pulled my knees to my chin, and mulled over Doug's comments. Four years earlier, I'd briefly thought about applying to medical school again when I was back at Penn State. When John walked in after work, I followed him and waited for him to hang up his jacket, then broached my interest in applying because I'd completed my master's.

"So you're still thinking about med school, huh?" he'd sneered unpleasantly. You have a daughter now. Don't you think it's a little late to *play at* being a doctor?"

I'd dropped the topic, feeling guilty that I'd dared to bring it up.

Now I stared blankly at my closed bedroom door. I was free of John and in full control of my destiny. Doug had suggested that I jiggle open that door I'd padlocked shut fourteen years earlier. Over the past decade, I'd ridiculed the fortune teller's prediction to friends, laughing about it outwardly to cover up my bitterness about what might have been. Did I still have the brains to study my heart out for the medical college aptitude test (MCAT)? Could I handle rejection letters? And if, by some crazy chance, I did well and actually got in, it would be tough to slave over books for four more years. Could I handle that at age thirty-six and as a single mom? My parents were always there without my asking, and I knew they'd bend over backward to help. But, damn it, I wouldn't be a doctor till I turned forty! Ancient! On the other hand, wouldn't it be better to do something I loved at age forty? Like treat people so they didn't make it to my embalming table in the first place? I'd be practicing prevention, not preservation.

A framed photo of my daughters was on the wall beside me. Shermila had her arm possessively around Shanthi. My beautiful daughters stared straight at me with dazzling smiles and glowing eyes—a happiness poster. I imagined being gone long hours from their lives. What if those shining, trusting countenances turned bitter? Would they hate me, as John had suggested, for sacrificing time I could have spent with them? What if they crashed and burned? Their welfare meant more to me than anything else in the world. After a restless night tossing and turning, I woke up bleary-eyed but armed with a resolute plan: I would give it a shot.

First, I'd enroll in a KAPLAN course to help refresh my cobwebby science background. The course was ridiculously expensive, I'd heard, but I sorely needed a refresher. Many moons had elapsed since my undergrad days. The next step would be to take the MCAT. If I did well, I'd apply. Heck, I'd apply two years in a row. If not, it was a pipe dream, and I'd pick something else to do long-term . . . perhaps get a teaching credential or something.

I sat up straight and took a few shaky breaths, consumed with a new sense of resolution. A car honked outside the window, as if to sound a warning. The only snag was the impact of my decision on my girls. If they stumbled as I charged forward, I'd drop it all in a heartbeat. If I didn't leave the morgue soon, all the inhaled formaldehyde would surely fry my lungs. One of these days, I might trip in a puddle of formaldehyde and croak.

Determined to do something about this plan before I balked, I emptied two rickety drawers in the bedroom. Over the next few days, I filled one with medical school application information and the other with teacher credential program brochures. If drawer number one let me down two years in a row, I still had another option. Once I'd filled both drawers with research, I felt excitement about a new me with a new life. Shutting my eyes, I closed the drawers, then tapped the closed drawers individually three times to seal my commitment to following a new quest.

I'd heard that only one in fifty med school applications was accepted. Given all the hoopla about the fortune teller, I'd keep my med school plan under wraps from my parents as long as possible. If word slipped out, I could just imagine my dad broadcasting the news to the world with his "doctor of doctors" prophecy. Long after I'd given up on medicine, he'd often cautioned, "You can't give up, Lally, it's your fate." No, I wouldn't breathe a word to anyone as I embarked on this new and scary journey. It would kill me to have my dad raise his hopes again, only to have them dashed if I encountered rejection.

Kaplan became my home away from home. I studied any chance I could get, during lunch breaks at work, weekends, and nights after the girls were asleep. My MCAT scores came out decent, not stellar. The following August, in 1996, I applied to twenty medical schools all over the country. My top choice was, of course, UC Davis. By December, rejections filled the mailbox.

In early January 1997, UC Irvine invited me for an interview. My heart danced somersaults in my chest as I walked from the mailbox with the invitation in my shaking hand. Granted, it was just an interview, but at least it proved that I was a competitive applicant. Apparently, your odds of getting admitted improved from one in fifty to one in three with an interview. And Irvine was a great school!

On January 23, 1997, UC Davis mailed me a thin envelope. I froze, knowing this signaled bad news. With trembling fingers, I ripped it open by the mailbox, my heart pounding unsteadily. A chill ran down the back of my neck.

"Sorry to have to inform you that . . ." I read, but couldn't go further because the words blurred, and my heart was encased in spicules of ice. I crumpled the paper in my fist, a vice tightening around my chest, then grabbed the mailbox for support, tears raining down my face. I'd done all their body bagging for three years, yet they'd summarily rejected me, whereas Irvine had offered an interview. What a slap in the face! Damn, damn, damn! It was now crystal clear that my sole chance of getting into medical school this year now rested on my upcoming interview at Irvine.

Two days after UC Davis turned me down, I walked with my friend Tammy to the bike parking area after aerobics. Her face dripped with sweat, and she swatted at her face and neck with a small white towel.

As we mounted our bikes, she turned to me. "Oh, I forgot to tell you, Lally, I can't make it to that dance class thing at Freeborn Hall tonight. I have a presentation to finish before tomorrow."

"Oh, Tammy," I wailed, "we've been looking forward to this for weeks. I really wanted to go ballroom dancing for a change. I'm so bummed!" I sat on my bike with a mutinous face and pulled my backpack over both shoulders. Dozens of other students swarmed around us, their bike bells ringing out raucously to warn off pedestrians and other cyclists. The cacophony of sounds was deafening.

"You should still go, Lally!" she shouted. "Maybe you can teach me the steps after?"

"But darn it, Tam, I wanted to go with you," I said glumly, pulling a face.

"You don't need a partner, remember? Just go for it. Maybe you'll meet someone cute."

"Hah," I snorted disdainfully.

"Aileen will be there, won't she?"

"Nope, she's down with the flu. Maybe I'll pass too if neither of you will join me." I shrugged my shoulders.

"Go, Lally, you should go. Just live it up for us. Tell me about it tomorrow. See you!" She cycled off, waving cheerily.

I watched until she was obscured by the dozens of bikers around. I was crestfallen. With the stress of med school rejections, I'd wanted an evening of fun with my pals. I cycled back dejectedly to work, still not sure if I'd go.

Tammy was Japanese, my age, and one of the brightest sparks in my life. We'd met in the rat lab and had continued our friendship after I left. Not only did we meet for step aerobics twice a week, but we'd also gone to half a dozen "singles" events over the past few months at classy hotels in Sacramento.

I loved to step out of mom mode, doll myself in finery, and have her whisk me away to a venue where we spent fun evenings together. We shared a babysitter, drove to hotels together, then giggled all the way there and back. I especially enjoyed trading stories about men we'd met. We had prearranged signals for help, and she was adept at rescuing me from unsavory situations.

"Brown hair, headed our way, two o'clock. Looks like he's going to ask you to dance," Tammy chanted one night. He was a tall, slightly overweight, dark-haired Caucasian man with a big generous smile, and I stepped onto the floor with him.

"My birthday's on December twenty-ninth. Want to meet up again for a drink?" he asked after our dance was over. I was ready to leave, but turned back, startled.

"Did you say December twenty-ninth? Unbelievable! That's my wedding anniversary. I'm divorced, don't worry," I added hastily, noticing his eyes moving to my ringless finger and widening. "Wow! Can't think of a better day to meet up. Sure, let's do it. Want to meet up at my place?"

As the words came out of my mouth, I wanted to take them back immediately. There was no spark with him. It was such a dumb move that I didn't even share my stupidly impulsive offer with Tammy. Or the fact that he'd agreed, and I'd given him my home address—an absolute no-no.

On December twenty-ninth, I asked my mom if the girls could spend the night with her because I had a visitor. She readily agreed. He showed up later that evening, leaving his dark blue pickup parked in my driveway. Our conversation was extremely stilted, with stops, starts, and fragments of conversation that didn't go anywhere. I realized that we had literally nothing in common, and I beat myself up for agreeing to such a dumb encounter in the first place. With so little experience with men, I racked my brain to figure out how to get him to leave without appearing rude.

"Want to join me on the couch?" he asked, a little later.

"Er, sure," I mumbled shyly, torn between just wanting to be held by a man so I could assure myself I was still desirable, but also lamenting the lack of chemistry. I moved awkwardly to the living room and sat primly on the edge of the couch, leaving him to take the initiative. He sat beside me and enveloped me in a comforting bear hug that lasted forever. When, many eons later, he stopped to slip on a condom before he continued pawing at me, it was awkward as hell. The sex was almost as interesting as loading up the dishwasher.

It was boring, but also consensual, safe, and with zero commitment on either side. As a way to salvage the evening and send a final "fuck you" to John to desecrate the date of our wedding anniversary, however, it couldn't have been more perfect. Crazy as it was, I embraced this unfettered new me. I never learned his name, and he never knew mine. He left in the wee hours of the morning, and we never met up again.

Thirty-Two

Tim

Tonight's ballroom dance class was still on my mind as I parked my bike and walked into the morgue. I donned white overalls, then harvested, labeled, and double-bagged a pair of freshly cut ankles. As I carefully placed the bag on the bottom shelf in the swirling misty haze within my freezer, I focused on those bagged, severed limbs that would never hold a body up. The smell of cold meat was overpowering. I slammed the freezer door shut with unnecessary force.

That cemented my decision. I'd go dancing tonight without Aileen or Tammy. I'd better exercise my own ankles before they ended up in a freezer like this. The event was a romantic-sounding "Moonlight Ball," right on campus at Freeborn Hall. After an hour of instruction, there would be free dancing. No partner was needed. Dancing would help take my mind off the UC Davis rejection. Plus, my mom had already agreed to babysit the girls that evening, so it would be criminal to pass up a free, golden Saturday.

It was to be a fateful decision.

The one-hour dance lesson was an aerobic workout. They delivered refreshers on the foxtrot, rumba, West Coast swing, cha-cha, and waltz. I twirled around with multiple dance partners, some male, some female, in a figure-hugging, shocking-pink dress and heels. The boring Freeborn dance hall had been transformed into a magical escape venue. The ceiling was festooned with curly silver streamers. Dainty floral arrangements and candles livened up circular tables covered with long white linen tablecloths. Silver-and-black helium balloon clusters jazzed up the walls. I was mesmerized by the bubbles from the sparkling lemonade fountain near my seat. Whiffs of expensive perfume added to the spice and magic of the evening.

Most of the dancers now sat around drinking and watching as a small group of brave folks strutted newly learned moves on the dance floor. I'd have bet most of the onlookers were like me: too shy to ask someone, yet at the same time desperately hoping someone would ask them for a dance. Spectator envy is a bitch.

I so wanted to waltz. The lilting *boom-cha-cha* rhythm stirred my blood, reminding me of the Scottish waltzes I'd loved so much in the past. I scoured the room trying to pluck up the courage to find a waltz partner. My eye spotted a drop-dead handsome, tall, dark-haired guy with an angular Italian jaw, who looked to be in his early twenties. He wore an impeccable blue sports jacket and dark pants and was filling up his glass at the pink lemonade waterfall. He was easily the cutest guy I'd seen all night. Looked way too young for me, but surely he'd agree to a waltz? I rose from my seat but then froze. What if he refused? If there was one thing singles nights had taught me, it was that I needed a backup plan if my pride was wounded. I looked around him in desperation.

Right behind Handsome was a sweaty, stocky, fortysomething professor type, sporting an ugly tweed jacket over brown pants. He'd be the perfect backup if Handsome declined. The waltz stirred my blood and reminded me that if I didn't pick up my nerve soon, the music might end. With a deep gulp of air, I sauntered over lazily, my heart hammering in my forehead, until

Tim

I stood right in front of Handsome. He towered above me, easily over six feet to my five.

"Want to waltz?" Close up he was even cuter. I saw gorgeous dark brown eyes and long musician's fingers embracing his glass. Definitely Italian, with jet-black hair, and he was muscular with a concave stomach. His eyebrows shot up quizzically, but he gave me a heart-stopping smile.

"Sure, let me set down my lemonade. I'll warn you, I'm not very good at waltzing." He had a very deep, soothing voice that sat strangely on a person who appeared so young.

"I'll show you the steps. It's not that hard." My heart sang. He walked up to my table, placed his glass next to mine, then followed me to the dance floor.

He said "yes," he said "yes!"

And just like that, I had my Cinderella moment. He was graceful and a quick learner, and we talked as we spun around. The hall and all the other dancers faded into oblivion when he held me, his warm hand firmly anchoring my shoulder. When I smiled up at him, I saw an endearing, shy smile and dark brown eyes that brightened up my whole life.

A delicious thrill of anticipation blazed through my innards like a roller coaster as we twirled. It had been three years since I'd left John, plus John had two left feet and wouldn't have gone anywhere near a dance floor. Here was the spark that had been missing from my encounter with Mr. No-name last month!

As the final strains of the waltz trailed off, far too soon, there was an announcement that everyone should clear the dance floor for a presentation given by professional ballroom dancers. My heart beat like a jackhammer as we returned to my table. Rather than come up with an excuse to go back to his party, he sat with me as if it were the most natural thing in the world and sipped lemonade as we chatted. Time passed in a daze.

Hanging out with Handsome (I learned his name was Tim),

he told me both his parents were Italian, and he had been born in Los Gatos in the Bay Area. He was almost done with pharmacy school and planned to head to Santa Barbara or Orange County to find a job. He was thirty-two, not twentysomething, so only four years younger, which was a relief.

He said he played a multitude of musical instruments, including piano, banjo, guitar, violin, ukulele, mandolin, and trumpet. I was impressed that he'd apparently taught himself to play all those instruments. He said he was probably best on the trumpet and finger-picked the guitar. His taste in music ran from jazz to rock and roll and even to country. He told me that this very night he was supposed to have attended a *Star Trek* convention, but friends begged him to join their trio for a dance lesson, so he'd canceled his plans and driven out with them at the last minute. We marveled that we'd both been on the verge of not being there tonight.

"The funny thing is, I don't even own a car right now, so I couldn't have driven here from Stockton if they hadn't brought me. Working on getting myself some wheels. Might buy a car from a friend soon." His eyes sparkled at me, and again I wanted to drown in those soulful dark orbs.

"I don't have a car either, but I'm saving up for a second-hand jalopy." I took a deep gulp of lemonade. I was jittery for some reason. "Borrowed my dad's car tonight."

I'd never met a more unusual man. Rather than impress me, he instead regaled me with a recent relationship failure. He'd dated a girl for four years, they'd become engaged, but then she revealed that she was married to a doctor in the Philippines "on paper" and abruptly broke up with him. Tim had been an excellent student, even made the dean's list, but after the breakup, he failed multiple classes.

"So, yeah, I got kicked out halfway through the three-year program," he said, his eyes lowered. He tapped lightly on the table. "But, guess what? I'm stubborn, and I thought hard about it and decided to go back. I took prerequisites at a community college."

"Wow, now *that* took courage." I shook my head in admiration. "Then what?"

"Then I reapplied, and UOP accepted me again. I'll graduate in May 1999. Can't wait to make some money for a change. My loans are horrendous. Getting a job has been my Achilles heel all along."

His unwavering resolve and his bravery in sharing his failures with a stranger struck me. I've always been more impressed by those who dare talk about hardships they've navigated rather than attempt to impress me with all their money and possessions.

We talked till midnight, and I know I babbled way too fast the whole time, like a nervous schoolgirl, because our time together was short. When the lights finally dimmed, he told his friends to wait and gallantly walked me to my car in the pouring rain under his umbrella because I hadn't thought to bring one.

No, he didn't kiss me, and I didn't leave behind a glass slipper, but at the very last moment, just before he strode away, he returned to the car, asked for my email, and said he'd be in touch. And just like that, he vanished into the misty rain in that dreary parking lot, like a wraith I'd dreamt up. The glow sat on me for hours.

Before I fell asleep that night, I reflected on the fact that this collision with the gorgeous stranger happened because of a culmination of multiple different serendipitous paths set up by the universe. I'd almost bailed because my friends weren't going. He'd planned to attend a *Star Trek* convention and didn't even own a car for the sixty-mile trip to Davis. If I'd seen him minutes earlier with his group of friends, I wouldn't have dared ask him to dance, because I'd have assumed one of the two girls was his date. If *my* friends had been there, I'd probably have excused myself from Tim to return to them. The waltz had played at the exact moment I was desperate to dance, and right then, he'd come up near me to get lemonade. Had they not announced the ballroom demo, he might have returned to his friends. Instead he sat there with me, and we exchanged life stories. The whole magnificent evening was either a huge weird set of coincidences or set up by the gods. I'd like to think it was the latter.

"Tammy, I danced with the most gorgeous guy at that ball last night," I blurted out Monday at step aerobics. "We danced and talked the whole night. I'm so glad I went . . . soooo glad! It was magical. No offense, but I'm actually glad you guys weren't there!"

She chuckled as we laid our mats out on the gym floor. In the background, the lyrics, "All I wanna do is have some fun . . ." blared out.

"Wonder if I'll ever see him again?" I remarked, trying to sound casual, even though my pulse pounded and my throat was dry.

"Give it a week." She stood on her mat, stretched her body to either side, then turned to me, waggling her index finger at me to make the point. "If he doesn't email you, then *you* make the first move."

"Yessir," I announced, with a mock salute.

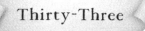

Thirty-Three

UC Davis

To my delight, Tim emailed me a few days later, telling me he wanted to meet again after he bought a car. I told him I was looking for one also. We exchanged emails several times a week. I told him about my upcoming UC Irvine interview. He wrote detailed missives about his roommate, classes, and future plans. It was riveting to enter the life of this handsome new stranger. The only weakness I discerned was his truly atrocious spelling.

With help from my credit union, I purchased a secondhand white 1991 Honda Accord station wagon that had already racked up 110,000 miles. In Ghana I'd become adept at changing a tire, but I knew nothing else about automobile maintenance, so I signed up for an auto mechanics course and quickly learned the nuts and bolts of car performance. By the end of the course, I was thrilled that I'd performed an authorized full service on my vehicle.

When the landlord told me he planned to sell the home I was renting, I located a two-bedroom condo a mile away. The rent was cheaper and the setup perfect. We had a carport and a tiny strip of garden space where we planted tomatoes. We got a kitten, and Shermila named him Rainbow because he had gray-and-white stripes. Sadly no other colors developed.

The Fortune Teller's Prophecy

A week later, I idly took a cursory glance at my email inbox during lunch, then choked on my peanut butter sandwich with a suddenly dry mouth. There was an email from none other than John Russell. Our divorce was still pending, so perhaps the courts had found a way to demand child support. Setting the half-eaten sandwich on my pile of unsorted mail, I focused intently on his words.

It was entitled, "US versus the US of A." That heading alone gave me the shivers, as did the pages-long email. The gist of his letter was that he'd decided that he would like to return to America to get back together with me. He laid out his demands for how I should handle his return, and how he planned to rekindle his relationship with the children. "They will have to get used to my being around again." He also mentioned, "Let's avoid descending into threats of lawsuits from your California social services." In one part of his email he noted, "Obviously, you have more earning potential over time, so I would seek a job while you worked. You would not mock me or make me feel bad because I wasn't working."

Either he was struggling financially or fearful that the courts would impose child support on him. I was well aware that if he arrived in the States without my cooperation, he'd be hit with bills for unpaid child support the moment he landed. As I read and reread his letter, a mantle of cold dread weighted my shoulders like a lead blanket. The sudden exposure to his demands left me utterly weak and helpless. I leaned back in my chair and shut my eyes tight. At a time when I was so close to absolute independence and a possible new romance with Tim in my life, John had resurrected himself. This was his playbook: to wheedle me, guilt me, and drag me back into the morass of sludge and control I'd worked so hard to escape. He'd done that with his prior wife . . . married her twice. These past three years, I'd built up considerable strength, resolve, and confidence, but his words still had the power to throw me into a mess of conflicted, unsettled, and fearful thoughts.

I don't know how long I sat there, but my heart was still racing when my office slowly came back into focus.

"John, you can't control me anymore," I said out loud. That sounded good, but shaky, so I repeated it even louder. The divorce was almost finalized, and he hadn't contested it. Nor had he responded to any of the court's requests for forms. My pro bono lawyer assured me that our divorce would go through in a month or less.

I smacked the table hard. What an entitled ass. Did he simply think he could snap his fingers, and I'd run back? I threw the half-eaten sandwich into the bin, satisfied with the *thwack* it made, as it became buried under several balled-up papers. Then I gripped the edge of my desk, shut my eyes, and took a long cleansing breath. I would not, could not, allow John to sabotage my hard-fought freedom. Would not. Could not. Never. Ever. I pounded both fists on the desk, stood up, and shrugged into my lab coat, thinking this would be the perfect afternoon to remove a head.

The next morning, I responded to his email. Using a measured and careful tone, I spelled out that I was happy, had moved on, and was not interested in getting back together. My final, and probably the most damning line in my response was, "I'm sorry to tell you that I haven't missed you a single day you've been gone." Perhaps it was a little harsh, but it really was the truth.

He never responded.

As the date for the UC Irvine interview drew closer, the Davis rejection sat heavy on my heart. If I were accepted by Irvine, how could I manage being 450 miles away from Davis and the challenge of medical school without my parents nearby to help with the girls? I'd have to uproot my daughters from their friends and schools as well.

Doug Gross joined me at the dissection lab one morning as I laid out a half-dozen heads on trays for an otolaryngology demo for the surgery residents.

"Any word on your med school applications, Lally?" He placed a circular yellow sticker on the skin covering the crico-thyroid muscle.

"One interview coming up with Irvine." I shrugged. "Davis told me no."

He looked up sharply with a frown on his face. "Davis said no? I'm surprised. I always thought you'd be a strong candidate." He turned to face me. "Lally, I have a suggestion. Our applications are still open. Why don't you tell our admissions office that Irvine granted you an interview? You might ask if they'll take another look at your application and reconsider."

"Reconsider? Is that even possible?" I threw my gloves in a bin and walked up in front of him. In my temple a blood vessel pounded.

"Who knows?" He shrugged. "The way I look at it, you have nothing to lose by asking." He tapped the forceps on the gurney, then smiled and added, "And here's what I can do for you. I'll write a separate letter to support your request."

"That's so kind of you . . . thanks so much," I stammered, speechless.

That night I wrote a carefully worded email to UC Davis, asking if they'd reconsider my application. I explained that although I had an interview with Irvine, Davis was my top choice because I'd worked in their anatomy department for three years. I added that Dr. Gross supported my request for reconsideration.

Less than two weeks later, a fat envelope arrived in the mailbox from the Davis med school. *A fat envelope!* My audacity had actually scored me an interview at UC Davis. Thrilled and nervous, I warned my heart to hold on and to prepare for possible disappointment. The interview was scheduled a few days later with a slew of faculty members. Several of the interviewers had seen me walking around the med school over the past three years. Rather than focus on my scores, they appeared fascinated by how I'd navigated a path back to medical school after facing so many roadblocks in other countries. A couple of them wanted to hear about the gory world of the embalmer. One told me he'd visited Ghana. From my interview day research, I'd anticipated cold hostility or trick questions, but nothing like that materialized.

For two torturous weeks, I was in a state of nervous anxiety until the fateful day I got the call I'll never forget. Ed Dagang phoned from the admissions office while I was seated at my desk in the basement having a sandwich.

"Ed?" My fingers shook on the receiver.

"Congratulations, Lally, you're going to be a doctor!"

For a few moments after I hung up the phone, my head collapsed on my arms on the desk and I remained there, paralyzed. A high whine sounded in my head as a feeling of exultation took hold. I jumped up, raced to the morgue, and turned off all the lights. My brain was on fire. Working any more today would be impossible. I'd bag that embalmed body tomorrow. He wasn't going anywhere.

"I'm going to be a doctor. I'm going to be a doctor!" I shouted out to the rows of dead bodies as I skipped past them in the murky gloom. "The fortune teller was right!" They didn't so much as blink. I returned to my office, my brain still whirling.

My mom was teaching, my siblings were in class, and my dad was in Southern California. I raced into the parking lot and drove like a maniac to a craft store, hunting for something that looked vaguely "medical" and finding only a shaggy four-inch monster apparition, like something out of *Where the Wild Things Are*. The medical connection was that he held a black doctor's bag. I dropped it off for my mom at her junior high school front office, then drove to my condo, screaming out with joy at the top of my lungs.

I hung out at my parents' house and grabbed my mom in a tight hug when she had barely exited the car. She held the troll doll in one hand and shot me a confused look.

"What is this, Lally? Is this . . . is this?" I loved the moment when her bewilderment gave way to a dawning understanding and joy filled her face.

Without breaking the bone-crushing hug, I whirled her around and around in the garage, watching her black braids fly around in careless abandon.

"I got in, Ammah, I got in!" I chanted. "I can't believe it. They told me today."

"Lally, we always knew you'd do it one day, girl. Well done, girl, well done. We have to tell Appah," she murmured, wiping tears from her eyes. Finally, she set me apart, holding my face tenderly just inches away from hers. "Lally, I've always believed good things happen to good people. You deserve this, after all these years of hard work and all the struggles you've gone through. Come on in, Lally, let's have some tea."

My dad sputtered on the phone when I shared the news and uncharacteristically fell silent. I imagined he was crying. As expected, when he finally recovered, he brought up the fortune teller's prophecy repeatedly, lecturing me to have more faith in providence. The moment I hung up, I knew that he'd share my news with every soul in the universe.

I set down the phone and walked into the back garden, rocking gently on the swing under the giant oak. I sipped my mug of cold tea. What a magnificent end to my crazy quest. Nothing and no one could take away this moment of pure, unadulterated joy. I was suffused with the same exhilaration that always hit me at the summit of a mountain when I solemnly added a stone to build up the cairn at the peak.

The blinding radiance of the sun's rays filtered through the dark green leaves above me. I imagined a new road opening up to this scary new destination, ablaze with a saluting lineup of flags from Sri Lanka, Ghana, and the United States. A cold, refreshing breeze lifted my hair off my forehead, and the slight chill in the air took me back to Pennsylvania. If I shut my eyes and listened hard, the pulse beating in my temple morphed into a clanging that grew louder and more insistent each second—the frenzied tolling of my old friend, the Liberty Bell.

Thirty-Four

Complications

Tim called to congratulate me. "I knew you'd get in," he said airily.

"You did?" I was a little irritated by his smug endorsement.

"Yeah, Ma does stuff with astrology and charts and all that. She says I've got a sixth sense. I just know some things are going to happen before they happen," he responded cryptically. I imagined him shrugging his shoulders. "By the way, I have wheels, a Volkswagen Jetta from a friend. You free Saturday?"

"Going to the zoo with the girls, but I'm sure my mom will babysit for me later if you'd like to meet up."

"No, that's okay, don't bother with that," he said. "How about I meet the three of you at the zoo?"

I was deeply touched that Tim could have had me to himself for a first date, but he'd accepted my "mom" status from the get-go.

When I set my eyes on tall, dark-haired Tim as he entered the entrance gate to the Sacramento Zoo, my breath caught in my throat, and I was suddenly very shy. It was our first meeting since the ballroom dance class, three months back. He looked relaxed and gorgeous in his loose-fitting Hawaiian shirt, immaculate khaki shorts, and a straw hat. After the first few awkward moments when I felt inordinately self-conscious, I was able to relax because he instinctively knew how to function with small children and wasn't pretentious or awkward; he was more like a big goofy kid himself. I've always felt that dogs and children really do know how to sniff out garbage.

He talked as we strolled past the animals. Like me, he was the oldest of four and had helped his mother take care of his young sisters. Shermila and Shanthi smiled up at him in rapt attention as he pointed out where monkeys were hiding in their enclosure. He raised Shanthi up on his shoulder so she could watch over the railings. Tears pricked at the corner of my eyes. John had left when Shermila was two, and my dad was the only person who'd come close to being their father figure.

A couple of weeks later, we met at Sacramento's Tower Theater to watch *Shine*. I held Tim's hand during the scary parts. He didn't pull away, but neither did he respond in kind, so it wasn't clear how he felt. I spontaneously hugged him in the car park after the movie, but he froze. It was like trying to hug a coffin, so I pulled away, embarrassed. I mumbled good-night and kicked myself all the way home, worrying if I'd come on too strong and fast.

Days of intense trepidation followed. I kept a nervous electronic silence, determined that I would leave the next move, if any, completely up to him. A few days later, he apologized if he'd hurt my feelings, but that my spontaneous hug had taken him by surprise. We continued email and phone conversations, and the weeks simply flew. He visited us at the condo some weekends. After I put the girls to bed upstairs, we had dreamy, lazy conversations that extended late into the night. I stretched out on the couch while he finger picked guitar chords.

At first, because of the natural and spontaneous way he interacted with me, we were simply like two very close friends, but when he stood in close proximity, my traitorous body swayed, as if it wanted to crush itself against him. My heart fluttered like crazy, and at times I willed him to make a move, but at the same time I was terrified that he might actually touch me and make me melt.

He used the living room futon when he stayed over, and we stayed up talking till late at night. One night I fell asleep on the futon beside him while he was playing his guitar. The next morning I woke up with a delicious sensation that I was getting a back rub. Tim had me pressed up against him, and he placed his finger on his lips to quiet my stiffening body as he continued to slowly rub my back with long strokes, all the while intensifying our whole-body embrace.

The girls were still asleep upstairs, so I relaxed and gave myself up to this new and welcome shift in our relationship. It had emerged organically from a firm friendship that deepened over five months of increasing warmth and trust. I lost myself in the reassurance and promise of his lovemaking. He was truly a master of the craft. I'd been with John for ten years, but unlike John, Tim was most focused on holding back and meeting my needs first and foremost. A skillful and exciting lover, he made my body resonate like one of his beloved instruments. As I faced a mind-blowing release, muffling a scream into my pillow, followed by a languorous comedown, I reflected that had I not met him, I would never have realized that a woman could feel such ecstasy with an unselfish partner. My world was absolutely complete.

Tim's transparency and lack of pretense were endearing. There was a genuine sweetness and sensitivity within him that drew me in. Unlike the previous domineering relationship with John, here was a friend and equal—a person who was extremely sensitive to what I wanted and who communicated his own needs so well. He never attempted to be controlling. I'd been incredibly nervous about allowing anyone to enter my life again, but now the gates to my treacherous heart were daring to swing open whenever that bronze Jetta showed up outside.

There was so much that should have made our relationship falter. I was a world traveler, steeped in multiple rich traditions and cultures, and he'd spent his life in Los Gatos, California. He'd never left America except for a day trip to Mexico. As a committed thrower-outer, I've learned not to care too much for material possessions. Tim, on the other hand, came with a vast garage of meticulously preserved childhood treasures. All his kindergarten toys were in pristine shape in their original boxes. I lived for the magic of each day and made wild decisions on the spur of the moment, whereas he was future-oriented, organized, and disciplined, especially with finances.

Yet we were similar in the ways that mattered. We each had three younger siblings we'd helped raise, and family was number one. I loved that Tim regularly made it a priority to visit his parents in the Bay Area, even though they had separated. Our quiet moments did not have to be filled up with chatter. We were at one with animals, nature, and the environment. We owned copies of the same CDs, from John Denver to Yanni! I'm never one for fakery and pretense, so his lack of artifice was the biggest plus in our relationship.

Med school began with a clanging cymbal of joy and proud expectation in the fall of 1997, but within weeks, any hope that it might be smooth sailing disintegrated faster than the chest wall I was dissecting. I'd gone this route before and expected a challenge, but I was completely unprepared for the way the curriculum sucked up and devoured every ounce of my brain the entire day and night. With two girls, ages three and six, I couldn't be purely selfish and study all the time. Plus, I wasn't nineteen anymore; retaining knowledge took way more discipline.

The Fortune Teller's Prophecy

Guilt was my constant companion. Guilt that consumed me when I lingered over dinner with my daughters after daycare ended. I held sacred their bath and bedtime routines instead of studying all evening. As a single parent, I relegated my studying to the wee hours because I could never turn my back on their beseeching pleas, "Please, Mom . . . one more chapter, pleeease. . . ." Many a time, I shrugged myself awake in the early morning hours, having fallen asleep on the floor of their bedroom with my back braced against the wall. I got zero studying completed on nights like that, and slowly but surely, I fell further and further behind in both review and school prep.

On weekends, my mother willingly offered to babysit the girls while I studied. She spoiled them at the Davis farmers market, bringing them home with intricate face paintings I knew she couldn't afford. I was profoundly grateful for her amazing support, but it was always shrugged off as "no big deal . . . I love my time with them." Tim was tied up with pharmacy rotations all over Northern California. I loved his visits but sacrificed more study hours when he was around.

Having dealt with dead humans for three years, it was shell shock to be thrust among ninety-two breathing classmates all day. They came from incredibly diverse backgrounds. A brilliant Libyan boy, only seventeen, must have coasted through undergraduate studies shortly after graduating from diapers. At the other end of the age spectrum was Gary, a forty-eight-year-old accountant who wanted a more fulfilling second career. Then there were the straight-shot "gunners" who'd decided at birth to be doctors and blasted every obstacle out of their path. We even had a retired professional model from Sweden. Despite tresses of lustrous silver-blond hair and an hourglass figure, she destroyed all conventional doctrines about dumb blondes by rising to the top of the class within weeks.

Previously, studying for tests and floating to the upper

echelons of my class had been like breathing to me. It was disconcerting, to say the least, to be thrust among dozens of others whose brain power rivaled or surpassed mine, making me feel slow and dumb. With undergrad studies far behind me, capturing and consolidating so much new information took both dedication and strict time organization because it was disseminated at a frenetic pace.

In undergraduate physiology, for example, it took us a full week to master Kreb's citric acid cycle. In med school, Kreb's was reviewed in an hour. If you skipped that golden hour, you were way behind.

Then things got worse. Shanthi developed frequent urinary tract infections, and I had to carry her, screaming and writhing, into the ER on multiple occasions. I watched, helplessly, as my usually tough-as-nails daughter shrieked inconsolably. A gazillion specialists, pills, and antibiotic treatments ensued, including painful investigative procedures. She was diagnosed with pyelonephritis caused by urine backing up from her bladder to her kidneys. Although surgery was floated as a treatment recommendation, I opted for a conservative approach, and she was placed on a year of antibiotics to ward off the repeated infections.

She gradually improved, but all the sleepless nights and ER visits took a further toll on studying. I visualized that I'd fallen to my knees on a trail with my girls and had to lie there, watching in desperation, as my classmates forged ahead of me, then turned around a corner so they were no longer in view. A veritable mountain of skipped study material piled deep and high in front of me, blocking my view of the trail completely.

"Who knows the four birds that live in the posterior mediastinum?" Dr. Erickson's booming voice thundered out during anatomy. His curly gray hair shook as he scanned the lecture hall with a twinkle in his eye. "No one? Okay, let me tell you about them: We have the esophaGOOSE, vaGOOSE, azyGOOSE, and of course, the thoracic DUCK."

Muted groans sounded around me, and a few people clapped. He was famous for his bad jokes.

"By the way, your midterm grades are posted in the main hallway across from your lockers," he added.

I was at the very back of the steeply angled, cavernous hall but froze in my ugly orange bucket seat after the word "grades." Acid flooded the back of my throat, and every neuron in my head turned on in high alert as I drew squiggles on my notepad with shaking fingers.

Lorraine nudged me with her elbow. "Hey, want to check grades with me, witch?" she asked. I'd donned a wig and tall black hat because it was Halloween.

"No thanks, I have to rewrite notes," I lied. "Go ahead—see you at dissection." I waved her away. My heart thumped out of my chest. I was absolutely terrified to learn my grades. I'd crammed like hell the weekend before midterms, but nothing had stuck.

I pretended to write until the lecture hall emptied, then rested my head on my folded arms and stared at my shaking knees until I could delay no longer. I hoisted my heavy backpack on my shoulder, shuffled outside, and crossed the empty quadrangle to Tupper Hall. Classes had begun, so the lobby was empty. As I reluctantly headed down the deserted hallway by the student lockers, my heart thudded. With nervous glances sideways, I crept to the chart with our grades as if it were a monster ready to pounce, then ran a trembling finger down the list of student ID numbers.

My grades weren't just bad, they were *appalling*. With horror, I learned that I'd landed at or near the bottom of the class in every single subject. I checked again and again. There was no mistake. Overwhelmed, my eyes flooded with tears, and I placed a hand on the wall to steady myself because the hallway spun around me. *Stupid, stupid, stupid!* I was an impostor among my illustrious colleagues. I didn't belong with them. I didn't belong in med school. I should have stuck to embalming dead bodies. I was a fool to think I could make it, just because some stupid fortune teller said I could over thirty years ago.

I couldn't bring myself to face anyone that afternoon and stumbled blindly out of the building, heading for the bike racks. I cringed at my reflection in a window en route: A witch with red hair and red eyes to match. Happy Halloween!

The next quarter was almost the same. Try as I might, I couldn't find a good fix for increasing dedicated study time, and the instruction carried on at a frenetic pace. The morning before my pathology final exam, I parked the girls at my parents' home and sat at my study desk, terrified that I had to cram two hundred pages of Robbins and Cotran's *The Pathologic Basis of Disease* before daybreak.

Instead of taking my customary single cup of coffee in the morning, I opted for an all-nighter and drank nine cups of coffee throughout the day. I'd never done anything that stupid before. Shortly before dawn I shut the textbook and snatched an hour of uneasy sleep. Photographs of cancer cells and prostate cancer statistics played leapfrog in my brain.

I floated into the exam room like a zombie and took a seat right at the front, so I wouldn't freak out seeing colleagues in front of me during the test. The dread intensified as I ripped the seal on the blue question booklet. Sweat burst out at my temples as I thumbed through pages of questions. The words jiggled around and became hieroglyphics. A monstrous deity had gobbled up my memory retrieval system. I'd taken hundreds of tests but never encountered total brain blockage like this.

When I tried to summon a response to the first question, my

brain whirled in a terrifying snowstorm of whiteout conditions. I flicked pages forward aimlessly as the panic built, but my anxiety had ratcheted up so high that I couldn't answer even the simple "fill-in-the-blanks" prompts at the end. It was time to call it a day. I bubbled in my name and social security number on the Scantron sheet, then briefly laid my head on my booklet. Shutting my eyes was like immersing myself in a tempting warm bath. Terrified that my severe sleep deprivation might make me doze off, I took a bathroom break.

At the sink, I doused my face with handfuls of cold water. A staring, bloodshot-eyed ghost with a dripping face confronted me. I sternly exhorted my pathetic reflection to quit stalling and get back to the test. Back in the exam hall, I shut my eyes and counted slowly to ten. I resolutely thumbed through the booklet again, but my brain was still full of snow. That hateful clock ticked away, as if sneering at my incompetence. An eerie whine now sounded inside my head—an arctic wind blowing over a frozen lake.

I wondered if I was going crazy. The combination of poor test prep, no sleep, caffeine, and heightened adrenaline had all conspired to ratchet up totally fucked-up memory recall. The gray-haired proctor sat in front of me, his head bent over his computer screen. For some illogical reason, I wanted to smack him out of his indifference and make him aware of my spiraling deterioration. When I glanced sideways, my stomach lurched. My classmates feverishly bubbled in their answer keys with bobbing yellow pencils. Twenty minutes into the two-hour test, I hadn't blacked out a single bubble.

Defeated tears dampened my Scantron answer key. Lowering my head so the proctor would not see my tears, I handed in the empty booklet, intercepting curious glances from several students as I walked out. It was tricky and surreal to make it to the exit door. A dark gray fog lay in front of me, and the path

Complications

I took had blurry margins and kept narrowing. I focused on the glimmer of light from outside as if my life depended on it and limped out of that accursed exam hall. With each faltering step, my dreams of becoming a doctor bled out in my wake.

As I hoisted myself up on my bike and began pedaling home, the rising pressure in my chest reminded me of a time when I'd struggled with paralyzing anxiety, in Ghana eighteen years back. Snippets of troubling memories from the past tumbled out in heedless abandon all the way home.

I was back in Ghana, age seventeen and a half, when the whole nightmare began.

Thirty-Five

Helter Skelter

We'd had to move to a temporary home on the university campus for six months. The day of the move, the six of us piled into my dad's car, drove under the gigantic white Ashanti stool inscribed with KWAME NKRUMAH UNIVERSITY OF SCIENCE AND TECHNOLOGY, and turned off at the Warden's Close driveway.

At first I was tremendously excited. Down the tree-lined, paved driveway was an elegant, spread-out white colonial bungalow with a postcard-perfect sparkling white veranda. Trees shielded the neighboring houses. As I got out and twirled with delight, an unexpected feeling of dread encompassed me with no warning. It was as if the leaves whispered a warning that only I could hear.

"Get back. Don't go inside."

My pulse raced and a frisson of fear took hold. Internal cartwheels of anxiety began to roll. I figured I'd simply watched too many scary movies where bad things happened to new occupants, but my panic only intensified when I walked into the long, narrow bedroom that was to be mine. I dumped my suitcase by the single bed, then whirled around back to the living room. Viji had put on her Earth, Wind & Fire record at max volume, and the haunting refrain of "Fantasy" filled the home.

I walked outside to the veranda again because the tune was inexplicably stirring up shards of dread. When I stepped back in, she'd started the record again.

"No, no! Enough!" I shrieked as I ran to the record player. "You played it already. Play something else. Ugh!"

She shot me a what-the-heck-is-wrong-with-you glare but put on Chick Corea instead.

Laddie entered our lives the next morning—an adorable short-haired brown-and-white terrier mix with a cute white triangular beard. He trotted down the driveway, greeting us as if we were his long-lost family. He had gorgeous, melting dark brown eyes but no collar. His ribs stuck out, so my mom allowed me to give him scraps of bread mixed with milk. He gulped down the food as though he hadn't eaten for a month, then contentedly stretched himself out in the sun on the front veranda. My mom warned that he was a stray and could never come in.

It warmed my spirits to see that cute, skinny white tail wagging when I returned from school. I lay beside him on the front veranda to read my novels. Laddie grew fatter and became part of our family as the days drew by. We must have passed his litmus test for being nurturing, because about a couple of weeks later, he introduced us to his entire family—four adorably cute brown-and-white puppies, still nursing from their mother.

We played with that lovely dog family any time we could. After meals, the puppies grunted, squished their fat puppy bodies against each other, and contentedly cuddled up snoring in the sunshine.

And then I bought *Helter Skelter*. A quarter of the way into the book, I kept turning to the crime scene photographs, imagining all those lives ending so horribly at the hands of the Manson clan. Those poor souls had simply been in the wrong place at the wrong time. Sharon Tate's murder affected me the most because she was pregnant.

The Fortune Teller's Prophecy

Our English literature teacher, a descendant of H. G. Wells, was on maternity leave at the time. Supposedly she'd been assaulted by her husband during her pregnancy. After delivery, apparently suffering postnatal depression, she dressed her infant son in "his best baby clothes" and drowned him in her bathtub.

But that wasn't all. After the drowning, she had apparently succumbed to severe remorse and attempted suicide by jumping off her third-story apartment balcony. Showing that truth may be stranger than fiction, an unsuspecting adult male stepped outside beneath her and cushioned her fall, inadvertently saving her life. She survived with a broken leg and returned to teach at our school, walking around campus with a pronounced limp and a cane.

No murder charges were made. With typical Ghanaian acceptance, the prevailing sentiment was, "Ah, but what do you expect? He beat her, paaa. They will divorce. It is finished." My brain was not able to let go so quickly. When she traipsed around campus, details of the Manson killings blended with her murder–suicide attempt. I began having vivid nightmares of murdered children, with the Earth, Wind & Fire song playing in the background. A persistent fear sat on me like a lead cloak.

I went to great lengths to avoid being alone in the house. If either parent left to run an errand, I made up some reason why I had to tag along. I was unable to share this new and unwelcome companion, dread, with anyone. As the eldest, I had way too much pride to let anyone in. For the first time in my life, the acrid taste of acid in my throat was my perpetual companion. I woke up with a pounding pulse and had a premonition that something bad was about to happen.

Matters got worse. I was doing homework in my bedroom one night when my stomach suddenly took a nosedive. My eyes blurred, my heart went nuts in my chest, and breathing was painful. Rooted in my chair, I glanced at the *Helter Skelter* book on my nightstand. I didn't know it at the time, but I'd just experienced my first panic attack. I shut my eyes and tried to count to five, but the ball of fear didn't dissipate. I had a bizarre feeling that a force was heading from the book to me.

Spooked, I left the room and fled to the comfort of the living room, where my eight-year-old brother, Vim, scampered around giggling as Nimi gave chase. Viji was leafing through a magazine, and my parents were watching a boxing show. I pretended I needed a study snack break, prepared a plate of Ritz crackers with cheese, and sat with the family in the living room. I envied my siblings' careless abandon, wanting so much to lose this choking feeling of anguish. I pretended to read till all my siblings went to bed and my parents retired also, then I grabbed a sheet and pillow and fell asleep on the living room couch.

I turned eighteen a week later. My dad set up the university swimming pool for the evening's celebration. The anxiety I'd harbored for weeks had magically evaporated. That night I drove home well after midnight. When I got home, Laddie ran up to me, wagging his tail. Something was wrong. He was anxious, whining. He scratched at the front door, begging to be let inside, then made a dash into my bedroom. I followed him inside and found him cowering under my bed. Puzzled, I carried him back outside, apologizing firmly to him as I put his trembling body out on the porch.

"Sorry, Laddie, not tonight, okay? I'll play with you tomorrow, okay? I'm sorry."

He continued to whine and scratch at the front door glass for several minutes, as if wanting to tell me something. I hated to turn away from the pleading look in those trusting brown eyes.

The next morning, I was the first to wake up. I'm not sure what made me head to the front porch—perhaps it was guilt that I'd turned Laddie away. The horror of the spectacle that greeted me on the porch is one I can never erase from my mind.

In the misty early-morning sunlight that slanted through the trees was a scene that imprinted itself on my brain—a scene of absolute carnage. I grabbed hold of the front door and screamed with every ounce of power I had.

On the front veranda lay the entire dog family: Laddie, his mate, and all four puppies on their backs. The awkward angles of their precious little bodies, their stillness, their bloated stomachs and glazed eyes kept me riveted.

My mother raced out, and I could do nothing but point with a shaking finger. She held my face to her chest, gently pushed me back into the living room, and called our houseboy, Sam, to help.

I cried out huge heaving sobs and collapsed on the couch, too weak to function. Blurred movement was all around, but I was too upset to register anything. Who could have done this? Who killed those delightful, wriggly, snuggly puppies? Never again would those trusting dogs wag their tiny tails and rush to greet me as I fed them breakfast. Never would we all lie nuzzled together when I read my books while they slept on my lap. Never would Laddie turn his head sideways to cock his ears in that beloved way when he was called.

He'd tried to tell me something last night, but I'd put him out. This was my fault. I felt like a murderer. It didn't help that my mother told me later that it was likely that someone had given the dog family poisoned meat. Most likely he'd acted strangely last night because he was already dying. I squeezed my eyes shut tight to erase the memory of his beseeching, pleading brown eyes.

That night, I lay in my bed and stared up at the ceiling convulsed with sadness and anxiety. My mind played out different horrifying scenarios that might have led to that massacre. I imagined the pain those innocent puppies felt. I wished I could inhale that delicious, earthy doggy smell and clutch those puppies close to my chest for one last time.

And then I wondered if someone was planning a home invasion soon. Maybe we'd all be victims soon, like in the Manson murders. That was it. Unable to tolerate the fearful images anymore, I plucked up all the courage I possessed to grab my pillow and tiptoe into my parents' bedroom. After staring at their sleeping forms for what seemed like an eternity, I gently shook my mom awake and asked if I could share their bed. Without hesitation, she immediately created a space for me on her side. My dad saw me lying there the next morning, but he acted like it wasn't a big deal. I could have hugged them both for their sensitivity.

I slept in my parents' bed for the remaining weeks at Warden's Close. At first, I snuck back to my room early in the morning before my siblings woke up, but of course, they eventually caught on, and I became the butt of intolerable jokes.

We left the home shortly afterward. It wasn't till after we moved out that I learned that a previous Warden's Close tenant had been murdered. Worse still, *he'd been murdered in my bedroom*! From day one, I'd had a premonition that something about that house was evil, and then I'd faced a succession of terrifying events.

My current fearfulness paled in comparison to the angst I'd felt at age seventeen. Somehow I'd managed to move on from it, hadn't I? With a start I realized that I had cycled the whole way home from the pathology exam on autopilot. Surely this current upset was no more than a pebble in my road. I braced myself for the next challenge.

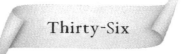

Thirty-Six

To Be
or Not to Be

I received a summons to meet with the student progress faculty team the week after the exam in a large hall on campus. Shafts of sunlight caught fine dust particles trapped in the air as I took my seat within a circle of a dozen or so frowning faculty members. It was deathly quiet. I looked around apprehensively, noticing a few tight-lipped smiles that tried to look reassuring but failed dismally. I clutched my fingers together on my lap till my nails made indentations in my palms. To my horror, tears spilled out before we could even get started. They did most of the talking, then I was given a chance to explain my unsatisfactory performance.

Only fragments of our twenty-minute discussion registered when I traipsed out afterward.

". . . So sorry to hear about your daughter's health . . . how about a leave of absence? You failed pathology, so you'll have to retake the course. You're struggling in not just one but several courses. We can offer you a chance to extend your medical training by a year if you like. . . . We took a vote on whether your performance qualifies you for dismissal, but our committee is prepared to give you one final chance . . . if you want it . . . if you want it . . . if you want it. . . ."

I cycled home, unsure if I could handle this level of stress for a week, let alone a whole extra year. A pedestrian walked partly into the bike lane, and I screamed at him loud enough to wake a sleeping vampire.

"What's wrong with *you?*" he swore loudly, jumping aside.

I knew what was wrong. Once again, I had hit a wall, and it was time to make a decision of significant consequence for my future life. Did I want this purgatory to continue? If so, I'd have to better navigate single parenthood and study more effectively to avoid last-minute cramming. Could I envisage spreading out training into five or even six years for a lighter schedule? Or was it time to throw in the towel?

That night, I went with my daughters to my parents' home for dinner. My brain was clouded in a fog of anxiety. I sat on the edge of my seat with a forced smile as I watched the girls play with Play-Doh. My innards were hollow, as if an alien monster had sucked out all my organs. In the kitchen, delicious smells wafted out as my mom put finishing touches to the meal, but I was unable to summon an appetite.

I wandered over to the kitchen, unsure how to begin the conversation. She was stirring garlic and ginger, and the aroma was delicious, but I had no appetite. I shifted my weight from one foot to the other and cleared my throat.

"Ammah, there's something I have to tell you—in private. . . ." I angled my head toward the hallway leading to the bedrooms when she looked up. Hearing my tone, she immediately turned off two burners and followed me into the first bedroom. Shutting the door, I leaned against it and motioned for her to sit on the bed. She sat ramrod straight, and there was a question in her eyes, but she waited silently.

I tried to speak a couple of times but choked up. What words should I use, when I was about to hand my beloved mother the biggest disappointment of her life? I couldn't even imagine how

I'd summon the courage to tell my father. It would break him even more.

"What is it, Lally? Huh? What is it, girl?"

A deluge of silent tears poured from my eyes at the concern in her voice. I sobbed, leaning further into the door for support. She started to get up, but I waved her away.

"Something bad happened, didn't it?"

I nodded mutely, with a roaring in my head.

"Tell me. Lally. Don't cry. It'll be okay, girl." Her voice softened.

"I don't know how to start," I mumbled, then took a quick breath. "I went to the student promotions meeting today. . . ." I took in a deep shuddering breath.

"Okay."

"I'm right at the bottom of many of my classes. They've put me on probation. It's disgraceful. They'll give me one more chance if I want, but . . . but. . . ."

"But what?"

"I've thought so hard about this . . . and . . . I can't do this anymore, Ammah. It's too much. I can't. I can't!" I spat out the words and shook my head vehemently, tears still cascading down. "There's too much studying . . . there's never enough time each night. It's ridiculous. I'm failing class after class, Ammah, and . . . my self-confidence . . . is all gone. . . ." I reached for tissues, blew my nose, then continued, "I'm so stressed that I can't even sleep. Plus, I'm already feeling so guilty about not spending enough time with the girls. This whole thing is . . . this is killing me. I was crazy to think that I could do this . . . I can't . . . ."

She opened her mouth, but I put my hand out to stop her.

"Don't! I've thought about it, Ammah, and I've made my decision. I'm dropping out. I'll tell the dean tomorrow. I'm sick of all these meetings. I'm sick of feeling so blooming stupid all the time. . . ."

Her head was bowed, as if she were far away, in another place.

"Ammah? What? What are you thinking? I know you're upset . . . I'm so sorry. . . ."

She gnawed at her lower lip and absently worked the seam of her black pants.

The silence became so unnerving that I rushed to fill it. "You and Appah always believed that crazy fortune teller . . . you thought I'd be . . . I'd be the first . . . first doctor in our family . . . and now here I'm letting you and the whole family down. . . ."

She lifted her head and looked straight at me. The whole room vanished, and only her warm brown eyes anchored me to reality. I thought of the hundreds of hours she'd babysat while I studied. All for nothing. Nothing.

"Lally. . . ." She reached out a hand, and I sat beside her. She laid an arm around my shoulders, and I sank into that warm, loving embrace and mom smell. My hiccupping sobs were the only sound in the room as she held me tight in her arms.

After a few seconds, I pulled away to face her. "Ammah? You haven't said anything. Say something."

I'd expected sadness, but she had a faint smile on her face.

"Lally, don't worry about it anymore. You've made the decision—you'll be fine, girl, okay? You got into med school, didn't you? You're clever; you have a big brain. I know it's been hard, so if this is really too much for you to handle, you should stop, Lally. You'll find something else to do. Don't worry how we feel. This is about *you*." She leaned forward to squeeze my hand gently. "Lally, there are so many other jobs out there. And you're so clever. You'll work hard. We'll be here for you, and I'll help with the girls, no matter what happens. Don't worry."

I blinked at her in amazement. She hadn't played the "I'm sure if you just try harder" or "Don't give up on being a doctor" cards—she'd just accepted my decision unconditionally. Of course I'd expected she'd be supportive, but nothing had prepared me for her total, unreserved acceptance of my decision. At the very least, I figured she'd tell me about how much time I'd invested and that I should keep trying a little harder because she'd take the girls on for even longer hours. Instead she was actually giving me her blessing to try something else for a career!

My battering heart calmed down with the soothing balm of her words. Like a desperate, thrashing swimmer, I grasped her lifeline, now overcome with a tremendous surge of love for my incredible, understanding, nonjudgmental mother. The intensity of the love I felt for her at that moment shocked me. I couldn't recall ever feeling such intense appreciation for the pillar of support she provided when I needed it most.

She believes in me! She believes I can haul myself out of this mess. She thinks I'm clever. She'll support us, no matter what! She's saying I can quit med school if I want!

And in that moment, armed with my mother's unwavering belief in my capabilities, I discarded and dismantled the baggage of guilt, self-doubt, and fear of failure that had shackled me ever since the start of med school. I took a long, deep drag of air and looked blankly out onto the street from my window. Instead of the dark street, I saw a sunlit beach that stretched forever to the sun, teeming with endless possibilities.

After a few moments of companionable silence, it hit me that it was quiet in the other room. Too quiet.

"Uh-oh, the girls aren't talking. That's trouble. Someone's going to cry very soon. I'll check," I announced.

We exchanged smiles like coconspirators. I made it to the door, and then, with a hand on the knob, I turned around. "Ammah, thanks for what you just said. You have no idea what your words mean to me. Thank you. Thank you!"

In the living room, a huge mess of Play-Doh littered the carpet. The girls were playfully wrestling but squawked "Mamma" in delight when I approached. There was no sweeter sound in the whole world. We did not discuss med school any further that night. I picked at a bowl of food to please my mom, but the girls feasted on rice, mutton curry, and eggplant curry. Dessert was cardamom-flavored tapioca pudding, which soothed our scorched palates.

On the drive home, I caught myself humming a song and smiled when I realized later that it was Gloria Gaynor's "I Will Survive." Later still, as I closed *Clifford the Big Red Dog* and left the girls' bedroom, I reflected on how my mom had reignited a spark that I thought was extinguished. Deep inside, petals of hope were daring to unfurl. Could I go back in there and do it? Accept the committee's offer to spread out classes over an extra year? Claw my way back into good academic standing? I honestly didn't know. All I knew is that my mom unconditionally believed in my abilities, no matter what.

I'd be damned if I'd give up. If she believed I could do anything, why shouldn't I? If I failed, I could do something else because I was "clever". I'd show my girls. I'd show the whole damn world! I was a Tamil Tiger inside, wasn't I? Every past obstacle I'd tackled, I'd come out stronger. I'd become a *doctor of doctors* if it killed me!

If I crashed and burned in the process, my mom and I knew I had the guts to shake myself off, grieve a little, and then chart a new and exciting course. I tossed *Clifford* on a table beside me, turned off the lamp, walked to the bedroom window, and stretched out my fingers till they touched the sky.

Thirty-Seven

Specialization

I extended med school training to five years, then six, clinging by my fingernails at the start, then developing a newfound confidence. Abandoning prior study habits of reading hundreds of pages of textbooks, I instead reviewed old exams for test prep, just as my classmates were doing. This helped me focus on the most important principles, and my grades improved markedly. I learned to harness my anxiety so it was no longer paralyzing. With the more relaxed schedule, I could spend more time with my girls, rather than become paralyzed with guilt that I'd failed at both being a mother *and* a med student. It was a tremendous relief to pass USMLE Step 1, the first of three national medical licensing exams. I held that cherished badge close to my heart, for it proved to the whole world that I'd acquired the book knowledge to become a physician—a special treasure because I'd come so close to dropping out.

While I was finding my path through medical school, John Russell continued to avoid parental responsibility. True to form, I discovered from internet searching that he'd continued to flit around the world. I'd tracked him down in Canada, Kazakhstan, and even Kuwait. Each time I located him, I reached out to him, threatening to contact his university for court-mandated child support. Occasional payments trickled in, but they'd abruptly stop when he absconded to another country, and I had to find him and beg for support all over again. The process was frustrating and psychologically exhausting.

Tim graduated as a pharmacist in1999. He left Stockton and moved to Davis, where he found a three-bedroom rental home for us, and the girls and I moved in with him. He was such a rock—always sensitive to my needs—and my love for him had only deepened over time. I could bank on his quiet support when med school tested every fiber of my being. It was my personal oasis to sit with him in front of a crackling fireplace with the girls goofing off while Tim strummed his guitar. The whole world stopped for me as I breathed in the magic of those moments.

State medical insurance was a blessing for us, along with the continuing county and city programs that helped subsidize our costs. Because I'd extended my training, I continued to borrow money to finance med school loans. Together, Tim and I now owed a staggering quarter of a million dollars!

The last two years consisted of rotations at various hospitals and clinics to provide more direct patient contact. This was the time to immerse myself in various medical specialties and figure out what field of medicine to specialize in during residency training after I graduated.

I set my heart on pediatrics. Even before I had kids of my own, children always warmed up quickly to me. I enjoyed their simplicity, those inquisitive minds, and their zest for life. How cool would it be to influence the lives of the next generation of humans to populate the planet?

As for other specialization options, I ruled out surgery as too physically demanding. Internal medicine was scratched off too. I'd never enjoyed number-crunching electrolytes and labs. Pathology and radiology were on the chopping block, because after three years up close and personal with death, I sure didn't want another day in a dark room poring over body parts and

X-rays rather than living people. I rejected Ob/Gyn, because, like pathology, I'd spend much of my working life peering into places where the sun didn't shine.

Psychiatry was definitely out. I'd worked so hard for my white coat that I simply couldn't imagine having to hang it up.

And how could I forget that Kwasi incident back in med school? In the summer of 1981, I'd stayed behind in Kumasi with our German shepherd, Rocky, while the family headed off to Sri Lanka for the summer break. As if portending an unsettling start to spending two months alone, a blinding flash of lightning ripped open the sky.

My footsteps sounded hollow in the large empty spaces in the empty house, devoid of the usual family banter. I was also jittery because of a conversation I'd had earlier in the morning with my classmate Michael. After anatomy lecture he'd pulled me aside, glancing around surreptitiously as the hall emptied.

"Lally, I'm worried about you. Kwasi is in my dorm, and he's been talking about you. Nonstop. Something's not right. Watch out for him."

Alarm bells rang, and a shiver went down my back.

"What do you mean, something's not right?"

"Don't know how to say this." He cleared his throat, and his voice dropped. Again, he looked around. "He told me you're sending telepathic messages."

"What? Telepathic. . . ?"

"Yes. He says you're calling to him. I think he knows where you live. Take care. I think . . . I think he's dangerous."

Back in my bedroom, the howl of the wind and the intermittent claps of thunder made study impossible. Loud, fat raindrops splattered against the aluminum roof. I shut Guyton and Hall's *Textbook of Medical Physiology* with a bang to stare blankly at a smiling family photo on my table. Gone just five hours, and yet I missed them so much. The house was a mausoleum.

Specialization

The thunder grew louder, so I ran downstairs with Rocky at my heels to grab candles and matches, just in case. In Kumasi, if the wind blows hard enough to knock off a dandelion seed, the power invariably goes out. There's actually a sequence. It starts with the TV, and then the lights die. You survive on candles, but after two days without power, there's not even enough water to flush the toilet. The bathroom stinks of urine because you get to flush only after number two.

A bloodcurdling thunderclap shook the roof and set Rocky off on a spat of frenzied barking. I walked to the living room to read a novel. Within fifteen minutes, as expected, all the lights flickered and died. The phone was dead too. The house was now as black as the night, so I balanced a candle on a small saucer and wandered into the kitchen to hunt for something to eat.

I'd almost finished eating when I heard knocking on the front door. At first, I thought it was the rain, but it became louder and more insistent. Absolute terror chased up and down my spine like a spider dancing the macarena.

Probably the neighbors wanting candles or something. I held the candle up, grabbed my growling dog, and headed for the front door. There was a long rectangular pane of thick glass that ran the height of the door. As I looked through the rain-drenched glass I got the fright of my life. Blurred by the rivulets of rain was a thunderstorm-manufactured devil! A flash of lightning lit him up. Oh, dear God, it was Kwasi! I was starring in a personal horror movie. Just two feet away his rain-soaked face was grotesque in the dim lighting.

Kwasi pushed his nose and forehead against the glass pane, as if trying to peer inside. He made no attempt to wipe off the rivulets of rainwater that tracked down his face.

"My mother's dead, my mother's dead, Lally, open the door!" His words were barely decipherable in the torrential downpour.

Reminding myself about Michael's warning earlier that

morning, I took a deep breath. "Kwasi, I'm . . . I'm sorry. . . . I'm sorry your mother's dead, but I can't help you. Please go away." Despite my best intentions, my voice quavered. He cocked his head, listening for a moment, then smooshed his face back into the glass pane, as if he'd been thrown against it by a freak wind gust.

"What are you *doing?*" I shrieked. "That's *crazy!* Go away. Leave. Now!"

I wondered if he knew the family had left for Sri Lanka earlier in the day. The candle wobbled, and I winced as hot wax dripped on the back of my wrist. Turning on my heel, I staggered back to the kitchen, taking deep, shaky breaths. I blew the candle out and collapsed on the floor, trembling, holding Rocky closer. Brilliant white lightning continued to flash through the windows, turning night into day.

Knock, knock, knock. Silence. Knock, knock. Silence. The rhythmic pattern of knocks terrified me. They subsided into single knocks and then stopped altogether. Petrified that it could be a trap, I lay on the kitchen floor a few more minutes.

Silence. Blessed, magical, wonderful silence. I heaved a huge sigh of relief and grabbed Rocky. Sleep was a very long time coming.

The next morning, the whole ordeal seemed like a bad nightmare. Sunshine lit up a washed-out blue sky. I shared the previous night's events over tea and Marie biscuits with my friend Nana.

"Want to come over to my house tonight, Lally? What if he comes back?"

"I've got Rocky to watch over me. You'll watch over me, right, boy?" I stroked him gently behind his ears.

Rocky growled, and I stared at him, puzzled.

It was then that we heard it. A light knocking on the front door.

Nana grabbed my wrist, her long nails indenting my skin.

"Lally?" Kwasi called out.

I placed a shaking hand on my lips to shush Nana.

"Open the door!" His tone was commanding.

"Set Rocky on him," Nana whispered. I nodded, grabbed Rocky by the collar, and pushed the surprised dog out through the back porch door. "Get him, get him!" I whispered. Rocky bounded off around the house, but the stupid hound fawned at him, wagging his tail.

"Go away, Kwasi. There is someone here," I threatened.

"I'm not scared." He snickered a soft, sick laugh.

He moved to the first pane of frosted glass louvers, his framed face staring directly at us. Nana screamed. I slammed the louvers shut so hard that the glass almost shattered. Undeterred, his face appeared at the next panel, and I slammed it shut also. Nana joined me, and together we raced around the room shutting all the louvers to wipe out that crazy, demonic face with the strange halo of orange-brown hair.

I grabbed Nana's hand and half dragged her with me through the side kitchen door. We ran for our lives through the copse of trees to my neighbor's house. The neighbor, Uncle Shekhar, a burly black-bearded man, walked back alone to check the house.

"He's gone. Lally. Please keep your doors locked at all times. Come with me, girls, I'll walk you home."

I sped up the driveway in my car like a woman possessed for the next four weeks. When I fumbled with the key to the front door, I was always terrified that Kwasi might pounce on me from a perch in the dense foliage beside the house. In class I kept well away from him.

His behavior in the dorm was becoming increasingly bizarre. He continued to tell my classmates that I was sending telepathic messages. Clearly, he was suffering from some kind of mental illness. Michael talked Kwasi into getting an evaluation from our school psychiatrist.

The day of the evaluation Kwasi came to class decked out in a black suit and crimson tie. He held a Bible in one white satin–gloved hand. He proclaimed to anyone who asked, "Today, I'm getting married—to Lally."

And that's when we realized how severe his illness was. He was diagnosed with schizophrenia and dropped out of medical school. He was admitted to a locked mental hospital five miles from campus. I was sorry for him but profoundly relieved that I could finally relax after classes were out.

Two weeks before my family returned from Sri Lanka, a classmate sat beside me on the school bus after anatomy dissection. Her brows were furrowed.

"Lally, did anyone tell you about Kwasi?"

My heart flipped. "Kwasi? No, he's in that mental hospital, right?" I faked calm.

"His parents picked him up today. He's gone home."

"If he's discharged, that's good news, right?" Petals of unease opened up inside my ribcage.

"Yeah, but I'm nervous. Remember how he fixated on you? Take care, Lally."

"He won't be back," I reassured her, but my stomach lurched when I remembered how he'd insisted that I was summoning him with telepathic messages. I drove home singing loudly to distract myself from the dormant tendrils of anxiety that were now beginning to raise their heads.

As I turned onto our street, Ridge Road, my breath caught. A figure with unkempt hair was staggering down the street in the twilight. I registered orange-brown hair that stuck out in all directions.

Kwasi. It was Kwasi! Freshly released from a mental hospital. Today!

Specialization

I floored the accelerator all the way home, left the car in the driveway, and dashed through the trees to my neighbor's home screaming, "He's coming, he's coming!"

By sheer chance Uncle Shekhar was dining with a professor from the med school who knew all about Kwasi. They offered me water and waited till I could speak more coherently.

"If he really is coming to your house, it'll take him a good ten minutes. Come, Lally, let's walk you home," Uncle Shekhar said.

Dusk settled in as I headed home with the two men. I threw a frightened glance down the dark driveway, but thankfully no one was there. I ran in and bolted the door after the men. I shut Rocky into the pantry. The men sat on either side of me on the sofa.

"Here's what you'll do, Lally," Uncle Shekhar said thoughtfully, stroking his black beard. "Leave the lights off. If he knocks, just let him in."

"What? Let him—?" I turned in surprise.

"He won't know that we're here also. Relax, Lally, just leave it to us."

The three of us sat quietly in the semidarkness. Sweat trickled down the back of my neck. Eight tense minutes crawled by.

I thought I heard shuffling footsteps on the gravel but couldn't be sure.

Tap, tap, tap. Silence. Tap, tap. Silence.

I sat there petrified. The two men exchanged startled glances as the taps grew louder. Uncle Shekhar angled his chin, suggesting that I respond.

"Who is it?" I quavered.

"Lally, it's me, Kwasi. I have *urgent* news for you. Open the door, Lally, now!"

Turning to the men beside me, I raised my hands helplessly.

"Go ahead, open the door," Uncle Shekhar whispered in

my ear. "Pretend you're alone. I'll be right behind you." He squeezed my shoulder.

Taking a deep breath, I hesitantly opened the door a few inches. Framed by the black night outside, Kwasi was an apparition with protuberant cheeks and bloodshot eyes. His clothes were disheveled and smelled like old garbage.

I instinctively stepped back, and that's when he pounced. The door was flung open and it slammed into the living room wall, rattling all the glass louvers. I almost tripped against Uncle Shekhar's shoes as I backed up. A sound roared in my head, and my pulse raced so fast that I couldn't make out individual beats.

Kwasi's arms were outstretched and his sweaty face, stench, and staring eyes were mere inches away. He'd almost grabbed my shoulder when he registered that two large men were right behind me, and he dropped his arms. I raced for the stairs taking gasping breaths.

Uncle Shekhar shut the front door behind Kwasi and turned on the lights. He gestured for Kwasi to take a seat. Blinded by the bright light, I ascended to the landing and sat there to eavesdrop.

Over the next fifteen minutes, Kwasi brought up tales of Satan, devils, and witches.

"Lally is a witch," he told them. "She's been coming to my house and sending me requests to come here for sex. We'll be married soon."

The men made supportive statements and Kwasi allowed them to escort him outside. I ran downstairs to bolt the door. It was hard to believe he could be so delusional after he was cleared for discharge today! I learned he was readmitted to a different mental hospital, over a hundred miles from Kumasi. We would never again cross paths.

After this several-month ordeal, I'd be delusional if I chose to specialize in mental health.

Specialization

❤ ❤ ❤

Now, here I was, eighteen years later in America, pondering what field of specialization I should select. I'd rather go to hell than spend all day managing psychotic folks like Kwasi. Psychiatry was out. I scheduled psychiatry right at the start of my hospital rotations to get it out of the way.

The first month of psychiatry rotation was inpatient adult psychiatry at the Sacramento Mental Health Treatment Center. Spending so much time with patient interviews allowed me to polish and hone my interview skills. I wrote long, detailed notes. I learned how critical it was to build up trust. Without trust, patients shut you out completely.

Once the diagnosis was made, treatment involved determining the correct ingredients for a complex mixture of therapy, medication, and lifestyle/behavioral changes. Listening to patients' life stories and the creative ways they navigated stress was enlightening. With my relatively privileged life, complete with amazing family support, I was shocked by the extent of my patients' trauma. Many were homeless, low-income patients who received assistance from the county.

It was a true privilege to be entrusted with a ticket to the mind of a patient. During psychiatry ward rounds, I was introduced to manic patients who sang from the rooftop, anxious patients who'd witnessed horrible tragedies, and patients so despairing that they'd escaped committing suicide by a hair's breadth. Add to the mix patients like Kwasi who harbored florid delusions and hallucinations. Then there were those I liked the least: brooding and homicidal, with shifty eyes and ready lies.

I met Jenny, a homeless, middle-aged Caucasian woman who had damaged facial bones from a fall downstairs. She'd also struggled with long-standing alcoholism and depression. Something about those haunted green eyes and scarred face intrigued me. She was evasive during our interviews, and I wondered what secrets she was hiding.

One morning, she placed an emaciated hand on my wrist as I perched on the chair beside her bed. Shafts of sunlight fell on her pale, wrinkled face.

"Doc, you're so kind. I gotta confess something." She touched the dressing over her fractured cheekbones gingerly. "This *wasn't* no fall, y'know. Adam pushed me." She lifted her hand up at the concern in my eyes. "No, Doc, hear me out. Y'know, he was in 'Nam—he's a veteran, y'know—saw shit that really messed him up. Anyways, we was drinking and got in a argument. He got mad and punched me. After he got sober, he swore up and down he didn't mean to hurt me . . . said he was sorry." She gently massaged her injured cheek. "An' he promised he won't never do it no more, Doc, an' I believe him."

"Jenny, Jenny . . . you should report him to Adult Protective Services. What if he'd killed you accidentally? With all that damage to your face? He came close."

"Don't want no trouble on him."

My heart went out to that fragile, injured lady, with her limp gray hair tied up in a messy knot. Her disclosure was dreadful, but I was more shocked by the excuses she gave for the jerk who'd beaten her up. At least she'd trusted me enough to say what truly happened. She'd lied to all the ER doctors and the psychiatrists she'd seen. I was grateful for her trust, but it made me very uncomfortable.

During subsequent exchanges, she gave me a guided tour into the miserable world of the battered spouse. This was her third physically abusive relationship. When her face healed, she thanked me profusely but insisted that she would return to her abuser. His apartment was her ticket off street life. How could I blame her? If I took a walk in her shoes, would I really pick being cold and homeless over having a home? I thought about how I'd repeatedly ignored warning signs that I should leave John, only to go right back to him. I was struck afresh how, unlike the other specialties, psychiatry hovered in the gray area between black and white.

After three years languishing with book learning, building real-life doctor skills with these patients was unexpectedly rewarding. Halfway through the rotation, my supervisor knelt on the floor next to me as I charted notes at my desk.

"Lally, you have a special talent for psychiatry. If you'd like to consider specializing, say the word, and I'll write you a strong letter of recommendation."

I was stunned with surprise. "Thanks, but unfortunately I've set my heart on doing pediatrics, not psych. I *really* appreciate the compliment, Dr. Luo. Never thought I'd say this, but I'm shocked at how much I'm *loving* this rotation!"

He stood up and tapped the desk a couple times. "Well, okay, but I'll say it once again. I believe you're a natural, Lally. If you change your mind, my offer still stands."

I watched his departing back with a mixture of pride and regret. Dr. Luo was warm, empathic, and a fine role model. It was truly heartwarming to receive his endorsement, after all the times I'd wondered if I'd make it as a "real" doctor! The smile on my face and the glow in my chest stuck with me for the rest of the day.

Before I fell asleep that night, I idly wondered if I could imagine specializing in psychiatry. No. Psych was simply my first rotation. Maybe they would all be just as cool. If psych was this much fun, peds might knock me out of the ballpark!

Surgery was next. Before surgery rounds with the attending physician and team, I had to preround on my own. During prerounds at six o'clock one morning, I noticed a tall building on fire on many television sets. After rounds, I joined a bunch of medical students and surgeons, and we stared at the large ER television screen, watching in horror as the tall building on fire collapsed. I learned that it was called the World Trade Center. The building beside it was also on fire. My attending doctor stood right beside me, and tears ran down his cheeks.

"Doctor Roberts?" I asked, placing a tentative hand on his wrist, "Are you okay?"

"My brother . . . he works in that second tower—one that's still standing. Been trying to reach him for the last hour, but calls aren't going through." He was distraught.

"I'm sorry," I mumbled. "Hope you get through soon."

As we fixed our gaze on the screen, the second tower crumbled to the ground. I imagined his brother trapped in the rubble, gasping in all that smoke and dirt, then passing away. What a horrible way to die. Tears tracked down my cheeks, and it hurt to breathe. I swallowed, not knowing what to say.

"I pray that he's okay," I mumbled lamely.

When I learned, later that morning, that up to forty thousand people worked in those two towers, the pain in my chest became so intense that I could no longer think or function. My brain buzzed, replaying the terrifying images from TV sets turned on everywhere I looked. I excused myself from the second set of rounds and found a side room to cry for all those dead people. Later that afternoon, Dr. Roberts passed me down a hospital corridor. He saw the question in my eyes that I couldn't bring myself to ask.

"My brother made it. He stepped out for coffee before . . . you know, before. . . ."

The relief almost floored me. When I was dismissed from work that day, I drove like a maniac to my parents' house, ran inside, and enveloped my surprised mother in such a tight hug that I almost crushed her slight body. She smelled of meat patties. Of course. I inhaled deeply, every fiber of my being so glad that we were both alive.

"I don't normally say this, Ammah, but I had to give you a hug because I *love* you. I really, really love you." I pulled away slightly and noticed her bemused expression.

"What a thing," she said, shaking her head. Her eyes traveled over my shoulder at the endless replays on CNN. "What a thing. . . ."

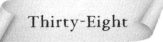

Thirty-Eight

Pediatrics:
The Awakening

Pediatrics, my long-awaited and anticipated rotation, was next. I was placed at Travis Air Force Base for the outpatient portion of the rotation. Although I loved talking with young kids, it was frustrating that, unlike psychiatry, our meetings were so abbreviated, and I was disappointed by the cookie-cutter treatment approach, with little chance to flex my creative muscle. Infected ears typically required amoxicillin. If the throat was inflamed, 95 percent of the time it was viral, which took cough syrup, fluids, and saltwater gargles. After a couple of weeks peering into the ears, noses, and throats of bawling kids, I wondered if I could handle taking this on for the rest of the month, let alone the remainder of my career. It didn't help that the sick children were invariably accompanied by anxious, irritable parents with frayed tempers who'd also been kept up all night.

Just as the glow of pediatrics was dimming, into the clinic walked Jaya, a petite thirteen-year-old Indian girl who'd tried to hang herself with a scarf in her closet. Her father found her in time. The physical exam of her body was fine, apart from an angry concentric bruise around her neck. She cried throughout the interview, generating a growing pile of tissues on her lap.

Although her father sat beside her, she scrunched herself far away from him.

"Doctor, I catch her smoking cigarette in house . . . again!" the belligerent pot-bellied, sweating father proclaimed, raising his hands up in the air. Then he waggled his finger. "I tell her, your punishment is no friends . . . no friends two week. So, she is running upstairs . . . and ten minutes later, she putting scarf around neck. What is this, doctor, huh?" He shrugged and mopped his receding hairline. "She want attention? Yes? My wife and I, we don't know what to do with her."

"I'd like to talk to her alone, please, could I?" I doubted she'd talk from the heart with her irate father there. Thankfully, her father was glad to leave the room.

After the door closed behind him, I pulled up close to the young girl, so the table was no longer in the way. She sat in a defensive posture, with hunched shoulders, and she played with a braid of jet-black hair that lay on her chest. We sat in silence for a few moments to allow some tension to drain, although tears flowed freely down her face. She stared at the floor, refusing to make eye contact. Her fingers were knotted so tightly in her braid that they appeared white, and they trembled.

"It's okay, Jaya, it's okay. You're safe now. Take a deep breath, okay? Like this. Watch me." I inhaled deeply then blew out the air fast. "Your turn, go ahead, try!"

She finally fixed her tear-ravaged eyes on mine and took a small ragged breath.

"Great job, great job, Jaya. One more. Let's do it together. I know you'll do even better next time," I encouraged. After several breaths in concert, her tears stopped, but her fingers still trembled on her lap. Her gaze was fixed on mine, as if I were the only anchor in her universe. Something in that look of desperation made me go out on a limb.

"Jaya," I leaned forward and touched a limp hand, "I don't think what happened to you—what you did—was just because of a cigarette. Am I right?"

She raised her eyebrows at me, then nodded almost imperceptibly before staring back at the floor. Her right foot tapped. I was getting warmer.

"When you're ready, just tell me. It's okay," I said quietly. I joined her in staring at the floor to give her space. Like a deer in the woods, she could startle at the slightest provocation, so I remained very still and nonconfrontational, all the time maintaining the light touch. The wrong word or any pressure on her might make her bolt, which would sabotage our tenuous yet critical connection.

My patience was rewarded. The story she eventually related was remarkable. She had been raped earlier in the day by a classmate she'd trusted. Unable to share what happened with anyone, she had returned home and smoked a purloined cigarette from her father's stash to calm her nerves. Her father caught her smoking and threatened to limit all contact with friends. The aftermath of the shame of the sexual assault, coupled with the prospect of being kept from her peers at a time she needed friends the most, placed her in an impossible, no-exit situation, so she'd attempted to kill herself.

I explained, gently, that this information was not confidential, because the perpetrator was on the loose. I would have to inform her father and social services. The police would help ensure her safety and perform the investigation. All she had to do was comply with their questions.

To my great relief, she accepted my assessment and recommendations, including hospitalization. Her only request was that I tell her father about the assault because she could not. Having deep roots in this Asian culture, I fully understood how difficult this was for her. The next hour and a half, I was embroiled in the fallout from her revelation, including notifying my supervisor, calling Child Protective Services and the police, and talking to a social worker. We recommended hospitalization and family therapy. I heaved a huge sigh of relief when her shaken father drove her to the hospital.

Halfway into my forty-minute drive back to Davis, I hummed along with the radio. I was relieved and lighthearted, despite the tangled mess with Jaya. She'd told me everything . . . *everything*, and we'd finally provided her the help she really needed. I felt like a *real doctor* today.

I didn't just *like* pediatrics, *I loved pediatrics!*

"I chose the right field!" I sang out as I banged my hands on the steering wheel in exultation. Unlike the exhausted-to-the-bone feeling that usually hit after work, today the adrenaline rush of accomplishment gave me a true energy jolt.

It was when I tried to determine why I was so jubilant that the realization struck me like a thunderclap. I gripped the steering wheel for dear life as I digested the enormity of my revelation, then pulled out onto the shoulder of a back road in Vacaville, generating a small dust cloud. Cars whizzed past, sending even more dust into the air.

You idiot, Lally, a small voice said in my head, *it's not pediatrics you're attracted to, it's psychiatry. Admit it!*

That was the day I ripped off my pediatric blinders. I may have helped Jaya a little today, but she'd bequeathed an even more precious gift. She'd shown me how much I reveled in work with the final black box, the brain, not the mechanical parts of the body—the various shades of gray, not black and white. Jaya's trust in me, followed by her complex work-up, was infinitely more satisfying to me than handing out the cream for her neck abrasion.

Dr. Luo had called me a "natural" for psychiatry, but I'd been so focused on a career in pediatrics that I'd missed all the signs. In every rotation so far, I'd naturally gravitated to the emotional side of treatment. Even in surgery, I'd instinctively focused more on allaying my patients' anxiety, not the actual discussion about surgical procedures. I wanted to find creativity in medicine. I wanted to use my skill to connect with each unique patient before I embarked on the real detective work. My personal exposure to severe, crippling anxiety as a teenager and the Kwasi situation would give me empathy for patients like this.

A large Safeway truck whipped past me, shaking my car in its wake. My epiphany was a shake-up for sure. I'd been jolted right out of my tunnel vision. I briefly rested my forehead on the top of my steering wheel to steady the whirling thoughts. When the road was clear, I eased the car back onto the highway and continued home. That very night, before I lost my new-found resolve, I sheepishly typed out an email. "Dear Dr. Luo," I wrote. "About that letter you offered to write for me . . ."

Thirty-Nine

Commitment

On Valentine's Day 2002, I woke up with only a warm indentation beside me. The early morning sunlight crept between the cracks in the slats of the long blinds, painting the wall across from me with vertical stripes. I wiped the sleep out of my eyes just as Tim walked into the room with a package and a nervous smile on his face.

"Happy birthday, Lally," he announced.

It was an exquisite brown leather Guess handbag with a long strap. He'd obviously noticed the tattered bag I'd hoisted for way too long. I turned it over and over, admiring the workmanship and all the cute zippered pockets. With Tim's meticulous attention to detail, every zip would slide perfectly, I knew. As I pulled out white paper stuffing from an inner compartment, a gold ring tumbled out. I gasped at the shimmering solitary diamond that protruded from the band.

"Wh—what's this?" I turned to Tim, my brain awhirl.

"Um . . . Lally, will you marry me?" He knelt beside me. His shy, expectant expression was my undoing. That, plus the intense stare of entreaty in those familiar dark brown eyes. My pillar of support was *kneeling beside me*, asking for commitment.

Unable to respond, I held his gaze, spilling tears of surprise. Our relationship had become so warm and comfortable that, for some reason, it simply hadn't dawned on me that he might want to formally tie the knot. From the first night that handsome stranger waltzed into my life, he'd provided unwavering security and assurance through every med school hurdle. He'd become the only father figure my girls had ever known. Not one day had I felt even the slightest flicker of indecision about unlocking my heart to this generous, quiet, sweet man now on the floor by my side.

Pushing the handbag to my side, I opened both arms wide to welcome him into my life. Burying my tearstained face into his soft navy dressing gown, I held him tighter than I'd ever held anyone before. His heart thudded loudly against my ear.

"I love you, Tim," I whispered.

We were married later that year at an outdoor gazebo on the UC Davis campus, with ninety friends and family in attendance. My two daughters, aged eight and ten, were flower girls. The sweetest moment of the ceremony was when Tim plucked the courage to strum his guitar and serenade me with *The Wedding Song*. I looked around at Shermila, Shanthi, my three siblings, and my parents—at all the people who'd carried me in their lives at different times along the way. In the grass by the gazebo, a wayward duck family waddled in a wavy line, the father honking from behind to keep them in check. I couldn't remember a time in my life when I'd been happier.

A few weeks later, I participated in the Match—a fiendish, legally binding process in which a computer program matches students with residency programs. My final coat of "doctor polish" would be applied during residency. It had already taken six years to become a doctor, but now I needed five more: three years of adult psychiatry, then two years of child psychiatry fellowship.

I prayed fervently that I'd get into UC Davis. I'd interviewed at both the San Mateo and Fresno programs, but they were three to four hours away. On Match day, crestfallen, I learned that I'd been accepted into the San Mateo program, not Davis. San Mateo was over a hundred miles away! What was I thinking? Would the girls and Tim move too? Tim worked at Raley's in Woodland, and the girls had close ties to their schools, their grandparents, and all their close friends. How could I strip them away and make them live in the Bay Area?

No question I'd loved the promise of the San Mateo program. It focused on Freudian psychotherapy and community psychiatry. Davis was more academic and medication-focused, but I'd placed it as my top choice to avoid uprooting my family. Like a doofus, I'd simply assumed I'd get in there, so here I was, crying like a spoiled baby. I should have been joyful, because some graduated doctors hadn't matched anywhere at all!

I walked around the room to clear my head, fished out the San Mateo materials from a drawer, and rifled through their shiny catalog. From hundreds of applicants, they selected only four doctors to train every year. What an honor to be selected! By entering into the Match process, I was legally obliged to accept the San Mateo residency spot.

I slammed shut the materials in the drawer and drove to pick up my girls from their after-school programs, imagining their faces crumpling if I announced a family move to San Mateo. I simply couldn't bring it up. The girls chattered happily in the back seat, but all I could hear was John's sneering words: "So, Lally, so you want to go ahead and play at being a doctor, huh?" Was I selfish to make my career path important enough to uproot everyone? The other option was for me to move a hundred miles away for three years. *Three years!* The timing sucked. I'd been married to Tim for only a few months.

When Tim came home that night, my blotchy, swollen eyes weren't exactly subtle. He became very anxious but honored my whispered request to wait to talk after the girls were asleep. As we cleared up the dishes, I shared the Match results.

"Can't leave you guys, can't drag you to the Bay Area. Just can't do it," I shook my head, "I'm going to postpone residency another year, Tim." I handed him a wet plate to stack in the dishwasher.

"Really?" He responded very calmly, focused on positioning the plate. He didn't appear outwardly frazzled by my bombshell, but I'd hoped for more of a response. I waited till he straightened up and looked me in the eye. "That's quite a decision, Lally . . . but sounds like that's what you want to do . . . so, what do you plan to do while you wait?" He was so expressionless that I could not put my finger on whether he supported my plan or not.

I shrugged. "Something. Anything. Maybe I'll just make some money for a change. Med school graduation's still months away. I have the time to find something."

"Yes, but you won't be fully licensed, dear. Listen, Lally, you're almost done with training. Do you really want to take a chance and throw it all away?" Now his tone was incredulous, which surprised me. I thought he'd be relieved and grateful that I'd made the "family" decision to remain with them in Davis.

"Lally, you'll have to do what you like, but personally, I think it's the wrong way to go," he said quietly. "What if you try and don't get into Davis next year? What then?"

"I've made my mind up," I said obstinately, deathly afraid he might be right. "Please let's stop talking. I need to clear my head." I pulled my apron off and walked out into the dark back garden. Ten minutes later, I returned to a spotless kitchen. Tim was strumming his guitar by the fireplace. He never fights with tears. I traipsed over to the easy chair next to him and flipped aimlessly through a magazine. The relaxing guitar chords soothed some of my angst, but the enormity of my decision made me feel as if a bowling ball had settled in my belly. Only time would tell if I'd made the right choice. I felt like crap. Only worse.

The next morning I called the San Mateo residency program director, Alan Louie, to withdraw. I told him that I couldn't imagine a program that would be a better fit for me, but I couldn't leave my family behind in Davis. I told him I'd accept the penalty for breaking the rules of the Match. Dr. Louie told me he was sorry to lose me but appreciated my dilemma.

"Family is all-important, Lally, but do you know that we have some really excellent elementary schools out here?"

I wished he'd been an unreasonable jerk instead of so darned understanding. His warmth made me feel like a traitor. Now he'd be in a bind because their program would have to locate a different doctor to take my spot. In the days that followed, I spent every spare moment working on my gap-year plan. Within two weeks, two other opportunities came through. I was offered a $40,000-a-year position conducting autism research at the UC Davis MIND center in Sacramento and was also accepted into the UC Davis master's program in public health (MPH). I mulled over these options the next few days. The MPH program would improve my portfolio for reapplication the following year, but experience in autism research would be a tremendous asset for a future career in child psychiatry.

I broached the topic with Tim at the dining table a week later. The pros and cons of my two choices were neatly tabulated on a large sheet of paper. I walked him down the list. He was uncharacteristically quiet for several moments, and then he tapped the table surface silently with a shuttered expression. I was mesmerized by those long, beautiful musician's fingers.

"Well?" I asked impatiently, exasperated at his long silence, "which should I accept, Tim? What do *you* think?"

"I don't think you should accept either," he responded flatly, avoiding my eyes.

"What? What are you talking about, Tim?" I turned to face him, startled.

"You asked my opinion, right? I think you're making a mistake, Lally." He leaned back and stretched before continuing. "Listen, you trained to be a doctor for six long years. You almost dropped out with all the stress, but somehow . . . somehow you clawed your way back. Now that you're so close to your dream—they handed you your dream residency—do you really want to throw it all away, hoping you'll match locally next year? That's nuts. There are no guarantees. What if you're stuck right in this position a year from now?"

"But . . ." I waved my sheet in the air. "But what about these two options, Tim?"

"Lally, listen, here's what I think. Accept San Mateo's offer. It's not like you'll be in a different state or something. The Bay Area's just down the road. I grew up there. Here's what you do: Stick it out for three years, and then you'll be back with us. Do the child psychiatry fellowship here in Davis with us when you're done."

I tried to talk, but he waved me away animatedly.

"Lally, listen! I'll look after the girls. Your parents will help me. This way they won't have to leave their schools or friends. We'll see you weekends. Every single weekend. Yes, it'll be tough, but we'll make it work somehow."

I gripped the table while my world did multiple whirls and flip-flops. Neurons fired like firecrackers on the Fourth of July. This was Tim, not John. John would have informed me that I couldn't leave for San Mateo. He would have forbidden that option outright, telling me that my place was at home with him and the girls. Tim's first thought, on the other hand, had been to focus on the best option for me! I'd thought I knew this terrific man, but he'd shown me how truly unselfish he could be. Tim, the love of my life, my new husband, was telling me that he'd hold the fort with the kids in Davis, and I should leave.

"Three years? Three full years? You'd really do that, Tim? They aren't even your own children." I walked over and stood next to him.

"It's what you've trained to do. We'll make it work, Lally. We'll be fine." Now he looked sad, so I leaned over to squeeze his shoulder.

"But . . . but I pulled out of San Mateo. They've probably found another doctor by now."

"So, call them tomorrow and ask." He stood up, reached out to me, and enveloped my cold hands in his warmth. "You've got to finish your doctor thing, Lally." His voice had a pensive tone, and I caught the faraway look in his eyes before he dropped his gaze to our clasped hands. My heart brimmed with love for this amazing man. He'd spoken his truth out loud and clear. He was probably right.

I pulled him into my arms very tightly, so my head was up against his chest. "Do you know something, Tim? I'm going to call Dr. Louie tomorrow. No matter what he says, I want you to know that John would *never* have supported me like you are right now. What you said means so much to me because . . . because . . . Tim, heck, we just got *married*, and now you're not only saying you'll let me go, but that you'll watch Shermila and Shanthi while I'm out there. I love you so much for this, Tim. You're so sweet. *I love you!*" I squeezed him closer still and, with one hand, gently stroked his dark locks. We were both trembling. I shut my eyes as we rocked in silence, and the loud thumps of his heart reverberated against my ribcage. When we were together like this, no impediment was unsurmountable. Tim's security blanket warmed up my entire world, shutting out every niggling doubt.

San Mateo hadn't filled their empty training program spot, and they accepted my about-face. I was in! We set up a family discussion, and I broached the new residency plan. The girls took it much better than I thought. They were adamant that they did not want to leave Davis. I explained that the next few years would be rough on all of us, but that I'd see them every single weekend by taking the train or having Tim drive them over. I told them I'd be only eleven miles from the ocean, so when they visited we'd get together at the beach. My final promise was that if anyone struggled with our new arrangement, I'd leave my program and drive to Davis to be with them at the drop of a hat.

A few months later, on June 13, 2003, I graduated from UC Davis School of Medicine. The unearthly, elemental sound of bagpipes rent the air as we shuffled slowly behind faculty decked in black graduation gowns. I peered sideways at the row taken by Tim, Shermila, Shanthi, and my parents, who all sat together. My breath caught as my eyes lovingly traced each silhouette. My dad beamed at me with pride, and his white handkerchief occasionally dabbed at his eyes. Nimi, Vimalan, his wife, Belinda, and my sister Viji were also seated, looking solemn. It struck me afresh that I'd dragged my family along on this ambitious and tortuous doctor journey, and my gratitude knew no bounds. My heart brimmed with dizzying exultation at this moment that was prophesized, this moment in time that no one could wrestle away from me.

I didn't feel like a "doctor of doctors," but today I had become a physician.

Forty

Psychotherapy

I hummed as I vaulted two stairs at a time to get to my third-floor Redwood City office. It was a truly special Monday. In just twenty minutes, I'd meet my very first therapy patient. After rotations in internal medicine, neurology, and geriatrics, I'd picked up the principles of psychotherapy, but today I could put book knowledge into action with my live therapy patient. I planned to take copious notes because later in the week I would present the patient and have my technique critiqued by my psychotherapy supervisor.

Seated on my black leather armchair, I pulled out a manila chart from my drawer and took a deep breath to quell my racing heart.

Rosie Johnson.

Caucasian, thirty-eight, single, homeless.

Referred for depression.

On the intake form, she said she'd consider medication. She'd agreed to weekly therapy sessions with me for the remainder of the year. I noted that she'd dabbled in substance abuse with methamphetamine and alcohol. Her medical history listed microcytic anemia. Details were sparse, so I'd need a thorough assessment to help with my formulation after our first meeting.

I shut the folder and glanced at the thousand-piece framed Thomas Kincaid puzzle to my right. The girls and I had completed it just three weeks back, and we'd scribbled our names on the right-hand corner in gold and silver. I'm addicted to jigsaws. The biggest one I ever completed was thirty-five hundred pieces, and it took a whole summer. People were jigsaws with infinitely more puzzle pieces. Maybe that's why I enjoyed mental health so much. The sunlight from my window lit up the charming cottage with the stream weaving by, bringing the entire scene to life. I blew a soft kiss to my girls' names.

My year as a weekends-only mom was manageable only because I spent every weekend with them, typically in Davis. I always broke down crying if anyone from work asked about them. When they did come for a visit, I always bawled when Tim's green Highlander pulled away on a Sunday night, and I watched two small hands waving me out of their lives for the week. Shanthi's piano teacher told me she was gifted. She brought the audience to tears when she played Chopin. I never missed a concert. If it was midweek, I left Davis at four the following morning for the three-hour train ride. They were both placed in gifted programs at school and developed close friendships with their peers, which lowered my guilt a smidgen.

My cellphone alarm sounded. Ten minutes. I'd been told to remove anything too personal so my office was a blank slate, a tabula rasa on which patients could lay their anguish. I scooped an untidy pile of lab request slips, papers, and Post-it notes into an empty desk drawer and adjusted the triangular black-and-white marble nameplate on my desk to align it perfectly. It was inscribed Lally Pia MD in gold letters on a black backing, a coveted graduation gift from my father. He'd joked when he handed it to me, "Use this when those crazy patients attack you, Lally!"

Psychotherapy

When my patient sat across from me in the cushioned armchair, she'd see my badge of honor lined up right below my face. My precious nameplate would help me build up my confidence as I learned more about therapy. It epitomized all the roads I'd traveled to claw my way to this black leather MD seat.

If all went well over the next few months, Rosie would lead me through her jungle of anxiety, depression, romance, pitfalls, and trauma. I'd be her safari guide. I still had five minutes. I was excited and also tremendously nervous. The clock was strategically placed just above the patient's seat, so it wouldn't be too obvious if I glanced slightly upward to make sure we didn't go over forty-five minutes. The boundary of the clock was a significant way to set limits from the start.

The strident ring of the telephone made me jump. My patient had made it to the lobby. My heart hammered as I ran a hand through my hair, took one final glance around the room, and took the stairs down to the lobby.

Patients filled the seats. When I called her name and came face-to-face with my jigsaw, my smile of welcome froze on my face. A frail and emaciated pale ghost rose unsteadily from her seat, clutching a faded black plastic garbage bag. A dog-eared, tattered brown cloth bag was slung over one scrawny shoulder. She looked closer to sixty than thirty-eight, and her weather-beaten and asymmetric face looked as if she'd lost a smashing contest with a brick wall.

"Good afternoon, Ms. Johnson, it's good to meet you." I took a step forward and smiled to relax her.

She gave me a weak nod of acknowledgment. Her sunken, faded blue eyes showed no animation whatsoever, and the skin on her face was stretched so tight over her skull that she was like an animated skeleton. Rosy, she definitely wasn't. Her shoulder-length, sparse, mousy brown hair was confined untidily at the back of her head with a faded blue ribbon. A slight shove and she'd likely keel right over. She trailed me up the stairs like a wraith.

Within thirty minutes, I learned that she'd had no contact with her birth family, had been in foster care, then spent a chunk of her adult life on the street where she'd amassed years of heavy methamphetamine use. She'd also experimented with just about every other drug known to man, including intravenous drugs and psychedelic mushrooms. She'd had stints in jail for alcoholism and disorderly conduct when intoxicated. Various physically assaultive males had added angles to her face. Her current boyfriend was her drug dealer. *Great*.

"Children?" I asked.

"One daughter. CPS took her from the hospital. Said she was positive for meth. Wouldn't let me keep her." Her eyes misted up, and her face looked wistful as she stared out the window. "S'right, Doc, it's on me. It's all on me. Ain't gonna make excuses for what I did, but after I held my baby girl close to my chest, it hurt so bad when they took her away. She was perfect, Doc, but she's gone. I'm here because I'm going to get her back." Tears flowed down her pale cheeks and dripped on her lap.

I looked around desperately for my tissue box. It was still in my desk drawer, so I snatched it up, walked over, and placed it beside her. "Help yourself. I'm so sorry."

I *was* sorry. I was sorry for her loss, sorry her mom had been absent from her life, and then she'd had her own baby wrested away. If her daughter had been exposed to methamphetamine in utero, I was sorry for the girl, because she'd likely have attention deficit problems. The system had dropped Rosie in a frustrating void with few viable prospects. If only she'd had parents like mine. How unfair that no one in her life ever truly cared about her.

She pulled out several tissues. I waited patiently for her to gather her composure.

"That's why I'm here, Doc," she sniffed, "y'know, I actually got my shit—excuse me—*stuff* together when she was six. Had her for a year." She picked at the seam on her tattered handbag. "She's a beautiful girl, Doc, just beautiful." A small smile of remembrance played across her face. "Yeah, I was good with her . . . and then I relapsed, went and lost her again. She didn't want to leave neither. We were both crying, and I was screaming for them to give me one last chance." She blew her nose, then turned to face me, and her countenance held a sense of purpose. "That's why I need your help, Doc. Lakiya's nine now, and I want her back. I'm here because I don't know if I can do it. . . ." She dissolved into tears again.

"Do you get to see her at all?" As the words left my voice, I realized I shouldn't have brought up visitation in case she didn't have contact.

"Yeah, but it's court supervised. That dang CPS worker had a big frown on her face the whole time we were at the McDonald's play structure. She says I need three random tox screens to be clean, one after the other. Gonna help me, Doc?"

"We're going to try together," I said, projecting a lot more confidence than I felt.

"She's growing up so fast, Doc. I'll do anything . . . *anything* to get her back with me."

"Mm-hm," was all I could come up with.

"Can't live without her no more. If I don't get her back, I want to die, die, *die!*" Her voice raised up to a crescendo, and then she dissolved into racking sobs. Tears welled up in my eyes also. During training, the general recommendation was not to hug the patient, but throwing caution to the wind, I decided there couldn't be a more perfect time.

I walked up to her, stood behind her, and gently held the shoulders of that fragile bag of bones for a full minute, saying nothing. She hiccupped and sniffed.

"And then, there's a part of me that says I don't wanna leave Bruce. Without him, all I got is homeless shelters. It ain't safe in those shelters. Turn your back and someone got half your stuff. Half those men are wasted all the time—they'll fuck anything in a skirt. I got a roof over my head with Bruce." She balled up her tissues in her hand, and her fingers trembled. "Thing is, he's got a bad temper, y'know. . . ." She fingered what looked like a faint purple bruise on her chin. Her halting delivery and the steadily growing pile of tissues made my heart sink into my heels.

She was off on a tangent now, talking about Bruce, so I returned to my seat, wondering what to do next. This was no thirty-five-hundred-piece puzzle! The fates had handed me a thirty-thousand-piece, three-dimensional nightmare to put together. I was a total fraud. How terrifying to take on the responsibility for another person's life into my inexperienced hands. I had a supervisor, but it was naive and stupid to think that this process might be manageable, or even fun.

She was now talking about a train. Something about not wanting to be alive. I leaned forward to listen to what she was mumbling. After a few strategic questions, it became crystal clear that my patient was seriously contemplating throwing herself in front of a light rail train right after we were done. I sure didn't want my first therapy session to end with my patient as roadkill, so I terminated the interview abruptly.

"I'm sorry, Ms. Johnson, but I'm sending you to the hospital, okay? I have to make a report, and the police will be here soon. If they agree with me, you'll be on a safety hold. They'll drive you to the hospital."

Her eyes widened in disbelief, and she half rose. "No, no, Doc. Please! Don't want no hospital. Got things to do tonight. I'll be fine, just fine. I'm not going to hurt myself, I swear. . . ."

"I'm sorry, Ms. Johnson, I don't feel safe letting you go. It's a judgment call."

"But. . . ."

I waved her to sit, and she complied, unsteadily. "Ms. Johnson, you'll be safe there. Safe from your thoughts. Safe from Bruce. Safe from getting hit by a train. And they won't have meth there, so if you were telling me the truth about getting your girl back, the hospital is the safest place to be. We didn't talk medication, but the good news is that they might start you on something in there. Maybe you'll feel better. Now here's what we *don't* want. We *don't* want you to relapse when you're feeling down. You told me you wanted Lakiya back, right? Isn't this the best way?"

"Maybe . . . y-yeah, but . . ."

"Listen, Ms. Johnson, trust me, it's the *best plan*. Even if we started pills today, they're not going to kick in for four to six weeks. In the hospital they can watch you—see how you do, make sure you're a lot better before you leave. Trust me, it's the best option to keep you safe."

"But . . . but I don't want to go. . . ." She hung her head, and tears dribbled out. She looked like an obstinate child.

I walked back over to her and held her shoulder gently. It was like grasping a fence post.

"Listen," I leaned over, so our faces were scarcely two feet apart, "I promised I'd walk this journey with you, right?"

"Right," she said, and nodded.

"So here's the deal. It's going to start with *you* trusting *me*. Our first step is to help you lose the meth and to treat whatever that down stuff is that you're taking the meth for. Once you're better, we can work toward getting your daughter back, okay? You going to give this a shot? For Lakiya's sake?"

Technically she didn't have to agree with me, because the cops would undoubtedly place her on an involuntary hold, but my gut told me that preserving our relationship was the most critical first step. We had a whole year to get something going.

She twisted and untwisted the strap of her purse for several seconds, then she sat up straight and looked me in the eye.

"'Kay, Doc, let's do it. I'll go." She let go of the strap and held her hand out, as if to seal our pact.

The flood of relief that hit me as I held her cold hand made me almost lightheaded. "They'll have food there too—it's like being in jail—three hots and a cot, you know." I winked.

She returned a weak smile. "I'll trust you, Doc," she said, simply. A beautiful smile lit up her sad face.

I asked the front desk to call 911, then walked her downstairs and waited with her till two burly cops arrived. They spoke to me briefly, evaluated Rosie in a small room by the lobby, and agreed to place her on a hold and escort her to the hospital.

She followed them outside to the waiting squad car, and I was struck by the haunted look in her pale blue eyes. Hopefully I hadn't scared her off forever. I hoped she'd return to see me. When I collapsed in my office chair ten minutes later, the wall puzzle appeared listless and flat. The sunlight no longer shone on it. I hoped to God that wasn't a bad omen.

Over the next two weeks, I couldn't stop thinking about Rosie. In a call to the hospital, I learned that she'd been started on Prozac. Although they set up a discharge date, I was skeptical that she'd return to see me. I was wrong. Not only did she surprise me with her first post-hospital visit, but she showed up fifteen minutes early! I felt vindicated.

Her cheeks had filled out, and as I ushered her upstairs, I observed more energy in her steps. She sat straighter and was significantly brighter. She began talking as soon as I shut the office door. "Doc, I'll be honest now. I wanted speed *so bad* at the hospital, y'know, but I couldn't get none, of course. It's been hard, but I'm trying . . . I'm trying, Doc. Been clean seventeen days and counting." She threw me a shy smile as she shot me a wavering thumbs-up. There was a magic sparkle in those faded eyes that knocked years off her age.

"Congratulations! I'm so happy for you. You go, Rosie!"

"Don't congratulate me. Not yet . . . my cravings are real bad. An' I'm back with Bruce. Scared I'll relapse any moment. Speed's everywhere you look, and hella cheap." She picked at the hem of her faded peasant skirt, avoiding my eyes.

I nodded. "Yes, Ms. Johnson, and if that happens, we'll work with it, okay? You need to quit at least five times before it actually works, I've heard. But the key is to stop beating up on yourself each time you relapse." I steepled my fingers and rested my chin on my fingertips.

"You don't know nothing about speed, do you, Doc? Ever try it?"

"Well, I don't know from personal experience, but I've read that—"

"Nah, you don't get it," she cut me off and shrugged, then shook her head. "I'm gonna try but can't make no promise."

For the remainder of our year together, she cycled. She kept going off her meds and went on meth and alcohol binges. Her depression then worsened, suicidal thoughts reemerged, and I sent her back to the hospital to keep her alive or get her clean. Replay. Repeat. If there was a surprise, it was that despite each attempt, she never actually succeeded in killing herself, and somehow she invariably returned to my office for her weekly therapy.

For my part, I never stopped telling her that I cared for her. I shared my helplessness in the face of the drugs that were destroying her life. She appeared to develop more insight into the damage to her psyche from meth and how the cravings fueled her depressed mood. She never gave up on her dream to establish a connection with her daughter. I, too, cycled with her. I cherished occasional glimmerings of hope when she was sober but became frustrated when hope was summarily extinguished each time she fell into yet another abyss.

Rosie taught me patience, restraint, and appreciation for all my own supports in a way I'd never learned it before. She gave me a tour into the seedy underworld in which she dwelled and described the ugliness that conspired to keep her trapped. I thought that I'd had it bad on welfare, but her misfortunes were a thousand times worse. Whereas I'd been aghast by mold on French bread, she'd probably have simply scraped it off and been grateful she had bread!

Working with dead bodies had given me immense appreciation for the gift of life. Now, Rosie's misery illustrated all the social supports I'd pretty much taken for granted. Sure, John had thrown keys at my belly. Rosie's partners hurt her so badly she'd needed surgery.

Her stories conveyed the precious fragility of society's fabric and the glaring holes in the weave. Time bombs awaited her every misstep. If she was a few minutes late, I never shook that jittery feeling that she might have overdosed or killed herself, perhaps without meaning to.

When residency training ended, our meetings had to end. I tried to link her up with a different therapist, but she politely declined. She said she didn't want to have to trust someone all over again. She said she was doing much better. Try as I might to stop them, tears filled my eyes as I gave her our final goodbye hug. Although she was also teary, her body was stiff in my grasp. We'd spoken for forty-five minutes every week throughout the year—more than I talked to some of my closest friends. I was headed to Davis, a hundred miles away, for two years of child psychiatry fellowship training, and it was highly unlikely that we'd ever cross paths again.

I wish I could tell you she became markedly better, or that I weaned her off medication, or that our work cured her

methamphetamine dependence. It didn't. I could take comfort only in the fact that we built up a relationship of mutual
respect and warmth at our weekly sessions. Her hospitalizations
decreased in frequency as we worked together, and I learned so
much from her.

As I followed her down the steps to the lobby that final
afternoon, I knew there was always the risk that she'd stop her
medications completely. She might actually kill herself! If so,
would *anything* we'd done that year have made the slightest difference—apart from buying her a little time? I'd never know for
sure. I crossed my fingers behind my back, praying that whatever happened to her along her road, she'd do us both proud.

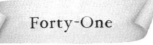

Forty-One

New Wheels

My trusty secondhand Honda Accord wagon was on its deathbed. I'd had a close relationship with her because she'd stuck with me a full nine years, through the rigors of medical school and residency training. The odometer reading was now at 201,000 miles. Unfortunately, my beloved vehicle had been vandalized multiple times when I'd left it parked at the Hayward Amtrak station and taken the train to Davis on weekends. Usually they took my license plate, presumably to reuse my registration sticker, but last week they'd severed the pipe that led to my gas tank. I didn't know that, so when I tried to fill up my car after driving from the Bay Area, I flooded a large section of the Chevron gas station. Thankfully, there were no sparks in the vicinity, or I would have blown up along with my car.

During my third year at San Mateo, several moonlighting shifts at Redwood City Jail had doubled my trainee stipend. I'd now saved up enough money to invest in a new car. It was such a thrilling proposition that at age forty-five I could finally purchase the very first new car of my life! I decided to go crazy and buy my dream car: a sporty metallic silver Lexus GS 300 sedan.

The day of the purchase, Tim and my dad drove me to the Sacramento Lexus dealership. After a flurry of paperwork that needed signatures, Tim snapped dozens of photographs of me next to my gleaming chariot. The lot was almost empty because the dealership was shutting down. It was pitch dark outside. I shivered in the chill.

I hugged my dad tight, then gave Tim an exuberant, bone-crushing embrace. I choked up when Tim reached into his jacket and pulled out my favorite Rondo Veneziano CD for my solo drive back. I'd splurged on a top-of-the-line, fourteen-speaker sound system for the car, and I fully intended to blast my music at the top volume all the way across the Yolo Causeway that led home. After Tim and my dad drove away, the salesman walked me to the car, handed me the key fob, shook my hand, and left also.

Completely alone in the parking lot with all the chaos behind me, I stared at this magical luxury car I now owned. The silver paint gleamed in the fluorescent lights from the showroom, and I touched the top of the car in wonder, relishing the cold metal texture. The car unlocked itself because of the proximity of the key fob, and discreet lighting turned on magically within. Once I sank into the black leather of the luxurious driver's seat, I shut my eyes and took a deep breath, salivating over the new leather smell.

Music. I needed music. I started the engine, popped my CD in, and shut my eyes in rapture as the violins and oboe began. The sound was so fantastic that it was like having my own private orchestra within the car. It was then that it struck me what a truly momentous occasion this was. A few years back, I'd been given a handout of moldy bread; I'd been on welfare, never had enough money, and got by on food stamps. I'd fed rats and chopped up and embalmed dead bodies for three years. But today, this incredible new vehicle now belonged to *me*.

I put my head on the cherry wood steering wheel and cried. I sobbed while raw feelings of sadness mixed with accomplishment engulfed me. I didn't know why I was crying, but the tears kept flowing. They dripped off the wheel and splattered into my lap.

There was an urgent tapping on the window.

"Ma'am? Ma'am? Are you okay? Are you all right?" It was the worried countenance of the young African American salesman. He had a sheet of paper in his hand. I rolled down my window, hurriedly wiping tears off my face with the back of my hand.

"Sorry, ma'am. I forgot to give you a copy of the receipt," he said, offering the papers to me. "Ma'am, is everything okay?" He seemed very flustered.

"It's fine, everything's fine." I accepted the paperwork and threw it on the passenger seat. He didn't leave, just stood there, frowning, shifting around in obvious discomfort. I felt I owed him an explanation.

"It's just that it wasn't very long ago that I was on welfare, you see," I confessed, smiling through my tears. "And this," I said, patting the steering wheel, "this is the first new car I've ever owned." I sniffed again.

"Oh, I see, I see, ma'am," he responded, lowering his shoulders, visibly relieved. "We aren't used to people crying when they buy a Lexus. Most customers simply point and say, "I'll take one of those," and drive away with a smile. It's, er . . . quite refreshing to see your . . . your gratitude, ma'am. Don't get much of that out here."

Two weeks later there was a knock at my front door. My jaw dropped when the delivery man handed me a huge bouquet of two dozen roses in a cushion of green ferns—a gift from the Lexus car salesman. I was arranging them in a large glass vase on our kitchen table when Tim walked in from work.

"Wow, Lally, that's a nice gesture, but if you ask me, I think he went a little too far," he grumbled.

Forty-Two

Doctor of Children

F or my final two years of psychiatric training, UC Davis accepted me into their Child and Adolescent Psychiatry Fellowship program. I was thrilled. This meant I could join the family after three long years apart, years that had been incredibly tough on Tim and me, even though the girls had adapted well. Now twelve and fifteen, they'd become mature and independent in my absence.

For months after my return to Davis, the sound of the blaring Amtrak train horn sent chills to the pit of my stomach; for too long it had symbolized my departure from this family I loved so much.

Shermila threw her arms around me. "Mom, *now* can we get a dog?"

It was fun to work exclusively with children and adolescents at my Sacramento clinic. I saw everything from severe child abuse to autism. The most common conditions I encountered were ADHD, anxiety, depression, and substance abuse. One of the more interesting cases I inherited was a case of selective mutism.

"Juan's thirteen. Long history of sexual and physical abuse. Worked with him for months, but he won't say a word," Jean

Chowdry told me as she laid the patient chart on my desk. "He's yours now. Good luck."

"Wow, fat chart!" I opened the chart and began to browse.

"Yes, lots of abuse, poor guy. The judge mandated weekly therapy sessions for forty-five minutes. He doesn't want to be here but has to. I'll be surprised if he says a word, unless he swears at you . . . he's got a choice vocabulary of four-letter words." She hesitated, poised to leave. "Anything else?"

"If he refuses to talk, what do you *do* for forty-five minutes?" I thumbed through to her most recent note.

"I tried and tried, but I've given up. I type up my other patient notes while he's there. He just curls up in a ball and won't respond."

I shut the chart. "Tried playing a game?"

"Yeah, of course. He refuses. Won't engage at all. It's frustrating."

I love a challenge. There and then I decided that I would use *every* trick in my book to get Juan to talk to me. I flat-out refused to type notes while he was in my office.

"Hi, Juan," I said brightly when his mother dropped him off for his first session. I extended my hand, but he pointedly ignored it.

"Fuck off, motherfucker." He glared at me, a shock of uncombed black hair partly obscuring his eyes. He was a short, chunky Hispanic boy. Looked ten, not thirteen. He walked over to the long couch at the back of the room and stretched out facing the wall with his back to me.

Undeterred, I spent the entire session talking. I shared about my life in Ghana, trips I had taken, pets I had owned, and my love of dogs. Despite multiple attempts to get him to respond, he shut me out completely and ignored all my questions. When our time was up, he got up and silently moved to the door.

"Thank you, Juan," I called out to his departing back.

"Fuck you," he responded, without turning around. He slammed the door shut, and it rattled in the frame.

The second therapy session was almost identical. I talked about Sri Lankan holidays but was running out of ideas for our next session, so I decided on a new approach. For session three, I read him chapter 1 of the first Harry Potter book, taking pains to modulate my voice to dramatize the action and get him invested. As I triumphantly put the book down, I was mortified that Juan had fallen asleep! I had to nudge him awake gently to tell him our time was over. He wiped his eyes and yawned deeply, but this time he didn't swear at me.

"Guess I screwed up," I told my supervisor. "I thought I'd finally made a connection, but he fell asleep!"

"Lally, don't be so hard on yourself," she encouraged gently. "That poor, abused boy paid you the biggest compliment ever. He *trusted* you. He felt *safe* with you, so he slept. I doubt anyone ever read to him before. Most of the adults in his life have neglected him or sexually abused him. He fell asleep because he let down his guard. Keep it up, Lally!"

Bolstered by her support, I brought Harry Potter back to session four. "Chapter 2," I announced, prepared to read for another forty-five minutes.

Juan sat up stiffly and pushed wayward locks out of his enormous dark brown eyes.

"You don't have to read anymore," he said nonchalantly. "I'm ready now. Let's talk."

And just like that, Juan handed me one of the biggest gifts of my therapeutic life.

Two years later, in June 2008, I graduated from the Child Psychiatry Fellowship program in a simple ceremony at a UC Davis office. My truly amazing mentor, Dr. Harry Wang, guided me during my final year of training. When he offered me a job at his agency, River Oak Center for Children, a nonprofit in Sacramento County, I jumped at the offer. Just as I had received free medical care when I was on welfare, I would now serve impoverished families who received no-cost mental health services. Along with five other child psychiatrists, I would have a great team of dedicated and empathic therapists and case managers. The team approach, along with a strong focus on therapy, was a perfect fit. I signed up for three days a week in case I decided to set up a private practice clinic in the future.

It was twilight when I left the graduation ceremony to walk to my car. This final trek from the university building to the parking lot marked the end of formal school instruction. I'd been in educational institutions from ages five to twenty-two, twenty-five to thirty-two, and thirty-six to forty-seven—a full thirty-five years of schooling! I whistled out loud. Had it been worth it? Without a doubt. I didn't feel like a "doctor of doctors," whatever that meant, but tonight I had become a fully trained child and adolescent psychiatrist.

I jumped into my car and zipped down the street with a heart bursting with gratitude. Family, friends, and the financial support from welfare had helped hoist and propel me, Princess Lally, to this huge beckoning career gateway. My mission from here was crystal clear: I would give back, any way I could, to this wonderful society that had furnished every critical opportunity, just when I needed it most.

Forty-Three

Return Home

In early 2013, I was cleaning up after our family dinner one Saturday when Shermila asked if we could sit down for "a talk." Now twenty-one, she had moved into a shared apartment to complete her bachelor's degree at UC Berkeley. She'd majored in molecular and cell biology, with double minors in global poverty and Spanish.

Unnerved by her serious tone, I sat across from her on a sofa in the living room, marveling that my eldest had grown up in a blink. Several inches taller than me, she had cascading shoulder-length chestnut-brown hair with natural gold highlights. I'd been complimented a multitude of times for my "stunning" daughters. After looking around to make sure we were alone, she sat on the edge of her seat and nervously tucked her hair behind her ear.

"Mom, I've been thinking . . . I want to go to med school," she said, all in a rush. The fingers of her right hand trembled slightly, and she watched my expression closely.

"Med school? Really? Are you sure, Shermila?" I put on my blandest psychiatrist face to hide the surprise and elation that churned within.

"I'm sure, Mom." She pulled the gold pendant on her necklace from side to side. "Won't be till I graduate, so I guess, two more years. . . ."

"Did I hear *medical school?*" Tim walked in from his music studio. "How about art history, or something else? You sure have the brains for it, Shermila, but do we need *another* doctor in the family?" He had a crestfallen tone.

I jumped in hastily. "She's probably thought a lot about this. Shermila, if you've set your heart on this, you're facing a very tough road. My advice is to make sure you've got a backup plan that'll make you happy if you don't make it. But with your grades, and the Berkeley name backing you, I think you'll stand a fair chance . . . heck, I knew about Berkeley when we lived in Ghana!" I stood up and threw her a conspiratorial wink. "Plus, remember that fortune teller's spiel to Grandpa? If you get in, you'll make me a doctor of a *doctor*. Not quite *doctors*, but I say, go for it. If you make it, I'll be halfway there!"

While Shermila was considering med school applications, Shanthi received a piano scholarship to attend Willamette University in Oregon in the fall of 2013. With both girls now poised to pursue future careers, I decided it was time to seize the day and plan a mother-and-daughter escape.

I'd just recovered from a real scare with breast cancer and radiation treatments, so the timing was perfect to take three weeks off in the summer. Tim couldn't get time away from work, so off we went; the girls chose Sri Lanka and arranged the itinerary. It was poignant to think that the three of us were poised to trace a cultural path together, given that I'd been eighteen, Shanthi's age, the last time I was there.

I wasn't too surprised when the girls settled on Sri Lanka. They'd never been there and wanted to experience their Sri Lankan roots firsthand. On trips to England and Scotland they'd already familiarized themselves with their British heritage. We would visit family in the northern and southern parts of the island, then tour the center where we would watch the Perahera (the annual procession of decorated elephants in Kandy), experience the hilly tea country, and visit an assortment of ancient Buddhist temples.

When we flew out, it was a bittersweet pleasure to link up with cousins, aunts, and uncles after thirty-four years away from the island. Both girls adapted very quickly, like natives, relishing all the new spicy curries without batting an eye, while half the time I walked around with my mouth on fire.

Halfway through the trip, I completed the arduous ascent of 1,250 steps to the Sigiriya Lion Fortress. My girls had gone up ahead of me. At the top, a cool breeze wafted into my face. I stood on the top of the hardened magma plug, a breathtaking 660 feet above the landscaped gardens and greenery we'd traversed several hours back.

My girls were a hundred feet away from me, their heads bobbing as they explored the ancient castle ruins on that elevated plateau. Shanthi laughed and pointed at something. Her hair, several shades darker than Shermila's, lifted off her shoulders in the breeze. Their silhouettes could not have appeared more radiant to me, or the scene more magnificent, with a verdant patchwork quilt of my beautiful island stretching out 360 degrees in every direction far below. I drank in their youth, their camaraderie, and the incredible beauty of that magical moment, wanting to contain it in a time capsule, to cherish it forever.

Despite all the challenges, so much had come right for our family. I had no doubt that, despite every dart that fate could fling their way, they would navigate each future obstacle with grace.

A surge of thick emotion overwhelmed me. I thought back to my mother, grandmother, and great-grandmother, all strong, independent Sri Lankan women. Their blood, pride, and love flowed in my veins. It had helped me keep a positive outlook through a lifetime of adventures in Sri Lanka, Ghana, South Wales, and then America.

This glorious day, I had returned full circle to Sri Lanka after a long absence. I was on the idyllic island where my adventurous journey first started—where the prophecy was first made to my father. What the future held, I had no idea, but had I died at that very moment, they'd have discovered a ridiculous, fat grin of contentment that nothing could erase.

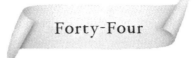

Forty-Four

Doctor
of Doctors

We were thrilled when Shermila was accepted at a medical school in Elk Grove called California Northstate University College of Medicine. During her second year in med school, I was recruited to join the faculty as an assistant professor. They wanted me to become the psychiatry course director for the third-year students. I'd always loved teaching, and they promised me flexibility so I could fit the teaching in around my current county clinic job. I asked Shermila what she thought.

"I think they'd be lucky to have you, Mom, but don't do it just for me. I know you like to figure things out. If you join the school, you'll be pioneering the design of the psychiatry curriculum for the third-year students from the ground up. You'd enjoy creating it. I say, go for it," she said with a big smile.

That sealed it. If I took it, I'd be a part of my own daughter's first real exposure to psychiatry. It would be a challenge to get the curriculum going, but I'd never run from a challenge. I became the psychiatry clerkship director. Groups of eight medical students would rotate with me each month as I provided tours of a career in mental health.

Shermila was right. I absolutely loved it from the get-go.

The Fortune Teller's Prophecy

At first it was a nightmare to set up the structure of the course, obtain speakers and sites, teach the students, and design the curriculum, all at the same time, but it was also very fulfilling when I received compliments from staff and students.

I created dozens of PowerPoint presentations and reached out to multiple hospitals and clinics to secure places where the students could learn the nuts and bolts of psychiatric practice. I even obtained a fascinating forensic training site, Napa State Prison, which housed prisoners who were criminally insane.

By the time Shermila rotated with me in her third year, the curriculum ran like a well-oiled machine. I arranged many different speakers, including survivors of sexual abuse and severe drug addiction. The medical students were riveted by these stories of endurance, and I relished playing a part in their mental health education. One of the biggest stressors to the students was the sudden death of Shermila's classmate who committed suicide at the end of her second year. This was a huge challenge to navigate, but as we worked through feelings of sadness and loss in our small group of eight students at a time, it was fulfilling to become part of the way they healed and grieved from a major loss.

I held on to this job for three additional years, until one of the proudest days of my life, when I walked in my long robes with other faculty members to witness the magic of the graduation of the inaugural med school class—Shermila's graduation as a physician.

As she accepted her diploma with a shy smile on her face, I reflected that I had become not just a doctor of my physician daughter, but also of all the other graduating physicians.

In that sense, I truly had become a "doctor of doctors"!

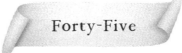

Forty-Five

Return
to Parkmill

In mid-July 2010, I flew alone to London for a friend's wedding and spent the week with my Kumasi friend Patricia in Essex. Her sister, Elizabeth, dropped by to see me, and one lazy afternoon, I sat with them on a backyard deck chair with a dog on my lap. We reminisced and laughed about the good old days in Kumasi. Elizabeth was engrossed in a knitting project, and the gentle rays of the setting sun made the day perfect. One could never rule out rain, given the vagaries of the fickle English summer.

Patricia set down her wineglass. "So, Lally, John Russell never got in contact with the girls after Shermila was two? That's pretty sad. Where is he now?"

"Last time I Googled him, he was a professor of accounting in Kuwait. They stopped asking about him years back. Shanthi was only two months old when he left." I shrugged. His memory had no power over me any longer; I registered only disgust at the way he'd abandoned all parental duties. I idly wondered if John maintained contact with his two boys, who were probably in their thirties now—they'd idolized him as kids. If only I had their contact information, I could have connected my daughters with their older half-brothers, but I'd never tracked them down. Presumably they lived in England still.

"How about the Claydens, Lally?" Elizabeth stopped clicking her needles and looked up at me. "Did you keep in touch after you got to California?"

I sipped my wine to give me a moment. Memories flooded back of golden evenings seated by the fireplace with them, accompanied with sharp stabbings of regret about the events of that fateful April Fool's Day so very long ago. The Claydens were unfinished business. I'd give anything to rewrite the script on that last wacky goodbye when I'd sped away in Yvonne's Mini, never to see them again.

I hadn't responded, so both Elizabeth and Patricia looked at me expectantly. My almost empty glass of cabernet glowed in the sun's rays, and I picked it up. The heady scent of lavender added a dash of magic to the English country garden. I downed the wine, exhaled slowly, and gently stroked the sleeping dog on my lap.

"I sent them several Christmas newsletters over the years but never heard back. Heard they were separated. I also heard Judy passed away unexpectedly."

"Passed away?" Elizabeth leaned forward, her mouth agape.

"Don't know." I shrugged. "Don't know what happened to John Clayden either. He was the same age as my ex—about twenty years older than me." I brought the wineglass to my lips, realized it was empty, and set it down again.

"Ray," Patricia called out, "we need more wine outside, please." She turned back to me. "Lally! You mean you don't even know if John Clayden's still living in South Wales? You *loved* the Gower, Lally, I remember."

"Yeah, it was a dream . . . that whole thing, me being stuck away from the family, happened . . . let me see," I rapidly did the calculation in my head, "that was twenty-six years back! Can you believe it? Ugh, that makes me feel old!"

A squirrel bounded across a flower bed, and Rusty jumped off my lap to give chase. "We had some issues at the end of my stay. John Russell was making moves on me, and they didn't like that, with my parents not there and his bad reputation and all that. Things got ugly." I shook my head. "So, yeah, I moved out, and we lost touch. All I have left are incredible memories. I'll never forget how they welcomed me unconditionally when I had nowhere to turn. John Clayden helped me extend my tourist visa the whole year. He was amazing." I twirled my finger around the top of my empty wineglass. "Plus, they paid all my expenses for the whole year." I smiled at Rusty's frozen pose by a rosebush as his eyes tracked a butterfly.

"Well, that was nice of them," Elizabeth murmured, her needles flying back and forth.

I shrugged. "It's pretty ironic, actually. The Claydens tried to warn me that John was a bad influence, but of course, I ignored their warnings and had to learn it the hard way, by getting married to him!" Rusty dashed around in circles like a small brown mophead. His antics mirrored the chaotic thoughts stirred up in my head. "I really wish I could go back to the Gower someday. It's just a magical place to me—you guys ever been?"

They both shook their heads. "No, I meant to but never did. It's quite a drive," Patricia said. "About six or seven hours, depending on traffic."

Ray emerged from the house with a half bottle of wine and replenished our glasses.

Patricia looked up at him thoughtfully. "Hey, Ray, want to take a couple days and drive to the Gower with Lally?"

My heart raced at her spontaneous suggestion, and I looked up at Ray. He ran a hand through his thinning white hair.

"Sure, why not? When do you want to go, 'Tricia?"

"It'll have to be tomorrow," Patricia said, "because Lally's going back to California next week."

The Fortune Teller's Prophecy

Ray straightened up, "Okay, let's do it, why not? Want to come, Elizabeth? There's lots of room for you, and you're all invited. We'll take the camper. What do you say?"

And just like that, five adults and two children decided to head for the Gower the following day. I loved that intrinsic Ghanaian spontaneity that I'd never lost either! They refused my offer to pay for gas, so I booked them a room at Parkmill's only bed and breakfast inn, the five-star Maes Yr Haf. The rest would crash in the camper for the night.

At the crack of dawn the following morning, Patricia and Ray's gigantic RV hurtled to Parkmill. The closer we got, the more my stomach churned. I hadn't seen John Clayden since he raced after Yvonne's Mini, pounding on it with a purple face. Was he living there still?

With the old nostalgia building up, I dreaded that the rugged, wild Welsh beauty might have been desecrated by tall apartment buildings and urban sprawl. I needn't have worried. As we left Swansea for the final thirty-minute stretch, I noticed that the tiny winding country road hadn't changed in over two decades. Our towering RV took up the entire road, so we had to pull into the shoulder repeatedly to allow oncoming cars to drive by. Sheep and wild ponies still abounded, and best of all were the luscious fields of green nothingness all around.

As we approached the curved road leading into Parkmill, my heart was racing so fast that I could hardly breathe, let alone talk. My chest ached with anticipation as I plastered my face against the window. We slowed to a crawl to drive into the tiny village.

As we inched past New Inn Cottage, I noticed that its whitewashed walls and terraced garden were still there, stirring jumbled memories of the birds I used to feed. Tears sprang to my eyes. With a flash of intense disappointment, I noticed a different car parked behind the house, then told myself off for hoping that John's green Renault would still be there so many years later. The dreamy stream still bubbled along on the opposite side of the road.

Although we'd faced astronomical odds that John Clayden still lived there, I'd hoped against hope that some miracle might have allowed us to connect again. The keen sense of loss sat on me like a weighted blanket. Shepherds, the village store, looked exactly the same. The monstrous RV dwarfed Maes Yr Haf's tiny parking lot. I was mortified and embarrassed at how it ruined the quaint charm of the picturesque village.

After check-in, I told my friends that I had to walk back to that wonderful house of my dreams. "I know John's not there, but I want to drool over the garden, for old times' sake." They insisted on following me at a distance, "just to make to make sure nothing happens." We made an odd picture, with me in front and the seven of them trailing a good fifty yards behind.

My heart lurched as I walked by the ancient gray walls of Mount Pisgah chapel, where I'd played the organ for many a Sunday service. It looked exactly the same, with the very same sign out front. The closer I got to New Inn Cottage, the drier my throat became, till I could barely swallow. I dragged my feet, my heart pounding in my ears.

Suddenly, I was no longer a confident child psychiatrist but a naive, stranded twenty-two-year-old, trying to settle an aching old wound that had never quite healed. I froze in front of the front door for several seconds, trying to summon up the courage to knock. The owner was probably home because of the car parked outside.

I thought of what I might say to a stranger. Perhaps something lame like, "I'm taking a trip down memory lane. . . ." I cast a desperate glance back down the road. My friends had stopped also. Elizabeth waved me toward the door, as if she sensed that I was on the verge of chickening out.

With a deep breath and all the power I possessed, I tapped timidly on the front door. A dog barked. I had my knuckle poised to knock again when the door swung open silently. And there, framed in the opening, stood John Clayden. His jet-black hair had turned white and thin. It was down to his shoulders, but I could never forget those unmistakable sparkling blue eyes.

"John?" I asked, with a catch in my voice, taking a half step forward.

His eyes widened slightly, and then he stepped out without hesitation to give me a giant hug. "Lally! Lally! Welcome, come on in," he said, as if I'd just returned from Shepherds with groceries.

All the dread evaporated at his unconditionally warm welcome.

"Did you come alone, Lally, or . . . ?" John asked, trying to look behind me.

I stepped back and pointed down the road at the others, gesturing for them to join us. "The entire Asare clan is here too, John. They're all dying to see you!"

The next five minutes were a chaos of hugs, barks from two overweight white Labradors, excited chatter, and a slew of introductions of the Asare girls' two husbands, the children, and John's wife, Sally. She was a Judy look-alike, complete with a hippie maxiskirt. Her long white hair was fastened into a ponytail. I saw from the dried flower arrangements and room decor that, like Judy, she was also into arts and crafts.

"How lovely to meet all of you," she said with a beaming smile of welcome. "If you give me a couple of hours, I'll fix up dinner tonight. You must come back and eat with us, please. It will make John's day."

I stared at the logs piled to the side of the antique fireplace, remembering how I'd sat cross-legged in front of the fire night after night, poking it to keep it from going out. The fire in our relationship was back. I sensed no rancor from John, only delight at this reunion. My heart was light and airy. Like the birds I'd fed in the garden terrace, I was a chaffinch who'd fluttered back to a beloved, familiar roost.

"So, you're staying at Maes Yr Haf for the night?" John turned to me, "Gosh, Lally, you must have a rich husband."

"Nope, he has me," I murmured, "I'm a doctor now, John."

Epilogue

In mid-February 2018, I walked through the crowded front lobby of my Sacramento clinic to pick up my lunch from the staff kitchen, when a voice halted me in my tracks.

"Dr. Pia?" Her voice was soft and gentle, but something about the excited tone sent chills of remembrance through the back of my neck and down my spine.

That voice! I know that voice! How do I know that voice?

I pirouetted with all the grace of a startled bison, my heart beating out of my chest.

There, seated in the lobby with a brown bag on her lap, was my old jigsaw puzzle, my first therapy patient, Rosie. Rosie Johnson! Rosie had stayed alive for coming on fifteen years! What was Rosie doing here, over a hundred miles from where I'd last treated her? I shook my head in disbelief, unable to speak.

She got up stiffly from her seat and walked up to me slowly. "Dr. Pia, it is you! I saw your name with the other doctor ones, and I wondered if it could be the same Dr. Pia! Can I give you a hug?" Without waiting for a response, she enveloped me in a giant embrace. Her body had filled out a little, but she was still pretty skinny. I disentangled myself gently, aware that several patients in the lobby were throwing us curious stares. My eyes were moist.

Epilogue

"Let's talk in my office, Rosie. Come, come with me."

I called out to the receptionist that I would be running five minutes late for my next appointment and turned back to Rosie. "I'm officially on lunch break now, so your timing couldn't have been more perfect."

Rosie picked up her belongings and followed me into my office. When the door closed behind us, she gave me another warm hug. I pulled away to look at her. The years had added lines to her face and gray to her sparse hair, but there was a softness and self-assurance about her that made her wrinkles beautiful. Motioning for her to sit down, I sat right beside her on another patient chair. Leaving my doctor chair vacant would emphasize that I was now a colleague, not her therapist.

After a few minutes catching up, I asked what brought her to the clinic.

"What are you doing here, Rosie?" Even as I asked this, my heart sang because Rosie had beaten the odds and wasn't lying six feet under, somewhere.

"I'm here with my grandson, Kyle."

"Your *grandson?* When I saw you last, you were trying to get custody of your daughter from CPS. Tell me about your grandson."

"It's a long story." She sighed, placed her bag on the floor beside her, and leaned back.

"I've got the time." I shot a quick glance at my office clock.

"Doc, so let me start with good news for a change. I beat meth. Yeah, I really did." She smiled at my bemused expression. "Did it—coming on ten years sober in August."

"Rosie, I'm so proud of you! Congratulations!" I leaned forward to squeeze her hand. "How did you do that?"

"I dunno." She shrugged and set her possessions on the floor beside her. "Meds, drug rehab, groups . . . stuff, y'know? Took parenting classes, lots of those." She leaned forward and spoke in an intense tone. "Biggest reason I stayed sober was because I wanted Lakiya back."

"How could I forget?" I nodded vigorously.

"Yeah, I got clean because I wanted my baby home with me. Got her coming on nine years back."

"Wow."

"Yeah, quit alcohol, cocaine, everything. Meth was the hardest, y'know." She smiled, revealing a few missing front teeth, and took a long, shuddering breath.

"So, my daughter . . . she . . . she was, like, seventeen when I . . . by the time I did my classes, and tested clean, and all."

"Okay."

"She'd been in several foster placements, but she was always asking for her mamma. She ran away from some of them. By the time I got her back from CPS, she was pregnant."

"Pregnant? Really?" I shook my head and reached out a hand and laid it gently on her wrist. "I'm glad you could support her at that time. What a story, Rosie."

"Yeah, her baby daddy weren't in the picture, so I left East Palo Alto and came to Sacramento to help her out. We got an apartment together, and get this, Doc," she leaned forward and her eyes sparkled, "I got a job at Denny's now. Helps pay the rent."

"Congrats, Rosie." I leaned back to hear the rest.

"Now here's the sad part, Doc." She stared out of my window and tears filled her eyes. "Lakiya got a heart attack when Kyle was, like, three. Happened right outta the blue. No warning, no nothing. Took her out. They couldn't do nothing. Never expected nothing like that . . . you always think you're gonna die before your kids, and she was only with me for a short time, Doc. . . ." She lapsed into silence and stared out my window. I sat back to give her space. Eventually she shook her head slightly, as if returning from a deep reminiscence, then turned back to me. "It was a shock, I tell you. Been years, but I haven't quite recovered from it."

"I can imagine," I murmured, shaking my head.

"After she passed, I got to keep Kyle. Didn't want him to end up in the system like my daughter, y'know. I'm all the family he's got now." She fished out a tissue from her purse and blew her nose.

I was stunned into silence.

"Yeah, Doc, so Kyle's fine, except he got problems focusing, trouble making friends, that sort of thing, so he's getting therapy right here at River Oak. Therapy helped me back then, so I figured, maybe it'll help him too. Anyway, that's why I was here, Doc. He's in with his therapist right now." She glanced at her watch. "He'll be out soon. I gotta go. But anyway, to end my story, out in that waiting room, I saw 'Dr. Pia' with all the other docs' names, and I thought, could it really be the *same* doctor . . . and it sure was!"

"Rosie, what a strange coincidence."

"Yeah, guess it was meant to be."

Before she left, she turned around with a hand on the door frame. "Doc, d'you know what kept me coming back to see you that whole year?"

I shook my head.

"You never let go of me, Doc. You showed me you cared, every time we met. I knew you were disappointed when I kept using. You threw in those long lectures to try to get me to quit. It was like . . . like someone was always there for me, holding out hope for a better life. That's what it was, Doc, you always gave me hope. You helped change my life and make a difference, and now I get to be a part of my grandson's life."

After she left my office, I leaned against the closed door and shook my head in disbelief. Once again, I was stunned by how we'd randomly reconnected. Had I taken my customary route to avoid the lobby, we might never have met. I thought about Rosie's life on the streets compared to the privileged one I'd led in four continents. In a strange way, Rosie and I had both extricated ourselves from multiple quandaries, found inner strength and self-assurance, and made life-altering decisions that led us to this moment of connection and enlightenment.

I've clung to the precious words she shared with me that magical day. I hold them close when the most challenging patients walk into my clinic and I feel the most defeated. Never have I truly aspired to be a "doctor of doctors." All I've wanted is to make a difference, forge a connection with others, and help kindle a flickering spark.

Most of all, I want those I care for to know that when life seems unsurmountable, there's always, always hope.

Acknowledgments

I want to thank my brother, Vimalan Mahadevan, who is my go-to critic whenever I want the truth.

Thanks to my sisters, Vijitha Mahadevan Eyango and Nirmala Mahadevan, for their emotional and financial support when life was rough.

To John and Judy Clayden, who provided a much-needed home to a lost and lonely girl.

To Sands Hall, who made a profound impact on my ability to write and improved my ability to create a sense of place.

To my Davis Writers Salon friends, especially MP Smith for her friendship and editing help, Robin Wing Dragoo for the psychological hand holding whenever needed, and David McLachlan and Lisa Montanaro, who toiled with me into the wee hours. Sincere thanks to Cindy Kiel for welcoming dozens of writers into her home for years and feeding us to boot!

To friends I can call on at 2:00 a.m. at the drop of a hat—Maria Tebbutt, Ingrid Abild Pedersen, Megan Lisska, MD, Ellen Moratti, Angela Haczku, MD, and Adele Mitchell, MD—your support makes my world a warm place.

Sincere thanks to Douglas Gross, MD, Alan Louie, MD, and Harry Wang, MD, who guided me professionally and held my hand when I almost gave up.

I salute Brooke Warner, Shannon Green, and my wonderful publishing team at She Writes Press, who recognized the potential of my manuscript and provided invaluable critique. Thank you for the publication deal that made this possible.

About the Author

Lally Pia was born in Sri Lanka, grew up in Ghana, and made it halfway through medical school before political turmoil closed down her university and she learned that her American Green Card had been bungled. She went on to work as a church organist, teacher, and ice cream decorator, as well as a scientist in a molecular biology lab. Her next stint was as the director of UC Davis's Body Donation Program, where she embalmed cadavers and maintained a freezer full of human specimens (a thankless job that she was glad to leave after three years). Lally is a mother, grandmother, and child psychiatrist who lives in Davis, California, with her husband, Tim.

SELECTED TITLES FROM SHE WRITES PRESS

She Writes Press is an independent publishing company
founded to serve women writers everywhere.
Visit us at www.shewritespress.com.

Feeling Fate: A Memoir of Love, Intuition, and Spirit by Joni Sensel. $16.95, 978-1-64742-339-1. A grief memoir with a paranormal twist, *Feeling Fate* recounts a fairy tale romance marked by a dark intuition of loss. When the premonition comes true, Joni—a woman torn between faith and skepticism—ultimately finds healing from and meaning in her grief through imagination and insights of the heart.

Fatherless, Fearless, Female: A Memoir by Mary Charity Kruger Stein. $16.95, 978-1-63152-755-5. In this tale of single mothers and fatherless children, a Rust Belt farm girl escapes poverty, weds, has a son, is widowed by her first husband, and then falls in love with a Jewish man whose mother opposes their relationship—just before she moves halfway around the world.

The Girl in the Red Boots: Making Peace with My Mother by Judith Ruskay Rabinor, PhD. $16.95, 978-1-64742-040-6. After confronting a childhood trauma that had resonated throughout her life, psychologist Dr. Judy Rabinor, an eating disorder expert, converted her pain into a gift and became a wounded healer—a journey that taught her it's never too late to let go of hurts and disappointments and develop compassion for yourself, and even for your mother.

The Longest Mile: A Doctor, a Food Fight, and the Footrace that Rallied a Community Against Cancer by Christine Meyer, MD. $16.95, 978-1-63152-043-3. In a moment of desperation, after seeing too many patients and loved ones battle cancer, a doctor starts a running team—never dreaming what a positive impact it will have on her community.

Finding Venerable Mother: A Daughter's Spiritual Quest to Thailand by Cindy Rasicot. $16.95, 978-1-63152-702-9. In midlife, Cindy travels halfway around the world to Thailand and unexpectedly discovers a Thai Buddhist nun who offers her the unconditional love and acceptance her own mother was never able to provide. This soulful and engaging memoir reminds readers that when we go forward with a truly open heart, faith, forgiveness, and love are all possible.